Meet the Food Radicals

MEET THE FOOD RADICALS

F. BAILEY NORWOOD AND TAMARA L. MIX

OXFORD
UNIVERSITY PRESS

OXFORD
UNIVERSITY PRESS

Oxford University Press is a department of the University of Oxford. It furthers
the University's objective of excellence in research, scholarship, and education
by publishing worldwide. Oxford is a registered trade mark of Oxford University
Press in the UK and certain other countries.

Published in the United States of America by Oxford University Press
198 Madison Avenue, New York, NY 10016, United States of America.

Library of Congress Cataloging-in-Publication Data
Names: Norwood, F. Bailey, author. | Mix, Tamara L., author.
Title: Meet the food radicals : / F. Bailey Norwood
and Tamara L. Mix.
Description: New York, NY, United States of America : Oxford University
Press, [2019] | Includes bibliographical references and index.
Identifiers: LCCN 2018034995 (print) | LCCN 2018046600 (ebook) |
ISBN 9780190620448 (Updf) | ISBN 9780190620455 (Epub) |
ISBN 9780190620431 (hardcover : acid-free paper)
Subjects: LCSH: Food supply—Political aspects—United States. |
Food industry and trade—Political aspects—United States. |
Agriculture and state—United States.
Classification: LCC HD9006 (ebook) | LCC HD9006 .N67 2019 (print) |
DDC 338.1/973—dc23
LC record available at https://lccn.loc.gov/2018034995

This book is dedicated to anyone willing to listen to a radical idea, ponder it, and extract its finest qualities, even if they do not accept the idea as a whole.

We also offer this work in memory of Jackie Dill, Oklahoma's favorite wildcrafter and one of our radicals, who passed away while the book was in progress.

Contents

Acknowledgments

A SPECIAL THANKS to the twenty-seven "radicals" we interviewed. They not only gave us the gift of their time, but shared the stories of their lives, their deepest passions, and their visions for the future of food. Their willingness to trust us is a responsibility we take seriously, and we hope they look back positively on their participation. We gratefully acknowledge funding support from the US Department of Agriculture and Oklahoma State University as well as the funders of our endowed chair positions (Barry Pollard and Laurence L. and Georgia Ina Dresser). Important thanks go also to our loving spouses and children.

Meet the Food Radicals

Introduction

DINING WITH FOOD RADICALS

YOUR FIRST QUESTION is probably: what is a food radical? A young American surfer might think the term "radical" refers to awesome people. Political junkies might think we are referring to people with unconventional ideas. A nineteenth-century British politician would assume we refer to people who wish a fundamental reform of the food system, one that gets at the roots of our food problems. After all, the term "radical" is derived from the Latin *radix*, which means "of or having roots." This is why one of the roots that we eat is called a "radish."[1]

So which definition do we use when we say "food radical"? All of them. This book is about food and agriculture from the perspective of twenty-seven individuals we interviewed, and they are all truly awesome people. Some do have unconventional ideas. Most seek to identify and rectify what they see as fundamental problems with our food system.

They are an eclectic group of people. The book will begin with farmers and end with a food meditation coach. In between are innovative companies, scientists, activists, radio talk show hosts, undercover investigators, and others. They are so diverse that the only thing they have in common is that they are fascinating people with something to teach. They do not represent a single perspective on the food system—in public, some of them are opponents.

Why write a book about such different people with varying perspectives? Because we follow the Latin proverb *hominem unius libri timeo*—"I fear the man of one book." We could easily write a book with a simple theme, attacking one problem within the food system and championing one solution. Such books abound, though. It isn't hard to find a book touting organic agriculture as a silver bullet to food problems. Nor is it hard to find a book championing scientific technology as the solution to those same problems. Such books are useful, but we contend there is no one single solution to any given food problem, and that those food problems are more complex than typically depicted. This becomes apparent after reading many books, and after conversing with many different people. Most people want to avoid the mistake of being a "person of one book" but do not have time to read lots of books. Thus, we wrote this book to reflect the perspectives of many different individuals, allowing the reader to develop the sophistication of a many-book person while turning fewer total pages.

Do not expect this book to champion one point of view or disparage another, at least not intentionally. If two of our food radicals disagree on an issue, do not expect us to say who is right or who is wrong. We simply wish you to meet these people and listen to them. What you conclude about food issues is up to you.

Think of this book as a friendly dinner party, one where a group of people meet to eat and discuss food. It is a polite affair, where each person patiently listens to others before speaking, knowing he or she will be heard likewise. All ideas are welcome, even if they challenge one's beliefs. Dinner parties and excellent food have a way of making people who are normally opponents behave cordially, listen to one another, and exchange ideas. Most guests will leave with the same opinions they arrived with, but all will have learned something.

How did we choose our radicals to interview? We thought about how we would make a guest list for a dinner party. We chose interesting people with a captivating story to tell, who would be likely to engage with others different from them and did not mind being in the same book as people from alternative backgrounds and views. A few we already knew personally, but most were initially unknown to us and were discovered based on their work and recommendation by others.

The first chapter of this book introduces each of these dinner guests, including a picture and a brief description. After this first chapter, the book is organized by subject. First comes items related to the production of food, second comes topics related to public policy and social issues, and third comes subjects about the eating of food. All of our interviewees transcend any one specific topic, and each person appears more than once in the book.

So join us for dinner and meet some of the most radical people in food. They are radical for different reasons, and all are radical in that each is unique. You cannot encounter these individuals without being exposed to new ideas.

We see the first course being served, so let's get started.

1

Meet the Food Radicals

Fergal Anderson. Food sovereignty advocate and owner of Leaf and Root Farm (www.leafandroot.org). Fergal taught us the importance of giving political power to peasant farmers and of the bold efforts made by small farmers worldwide to challenge the political power of transnational corporations. He also described the sustainable farm practices he employs on his own land and his efforts to reclaim food sovereignty for Ireland.

FIGURE 1.1 Image courtesy of Fergal Anderson

Ray Archuletta. Soil scientist, US Department of Agriculture. Ray is leading a new soil health movement based on using agricultural methods that mimic nature. He taught us the benefit of preserving organic matter in the soil, the role of faith in preserving farmland, and the importance of personal knowledge in educating others.

FIGURE I.2 Image courtesy of Ray Archuletta

Dominique Barnes. Founder and CEO of New Wave Foods. Dominique impressed upon us the urgency to protect aquatic life and how modern food processing technologies can aid this quest. The story of how she created her own company at such a young age is an inspiration to anyone wanting to improve the world through the private sector.

FIGURE 1.3 Image courtesy of Dominique Barnes

Dan Brown. Small farmer in the state of Maine. Dan taught us that the current food regulatory system is not well suited to small farmers. When regulatory agencies told Dan that he could not sell raw milk to local consumers, he fought them all the way to the Maine Supreme Court, and his struggle began a food sovereignty movement in his state. Small, local farms have enough challenges, Dan asserts, and the last thing they need is opposition from inflexible regulatory agencies.

FIGURE 1.4 Image courtesy of Dan Brown

Bill Bullard. CEO of R-CALF USA, an organization fighting for the independent US cattle producer. Independent poultry and hog farmers are mostly a thing of the past, as they found themselves increasingly under the control of powerful meat processors. Bill and the members of R-CALF USA are intent on making sure the cattle industry does not suffer the same fate. We learned from Bill that it isn't R-CALF USA that is radical. What is radical is how the US livestock sector has changed.

FIGURE 1.5 Image courtesy of Bill Bullard

Cody Carlson. Former undercover animal rights activist. Before he was a lawyer for Mercy For Animals, Cody went undercover as a worker on live-stock farms to capture cruel conditions on video. It is tempting to simply buy food at the store and not ask how it is raised. Cody's work reminds us that doing so is irresponsible and unethical, encouraging us be account-able for the food we purchase.

FIGURE 1.6 Image courtesy of Sarah Von Alt

Hannah Dankbar. MCRP in community and regional planning and MS in sustainable agriculture from Iowa State University. Along with Rivka Fidel, Hannah sought to hold Iowa State University accountable for human feeding trials research it performed with genetically modified bananas. Her story taught us that universities need to allow students to be both scholars and activists in their attempts to learn about, and improve, the world.

FIGURE 1.7 Image courtesy of Hannah Dankbar

Jackie Dill. Wildcrafter. Jackie is Native American and uses a lifetime of traditional knowledge to teach others how to forage for food in the wild. Our time with Jackie taught us the bounty nature can provide, our responsibility for being good stewards of the wild, and the challenges many people face in acquiring food.

FIGURE 1.8 Image courtesy of Jackie Dill

Dan Durica. Member of Dancing Rabbit Ecovillage, Missouri. Residents of Dancing Rabbit Ecovillage build houses out of straw and mud, and almost all the energy they use is renewable. They share vehicles, they have gardens instead of lawns, and their carbon footprint is only half that of the average American. They are members of an ecovillage in Missouri, and resident Dan Durica tells the story of why he calls it home.

FIGURE 1.9 Image courtesy of Dan Durica

Evan Ellison. Molecular biology student and farmer. Evan grew up farming genetically modified crops and can testify to the advantages of doing so. He also knows that plant genetics must continue to change for farmers to survive and food to be abundant. He sought to participate in the genetic revolution and improve crop varieties by studying molecular biology.

FIGURE 1.10 Image courtesy of Evan Ellison

Alex Evers. Karate instructor and food defense promoter. It is hard enough getting kids to eat well, much less convince them to practice mindful eating. Doing so takes someone with kid credibility—someone like martial arts instructor Alex Evers. Alex taught us the importance of taking radical ideas and transforming them into a form more palatable to the average person.

FIGURE I.II Image courtesy of Alex Evers

Rivka Fidel. Doctoral student in soil science, Iowa State University. Along with Hannah Dankbar, Rivka sought to hold Iowa State University accountable for the research it performed with genetically modified bananas. Her story taught us that universities need to allow students to be both scholars and activists as they attempt to learn about, and improve, the world.

FIGURE I.12 Image courtesy of Rivka Fidel

Aruni Futuronsky. Food meditation coach. Our struggle to keep a healthy weight usually involves changing what and how much we eat, but rarely do we consider the how of eating. Aruni's spiritual journey taught her not only how to live but how to eat, and she shares with us these lessons on how mindful eating can benefit us both physically and spiritually.

FIGURE 1.13 Image courtesy of Aruni Futuronsky

Jimmy Kinder. Farmer and no-till pioneer. Jimmy doesn't seem like a radical today because his system of no-till farming is used by many farmers across the United States. However, the first year he implemented his no-till system, people thought he was crazy. People predicted it would fail, and he would lose his farm. But Jimmy bet the farm and won! His story reminds us that it takes brave people to prove a radical idea reasonable.

FIGURE 1.14 Image courtesy of Jimmy Kinder

Karissa Lewis. Food justice advocate. A self-described black radical farmer and international twenty-first-century socialist, Karissa taught us what the US food system looks like through the eyes of a black woman raised in a food desert. As the current executive director of the Center for Third World Organizing, she champions a movement for social justice led by people of color, a movement based in part on local food production and community-owned farms and grocery stores.

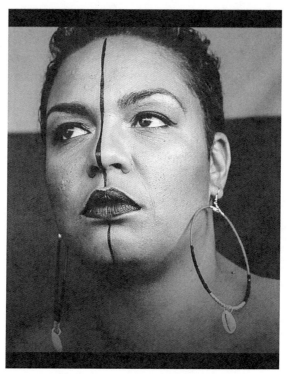

FIGURE I.15 Image courtesy of Karissa Lewis

Trent Loos. Rancher and radio talk show host. Many ranchers and farmers are frustrated with the rural-urban divide, where consumers who do not understand how food is produced seek to regulate how farmers produce food. While industry groups protect themselves through lobbying, Trent pursues a radically different strategy: reaching out to the urban public through his radio show and traveling to confront animal rights groups in person.

FIGURE 1.16 Photo by Zuhrah Alwahabi

Katie Michels. Former university ecovillage member. Rather than live in a dorm, Katie lived in Middlebury College's local food and environmental studies interest house, where the students decided for themselves what to eat. They cooked locally produced food from nearby farms using regenerative agricultural practices, including only non-GMO foods. Since Katie is a Type 1 diabetic and needs insulin produced from genetically modified bacteria to live, she provides a unique insight into the anti-GMO movement.

FIGURE 1.17 Image courtesy of Katie Michels

Bob Moje. School architect. Childhood obesity is clearly a major problem in the United States, but what to do about it is less clear. Parents can work to ensure their children eat healthy at home, but kids will spend a large portion of their day at school. Bob sees this as an opportunity to invest in school designs that promote health. His explanation of how this can be accomplished impressed upon us the profound ways our environment influences our behavior.

FIGURE 1.18 Image courtesy of Bob Moje

Jeff Moyer. Organic agricultural researcher at the Rodale Institute. Plowing harms the soil, but is necessary if a farmer wishes to raise food without the use of herbicides—or so it was thought until Jeff and others at the Rodale Institute invented a no-till organic production system. In Jeff's story, we learn both the values that drive research at the Rodale Institute and how those values lead to innovation.

FIGURE 1.19 Image courtesy of Jeff Moyer

Marc Oshima. Cofounder of AeroFarms. Ask anyone the three most essential things for plant growth. In addition to water, they are likely to list soil and sunlight. This isn't necessarily true. AeroFarms produces large amounts of beautiful vegetables with neither soil nor the sun. Marc tells us the story of how this is accomplished, and why the technology is only successful when paired with sound business practices.

FIGURE 1.20 Image courtesy of Marc Oshima

Katie Plohocky. Food justice advocate. Katie knows what it is like to experience severe challenges to food access. She also knows that many people today are in the same stressful situation. Katie converted a horse trailer into a mobile grocery store and set about hydrating the food deserts of Tulsa, Oklahoma. She also leads programs to reduce the cost of fruits and vegetables to low-income households. One person cannot change the world, but Katie has certainly changed the city of Tulsa.

FIGURE I.21 Image courtesy of Katie Plohocky

Christina Schiavoni. Food sovereignty activist and scholar. Christina has been studying food in Venezuela since the rise of Hugo Chavez, learning from its efforts to transform food sovereignty from a vision into reality at the national level. She corrects some misperceptions reported in the media about Venezuela and describes what other countries can learn from its food sovereignty movement.

FIGURE I.22 Image courtesy of Christina Schiavoni

Liz Specht. Scientist at the Good Food Institute. From a young age Liz was trained to seek practical solutions to urgent problems. Today we face environmental pollution, global warming, health problems due to poor diets, and animal suffering. Fortunately, Liz sees a common solution: a reduction in meat consumption—but how do you convince people to trade in their meat for quinoa? You don't. You create meat made from plant substitutes that taste just as good. Is this possible? Liz and the people at the Good Food Institute are working to make it a reality.

FIGURE 1.23 Image courtesy of Liz Specht

Amory Starr. Professor of sociology, alterglobalization activist, and underground restaurateur. No one appears in the book more frequently than Amory, and no one is radical in so many different ways. She taught the political economy of food before it was popular. She had the audacity to challenge industrial agriculture while working at an agricultural university. Along the way she became a chef and opened an underground restaurant—not to make money, but to encourage food literacy and develop a greater political culture on food issues.

FIGURE 1.24 Image courtesy of Amory Starr

James Underwood. Robotics engineer. He grew up programming his own video games, but he now programs robots to herd cattle, manage weeds, and monitor fruit production. Much of his work involves helping robots to see and think better, which includes developing better algorithms. James taught us that there are many ways to revolutionize agriculture, and his way is applying mathematics and programming to create farm solutions.

FIGURE 1.25 Image courtesy of James Underwood

Dan Voytas. Molecular biologist and plant breeder, chief science officer at Calyxt, and professor at the University of Minnesota. The debate about genetically modified food is controversial, but thanks to Dan's research, we can now edit plant genes without them becoming genetically modified organisms. His genetics research has created a healthier vegetable oil and has even saved the life of babies by permitting a new type of leukemia treatment. Our conversation with Dan revealed the importance of marrying advanced genetic research with financial backing from the private sector in order to create healthier food products.

FIGURE 1.26 Image courtesy of Calyxt

Taber Ward. Goat milk farmer. It is hard for small livestock farms to survive when they must compete against large factory farms, but Taber found a way. Rather than raising goats for milk and creating a for-profit business, she established a goat dairy as a nonprofit organization. Mountain Flower Goat Dairy sells goat milk and hosts summer camps, field trips, cheese-making workshops, birthday parties, and even goat yoga. The dairy is no petting zoo, but a working farm, and Taber is intent on educating the public about sustainable and ethical food production.

FIGURE 1.27 Taber Ward (right)
Image courtesy of Taber Ward

2

The Farm

Our Little Friends in the Soil

Archaeologists have found evidence of farming going back as far as 21,000 B.C. Confirmation consists of the preserved remains of weeds gathered in one area alongside the remains of ancient grains. An unusual accumulation of weeds is said to be evidence of agriculture because "weeds thrive in cultivated fields and disturbed soils." Proof of agriculture, then, seems to consist of a soil deliberately disturbed by humans.[1]

Ancient depictions of farming often show an animal pulling a plow, like that in the burial tomb of the Egyptian Sennedjem (1300–1200 B.C.).[2] When the Future Farmers of America organization chose an emblem in 1928, the image consisted of five symbols. One of them is a plow (see figure 2.1), "a symbol of labor and tillage of the soil, the backbone of agriculture and the historical foundation of our country's strength."[3] The American Farm Bureau Federation offers the prestigious Golden Plow Award, as "The plow is the most generic symbol of agriculture available."[4] Plowing is even an art, with the World Ploughing Organization holding plowing contests, crowning a world champion in four different categories.[5]

Even the ideal garden is said to need something akin to plowing. The book of Genesis notes that man was placed in the Garden of Eden to "work it,"[6] which can be interpreted to include digging into the soil.[7] It is a radical departure from traditional agriculture, then, that the plow is becoming increasingly unpopular. A new philosophy of agriculture is emerging that says one should disturb the soil as little as possible. A radical change, indeed.

FIGURE 2.1 Oxen pulling a plow in ancient Egypt (left) and a plow on today's FFA emblem (right)

Left image is in the public domain at Wikimedia Commons: https://commons.wikimedia.org/wiki/File:Maler_der_Grabkammer_des_Sennudem_001.jpg. The right image is courtesy of the FFA.

For most of agricultural history, plowing (digging deep into the soil, often flipping it over to bury weeds) and tilling (scratching, raking, or cutting the soil without flipping it) were seen as absolutely necessary. It was the only way to control weeds. Before planting a seed, a field might be plowed so thoroughly that no plants, living or dead could be seen. That is the point. A barren field allows the farmer to plant a seed with little worry that weeds will steal water and nutrients. Plant diseases from previous years will remain on plant residues. Burying those residues protects the crop from disease also. Weed seed and pathogens (like harmful fungi) easily travel through the air, so as the crop seed germinates, weeds are likely to begin growing with it. In response, farmers will often till the area between the rows of crops as the crop is growing.

Plowing and tilling have historically been necessary, yet the practice led to soil erosion. Most American children are taught about the Dust Bowl of the 1930s, when winds carried the loose dirt from plowed fields thousands of miles, stripping some areas of its land-growing potential and burying houses. A sense of urgency ensued, and studies soon found that in some locales land was eroding two hundred times faster than it was being replaced, and in some places three-fourths of the original topsoil was already gone.[8] Soil erosion problems did not begin in the 1930s though. In almost all regions where population pressures are large and plowing common, the soil has eroded and left civilizations vulnerable. They say

Rome wasn't built in a day. It didn't fall in a day either, and its steady decay stemmed partly from the persistent erosion of its soil.

Awareness of soil erosion problems is ancient. Plato and Aristotle both recognized what deforestation and tilling had done to the soils of ancient Greece.[9] Awareness of soil erosion problems still exist, so much so that we actually measure it. The United States continues to lose over a billion tons of cropland due to wind and water erosion each year,[10] and globally the land is eroding ten to forty times faster than it is being created.[11]

The transport of soil by wind and water is indeed a problem, but so is the deterioration of the soil that remains in the field. When the plow first pierced the American prairie, the carbon content of the soil was around 6 percent,[12] but through successive plowing and tilling, that content has fallen on many fields to just 1 percent. The organic matter containing carbon serves a vital role in the soil ecosystem. Soil is not just a physical medium, a placeholder for plants—it is alive. One teaspoon of prairie soil contains great numbers of microorganisms—between 100 million and 1 billion bacteria[13]—but also around 100,000 different species of microbes.[14] Microorganisms (especially fungi) mine the ground for minerals and transport those minerals to plants in exchange for the carbon and hydrogen the plants capture from the atmosphere. They not only transport nutrients from the soil to a plant, but between plants, and can even act as an immune system for the plant world, killing harmful pathogens—with the plants and soil microorganisms actually "communicating" through the exchange of volatile organic compounds to coordinate such attacks. These compounds are exchanged between plants through a network of fungi so complex and interconnected that it is sometimes referred to as an "internet of fungus." For example, one plant that receives a bite from a predator may send volatile organic compounds through its plant roots, into a network of fungi, and into the roots of a nearby plant. Once this nearby plant receives the compounds, it may begin producing a chemical that discourages the predator from consuming it. This internet of fungi needs carbon, so as the carbon content of soils falls, it degrades this unseen ecosystem.

Soil erosion and the health of soil ecosystems are not two distinct subjects, as a vibrant ecosystem is necessary to protect the soil from wind and rain. Only recently have we begun to understand this relationship, and many people who learn about it learn it from our first food radical, Ray Archuletta.

Meet Ray Archuletta

Ray Archuletta could see the consequence of erosion in the Snake River, and it concerned him. As the district conservationist for the US National Resource Conservation Service in Malheur County, Oregon, and resident in the region, he saw the naturally emerald-green Snake River turn into chocolate during the season farmers irrigated their crops. That alone was sad, but adding to the travesty was the fact that these farmers were financially struggling. Something was wrong, and worse, he felt that he was part of the problem. A component of his job was designing irrigation systems, which involved giving advice to farmers on how to manage their crops, and with the struggling farms and the muddy river, he started questioning all that he had been taught and all that he was teaching. This was all happening when Ray was in his forties, and he spoke of going through something akin to a midlife crisis, where he questioned whether he was positively contributing to the world. After all his hard work to help farmers, the Snake River was getting worse and farmers were going broke. Was he part of the problem? The answer seemed to be yes. The problem wasn't Ray, per se, as he was giving the same advice as all the experts—the same advice he was taught in college. When he looked at the Snake River and the struggling farms, it seemed the conventional wisdom about agriculture was not working. A new system of thinking was needed.

Thus began his intellectual journey to better understand the soil and his personal mission to restore soil health. He couldn't just consult the scientific literature or the universities to figure out the problem—that is where the problem seemed to originate. No, he had to discover new sources that recognized this problem existed and were not scared to seek radical solutions. The restlessness induced by this midlife crisis encouraged him to apply for a different position within the Natural Resource Conservation Service, moving him from the West Coast to North Carolina. Most of these new ideas came not from scientists, but regular farmers and contrarian thinkers who were developing new methods of farming. The new system of farming sought to work with—not against—nature. "We build agriculture on how to have dominion, how to control it, how to force it, how to manipulate it. How to force it with our tools. What I'm teaching is to learn how to understand it, to mimic it, understand its complementariness, and understand its synergies." He encouraged a system of biomimicry.

A plowed field is not natural. Neither is a monoculture, like the fields of Iowa, where corn and only corn is planted year after year. In a tallgrass prairie, soil is never disturbed, and in its natural state may have up to sixty different grasses, three hundred types of flowers, lichens and liverworts of over one hundred different types, in addition to the various trees, shrubs, and animals.[15] Of course, we cannot feed people with these natural prairie plants, but what Ray argued that is that our fields need to *mimic* the natural ecosystem. This means raising different plants at different times, allowing more than one plant to grow at once, not applying chemicals that kill organisms in the soil, and pierce the ground with farm implements as seldom as possible.

Ray is a YouTube star, so much so that Warren Buffet's son, Howard, once recognized him from the videos. Although Ray is energetic and charismatic, it isn't Ray himself who draws so many viewers, but his soil demonstrations where he proves that biomimicry is the best way to save the soil. One especially convincing video showed him placing two different soil samples in two different containers. One sample was from a heavily tilled field, and the other was from a field where a diversity of plants were grown and the field was rarely disturbed. The containers had a hole at the bottom for water to escape after it had percolated through the soil. He then poured equal amounts of water into each container.

Conventional thinking was that water would flow through the heavily tilled soil faster. It has been ground into smaller and smaller pieces, resembling sand. Farmers used to think that plowing would loosen the soil and provide more holes through which rainfall can penetrate the surface. Some even went so far as to refer to a stirred soil as a "dust mulch," much like mulch applied in a garden, keeping the soil from drying and conserving excess rainfall until it is needed by plant roots.[16] However, Ray's demonstration proved otherwise. The tilled soil was ground into such small pieces that they collapsed upon one another and hardened, providing few holes for the water to flow through the soil to reach plant roots—the water just settled on top of the heavily tilled soil like a pond. If this were a field, the water would not percolate the soil but would instead flow over the land and downhill, as in a parking lot, taking some of the soil with it. Conversely, the water flowed quickly through the seldom-tilled soil, and when it escaped through the bottom, it was clear. In seldom-tilled-soil conditions, the water does not run off the field, nor does it transport the soil on its way down.

In another video, Ray took a handful of those same two types of soils and just dropped them in two separate glass containers of water. The difference was stark. The heavily tilled soil broke apart and made the water muddy. The seldom-tilled soil stayed together as a clump and the water remained clear. Once again, the lesson is that a heavily tilled soil erodes faster.

Why the difference? In a sense, glue. Remember that Ray was teaching us to think of the soil as an ecosystem—that the soil is alive—and its members include plants, fungi, bacteria, nematodes, arthropods, protozoa, and others.[17] As these organisms interact, they produce a variety of molecules, like glomalin, which is a sticky substance that helps "glue" soil particles together.[18] This "glue" keeps water from breaking the soil particles apart and ensures water can infiltrate the soil by preventing the soil particles from collapsing upon one another. Glomalin is not something you can produce in a factory and apply to the field like fertilizer. It takes microorganisms to produce glomalin, microorganisms that thrive only in soil conditions mimicking those found in nature—no synthetic chemicals, no plowing, and an abundance of biodiversity.

What a radical message to an industry that uses the plow as its symbol! One might think that farmers are stubborn and are resistant to such a change, and some are, but these demonstrations are all Ray needs to convince many farmers. Seeing is believing. "Let the soils speak," he says in one YouTube video (with over twenty-one thousand views!).[19] Seeing is powerful. Farmers attending his workshops have cried real tears after observing what tillage does to the land. For "people in agriculture, that farm is their life. It's their blood and it's their identity—it's them. When you're going in there and you're changing their identity, their life, the way they've done things for all those years, it's a huge responsibility. . . . What this has done has completely transformed the people that have embraced it and understood it. Completely changed their lives."

Ray stressed the importance of *personal* knowing. It is one thing to hear a statistic about rates of soil erosion, but a very different thing to personally see Ray's demonstrations and ponder what it means to perpetually plow one's own fields. This is why Ray's message has resonated faster with farmers than university scientists and government agencies. Those outside of scientific institutions might imagine that scientists simply follow the data, changing their minds as soon as new experiments usher in new findings. We like to think of science progressing by one experiment building upon another, where the facts guide the scientific community. Sometimes this is the process, but often new ideas must exist as heresy first, for years being defended by a few individuals seen as radicals. Ray notes that "some of our best science has been people outside—outliers, some people outside the norm, which would be termed radical. Many of the farmers first turn to me and say, 'You know, Ray, when I first heard you, I thought you were crazy.'" Along the same lines, the great quantum physicist Max Planck once remarked that "science advances one funeral at a time," meaning the existing power-holders of the science community must be replaced before new ideas can be seriously considered. Before agricultural scientists adopt Ray's view of soil health—if they do—people like Ray may have to remain on the outsides shouting their heresies . . . being radicals.

Ray works for the Natural Resource Conservation Service (NRCS), which between 1935 and 1994 was called the Soil Conservation Service,[20] so you might think it eagerly joined Ray's efforts to restore soil health. It has, but it took a while. At first it took a lot of "kicking and screaming," as government agencies are not designed to evolve quickly. People at the NRCS eventually did listen. When they did, they liked what they heard. Ray says he is now very proud of the NRCS, as it has created a soil health division and invested millions in educational programming, sending Ray around the world to give talks.

What finally convinced NRCS to begin backing Ray's educational programs? It was farmers. Ray learned that you first have to take the information to the farmers and convince them by making it personal knowledge. He argued that "we got to take it to the people, to the foodies, to the general public, to the farmers themselves. They will change the government, and they will change the farm programs, because the farm programs do not help us."

As the farmers adopted the new system of farming without the plow and increased their plant diversity, they started forming associations, like the Missouri Bootheel Soil Health Alliance. The farmers started doing their own experiments on their farms and shared their findings with each other. Ray focused on building relationships, "from the farmer to the microbe, to the insects, to the plants, to their fellow human being. Even in some cases, taking in the person's understanding to the relationship with the Creator himself. . . . We're teaching people. What is your relationship to that soil, to those organisms, to everything around there? Everything you do impacts something. Everything is connected." Only then did the NRCS see the real value of Ray's program, and, to that agency's credit, now sees it as a tremendous public investment to help secure the ability of future Americans to feed themselves.

Personal knowing also involves understanding *why* something is important. Ray is an effective educator, and one of his inspirations was a TED talk by Simon Sinek called "How Great Leaders Inspire Action." This talk argues that to influence others, you not only need to know what needs to be done and how it should be done, but why. That "why" must be compelling and sincere and must tug at our heartstrings, beckoning our deepest values.

For Ray, the "why" of protecting the land stems from his Christianity and the Judeo-Christian Scriptures. In particular he cited a sermon titled "Lord of the Earth" by Timothy Keller.[21] The sermon begins with Genesis 9—the ending of the Noah's Ark story. God has promised not to create such a flood again and commands Noah to "be fruitful and multiply and fill the earth." Then in verse 10 God says, "I will remember my covenant that is between me and you and every living creature of the flesh."[22] Here God is demonstrating his concern not just for humans, but for the earth's ecosystem, Keller asserts. Going further, in an interpretation rarely heard elsewhere, Keller suggests that this covenant is made not just to protect humans from their sins, but to also protect the earth from the sins of humans. Using today's knowledge, God is telling humans that he loves his ecosystem and that humans are to be its dutiful stewards.

Mainstream Christianity has not made a bold move toward environmentalism, but there are many others who have used religion as a motivator for green living. Many Quakers adhere to a set of "testimonies" that include integrity, simplicity, equality, community, peace, and *care for the earth*. More recently, echoing Keller's sermon, Pope Francis has argued that exploiting the earth is a human sin.[23] The personal knowing Ray described can be more than just personal experience with the soil, but also a personal experience of the soul.

The argument that agriculture should mimic nature has led to a new science, but also a new social movement, called agroecology. Defined loosely as the science of ecology applied to the design, development, and management of agriculture, it is biomimicry in application. Though the term "agroecology" was first used in the 1920s, it is only now becoming a common term in the United States.[24] It is an idea often reflected in our interviews with others. Karissa Lewis once grew marijuana in a friend's yard, initially as a monoculture, meaning marijuana was the only plant she raised. Soon she encountered pest problems and was advised to increase the variety of plants in her plots. The first plant she brought in was a tomato, and as time went by, she added more plant diversity, until she eventually had more than a plot of marijuana—she had a garden, and that is what got her interested in agriculture and food. She quipped, "A lot of folks call it [marijuana] the gateway drug. I call it the gateway plant." A natural ecosystem always contains diverse life-forms, and Karissa needed to mimic this diversity to manage her pests.

When Hannah Dankbar, Rivka Fidel, and other Iowa State University graduate students opposed the banana genetically modified to produce vitamin A, they argued that an agricultural system that provides insufficient amounts of vitamin A lacks diversity. If diversity is the problem, then diversity is the solution—not genetic engineering. For instance, amaranth leaves provide high amounts of vitamin A, are easy to grow, and are as delicious as spinach. If your children are suffering vitamin C deficiency, what would you rather do, give them vitamin C pills or have them adopt a more diverse diet?

When the Dancing Rabbit Ecovillage first began, it purchased land on steep slopes that had been plowed extensively over the years, resulting in erosion and degradation of the soil ecosystem. The solution used by Dan Durica and others was to create gardens with minimal disturbance of the soil, use cover crops (crops planted by the farmer to enhance the soil but never harvested) to increase plant biodiversity, and introduce livestock. It is increasingly recognized that soils can be revitalized by grazing cattle, sheep, goats, and other livestock. After all, the virgin American prairie did not just contain millions of soil microorganisms and hundreds of plant species, but bison as well.

One of the most well-respected agricultural economists once remarked, "It is not an exaggeration to say that all of agriculture is intrinsically a struggle against nature."[25] There is no denying some truth to this. The earth will naturally produce some food for us, as our ancestral hunters and gatherers would have attested, but not enough to feed large populations. To do this we must dam rivers, domesticate plants and animals, and clear forests. Yes, we must fight nature sometimes, but we must pick our fights wisely. Nature is a powerful foe, if you make her a foe—so why not make her a friend? Why not work *with* nature whenever you can? That was Ray's point.

And the point is radical. His job is formidable because he is battling decades of entrenched thinking. Universities and the mainstream scientific community rely too much on engineering solutions rather than better systems that would prevent those problems in the first place, Ray asserted, and so in the last ten years he has become skeptical of most everything that comes from the mainstream scientific community. Young people call him frequently to ask where they should go to graduate school, and he urges them not to get an agronomy degree, but to get a degree in agroecology.

At a meeting of over two thousand people affiliated with organic farming Ray asked his audience for a show of hands if they were taught by a mentor, professor, a teacher—anyone—how to farm by mimicking nature. Fewer than 1 percent raised their hand. That is why Ray's approach to soil health is radical. Farmers have to be convinced by people personally committed to the cause—people like Ray. Farmers benefit from better land, but many industries would lose money, as improved soil health reduces the need for pesticides and fertilizers. In fact, the large agricultural corporations don't want Ray's message to be told. At the bottom of Ray's emails is a quote from Upton Sinclair stating, "It is difficult to get a man to understand something, when his salary depends on his not understanding it."[26] Agricultural scientists spend much of their research effort evaluating various pesticides, fertilizers, and new crop genetics. A reduced need for these inputs means a reduced need for the scientists' services as well. No company, and few scientists, would benefit monetarily from spreading the gospel of soil health, so the incentive must come from a personal calling, something Ray has in spades.

Jimmy Kinder Bets the Farm

Most farmers have not adopted Ray's philosophy of soil health, but many are going in his direction. Of all the US cropland planted to the eight major crops (88 million acres), about one-third uses a no-till system where the ground is never or rarely plowed.[27] One lesson from Ray Archuletta is that movements in agriculture often need radical farmers to lead the way, after which the universities and government organizations follow. This is the case for no-till agriculture, which first became a feasible agriculture practice on the hilly fields of Kentucky by a farmer named Harry Young.[28] Young pioneered the no-till system in the 1970s. It is surprising, then, that when Jimmy Kinder sought to bring no-till to Oklahoma twenty years later, he experienced considerable resistance from both other farmers and experts.

One of the proudest days in Jimmy Kinder's life was when he walked out into the middle of one of his fields, dug into the earth, and discovered an earthworm. He is the fourth generation in his family to farm that field, and decades of tillage had reduced the carbon content of his soils to a very low 1 percent. With that little carbon, there wasn't much organic material for worms to eat, which meant that the populations of other species in the soil had dwindled as well. Now that the earthworms were back, it meant his soils were returning to life. He knew that if this continued, he could pass the farm onto the next generation of his family in better shape than he received it. This was an achievement that other Oklahoma farmers, as well as agricultural scientists at Oklahoma State University, said couldn't be done.

The no-till system originally developed in Kentucky requires herbicides instead of tillage to control weeds. Instead of burying weeds by turning the soil, you kill them with synthetic chemicals. Before planting, fields no longer look like smooth sheets of bare soil, but messy fields of residues from dead plants (figure 2.2). New planters had to be developed that could plant seeds amid the plant residues. Herbicides control weeds, but using this no-till strategy means that fungal diseases remain on the fields in the plant residues. If a farmer raises the same crop every year, the plant residues increase the chance of fungal infections, decreasing yields and increasing the need for expensive fungicides. Fortunately for Kentucky, crop rotations were a typical practice, where one crop is raised one year but then a different crop is raised the next year. Because the same fungal infection rarely impacts different crops, rotation helps protect the farmer against disease in the no-till system.

Oklahoma raises continuous wheat, which is one reason why university scientists said no-till wouldn't work, and why their experiments attempting it failed. Moreover, no-till was a practice hardly anybody used in combination with the livestock-crop system popular in Oklahoma. (It

FIGURE 2.2 Heavily plowed field (left) and farmer planting in a no-till system (right)

Images courtesy of Oklahoma State University.

is a common practice in Oklahoma to plant seed in September and graze cattle on the growing wheat until March. The cattle are then removed from the field and the wheat is allowed to grow and form kernels, which are then harvested and made into flour.) Although there were only about five other people employing no-till methods in the entire state, none of them also raised cattle, so Jimmy was attempting something that had not been done—something everyone said was impossible.

Yet Jimmy had three things going for him. First, he conducted small-scale experiments on his farm, doing his own research. Second, though every sane person fears failure, he did not allow that fear to stop him from trying to improve. Third, he recognized that implementing no-till would require a change in his whole system of farming. It wasn't just a matter of replacing the plow with chemicals, but changing what he planted as well.

About the time he convinced himself that no-till might work, his farm machinery was wearing out and in need of replacement. Most of his equipment was designed for tilling, and it was too expensive to buy both new till and no-till machinery. It was either pull the trigger on no-till or stick with traditional farming.

If his plan didn't work, he could have lost the farm. Jimmy is bold but not arrogant, and he knew there was a chance his gamble could fail. This wasn't just a personal bet, as he farmed alongside his father and brother, so he needed their blessing. As he waited to see if the crops he planted under his new no-till system would grow, he kept fueled tractors hitched to plows, just in case he had to plow the fields to salvage the crop year. Those crops grew, though, and those plows never moved. "We were literally betting the family farm. . . . Today, I don't even own a plow."

Jimmy's foray into no-till agriculture made him unpopular with the farming community. He was socially ostracized by his fellow farmers. They thought he was crazy and foolish. At one point someone very close to Jimmy approached him, telling him that everyone else was talking about him and saying what a silly idea he was pursuing. No-till was referred to disparagingly as "trash farming." The plant residues remaining on the field were not considered good for the soil, insinuating that someone who didn't take the time to plow and till the fields was not being a diligent farmer.

Some farmers were openly hostile, with one even stepping closely to Jimmy (invading his personal space), asserting that no-till is cheating and also not biblical. Not biblical? The Bible is replete with references to plowing. Just as Ray Archuletta used the Bible to advocate for soil conservation, others were using it to justify plowing. Even though no-till strategies were being used in other regions of the United States, to Oklahomans, Jimmy was being too radical, and many resented him for it.

No-till in an Oklahoma crop and cattle system is not only possible, but as Jimmy proved, profitable. Jimmy's crop yields are about the same as when he used the plow, but his costs are lower. The money saved from not having to plow the fields more than compensates for the extra money he spends on herbicides.

Word got around that Jimmy had bet the farm and beat the house, and the invitations to speak started arriving. Other producers wanted to know how his system worked, and Jimmy didn't mind sharing his story. He worried that there weren't any scientific studies to support his efforts. Since the state had an agricultural college devoted to researching new farming methods, shouldn't they be the ones making the discoveries and disseminating the knowledge? When he attended meetings with agricultural scientists in the audience, he made this point, but as in the case with Ray Archuletta, the university just wasn't interested. Remember how science progresses: new blood replacing the old.

At the same time Jimmy was proving the feasibility of no-till in Oklahoma, a new crop of agronomists arrived at the university. Some of them came from other regions where no-till was in use. They were young and they had seen it work, so they were not opposed to studying the system on Oklahoma fields. One of these new arrivals (Jeffrey Edwards, the department's current head) saw how Jimmy had modified one of his fertilizer spreaders to cover more evenly and was impressed by his ingenuity. If anyone could figure out how to farm no-till in Oklahoma, it might be this guy, Dr. Edwards thought. New blood with more receptive minds consulted with Jimmy and started experiments to confirm whether his no-till system could work—and found that it did. Now, when farmers hear Jimmy's story of farming Oklahoma soil without the plow, they don't have to just take his word for it: the science backs it up. Today the Department of Plant and Soil Sciences is a leader in no-till research and sponsors an annual no-till conference. If you look at the list of presenters at the 2014 conference, you will recognize two of the names: Ray Archuletta and Jimmy Kinder!

Witness just how large of an effect Jimmy and the few other Oklahoma no-till innovators have had on preserving soil health. Twenty years ago, almost no Oklahoma farmer used no-till methods. Today around two-thirds do.[29] A field managed under a no-till system will experience around

90 percent less soil erosion than if it were tilled,[30] and over four million acres of land in Oklahoma are used in crop production. The rising popularity of replacing the plow with herbicides can then be said to have virtually halted soil erosion on more than a million acres in Oklahoma, and radical farmers like Jimmy Kinder deserve much of the credit. Not only was soil preserved on the field, but soil health was enhanced as well, all while allowing Jimmy to increase his farm's financial performance.

Is Jimmy's farm environmentally friendly if he manages weeds with herbicides instead of machinery? It depends on how you view the regulations. He can only apply herbicides that are approved by three regulatory agencies, and only in the manner they dictate. The chemicals cannot be applied without a license, and the regulations are designed so that, although some of the residues can be detected in food, they are at far, far lower levels than would cause any harm. For example, per milligram of active ingredient, the herbicide glyphosate that Jimmy applies is less harmful than caffeine. Just as you consume too little caffeine for it to harm you, regulators help Jimmy ensure his herbicide applications cause no harm either. So for those who believe chemical regulations are effective, the Kinder Farm is environmentally friendly.

Of course, not everyone has such confidence in regulations, and the synthetic input issue is bigger than just its direct effect on human health. Just as some people prefer not to drink caffeine, some prefer that food be produced without chemical inputs—but can you no-till farm without chemicals? It isn't easy, but Jeff Moyer of the Rodale Institute is proving that you can.

Jeff Moyer: No-Till without Herbicides

No-till agriculture has revolutionized how we produce food. No longer do we have to accept the plow as a necessary evil. The trade-off, though, is that it requires more herbicides, and while some believe that current regulations prevent us from harm, others believe that any amount of synthetic input use is dangerous. Wouldn't it be nice, then, if we could spare the plow and the herbicide at the same time?

The future of organic agriculture might depend on whether such a system is developed. Jeff Moyer researches organic agriculture at the Rodale Institute, and he first understood the necessity of such a system in the 1980s while speaking to a group of Maryland farmers. His presentation was about the benefits of organic farming and how conventional farmers can make the transition. At the end of his talk one of the farmers remarked that organic farmers plow too much, and that the Natural Resource Conservation Service told him that that if they plowed all their acres every year, there would be excessive erosion. The farmers resisted going organic because it was seen as bad for the environment—the opposite of organic agriculture's goals. The farmers were only going to consider organic if it could be done without the plow, so Jeff began the steps to make that possible.

To understand Jeff's sense of urgency we must understand the research philosophy of the Rodale Institute. It was founded in 1947 by Jerome Rodale, an inventor and businessman with an adventurous personality and an eager willingness to march to a different drum. At a time when the world saw chemical fertilizers and synthetic pesticides as the world's answer to hunger, Rodale was a lone voice expressing skepticism. Fertilizers and pesticides were akin to poisons, in his view, so Rodale didn't understand how applying poisons to the soil could result in healthy food. It was around 1942 that he is said to have written on a blackboard, "Healthy soil equals healthy food equals healthy people," and he bought a small farm where he began research on how to build healthy soils. The magazine known today as *Rodale's Organic Life* was first penned by J. I. Rodale in 1942, though it has changed names over time.

If the reader is surprised that organic agriculture existed in the 1940s, we remind them that before the twentieth century, organic was the norm. Before chemical fertilizers a field could only remain fertile through methods like applying manure and compost or planting cover crops (especially legumes). Prior to the development of synthetic pesticides, farmers managed weeds by plowing and tilling, and insects and disease by planting a diversity of crops. Chemical agriculture was implemented when synthetic pesticides began being produced in large factories and nitrogen fertilizer was extracted from the atmosphere using sophisticated chemistry. Farmers could then specialize in a few crops and produce great amounts of food from the field every year. Chemical additions gave birth to monocultures, where a field is planted in only one crop every year. Food prices at the store fell, but a few food radicals like Jerome Rodale feared we paid an ever higher price in the form of less healthy food and by compromising our ability to feed future generations.

When Jerome's son Bob took over the Rodale Institute in 1971, he charged the organization with not just pointing out problems in conventional agriculture but finding solutions. If organic methods are better than industrial agriculture, they would need to be proven so using legitimate scientific experiments. Thus began a long-term project comparing organic and conventional farming methods side by side, a project Rodale says demonstrates organic agriculture's ability to produce as much food as its conventional counterpart. "From a rural sociology aspect, from a human health aspect, from a soil health aspect, from an economic aspect, from an engineering aspect—no matter how we look at organic agriculture, it makes sense," Jeff remarks. If you hear people affirming the ability of organic farming to feed the world, they are likely referring to research conducted at the Rodale Institute.

To say that organic agriculture can feed the world is quite a claim, but the Rodale Institute is ambitious. Rodale is not merely trying to demonstrate how to garden organically. Rodale wants to change how the majority of cropland in the United States is farmed. Since most US acres are in corn and soybeans, those are the institute's crops of focus. When no-till crop production started gaining in popularity, people at Rodale knew that a no-till, organic system had to be developed if organic agriculture was going to be touted as a valid system for feeding the world.

Jeff Moyer has worked at the Rodale Institute since the 1970s, and developing a no-till organic system became one of his obsessions. One day he watched the gardeners at the institute work, and he contemplated how easy it was to achieve organic no-till on a small plot. Many gardeners control their weeds not by tilling the ground or applying herbicides, but by applying mulch. Spread a layer of straw around a tomato plant and that will usually keep weeds from sprouting. This was obviously unfeasible on a three-hundred-acre field of corn. Buying so much straw would be expensive, and applying it equally so.

Then it struck him: why would farmers need to buy straw? Being an organic enterprise, Rodale already used cover crops, crops that are planted and allowed to grow between the harvest of one crop and the planting of another. The key distinction between a cover crop and a production crop is that a cover crop is not harvested. It remains on the field to keep the soil from eroding, to increase plant diversity, and to help revitalize the soil's fertility. As an example, wheat may be harvested in June, but before corn is planted in May the field may be planted in a "cocktail" of cover crops including vetch, clover, legumes, turnips, and the like.

The selected cover crops "are quick germinating, fast growing cover crops that cover the ground with something green and growing. So it's my way of apologizing to the soil for that tillage operation. Sorry guys,"

Jeff says to the soil, "it's something I had to do in the rotation to break the cycle. Tillage for me is like hitting the reset button on the computer."

Why, Jeff wondered, couldn't farmers simply mow the cover crop when it is thick and tall, immediately before planting the next production crop? That would create a layer of mulch to control weeds. The problem was that mowing detaches the cover crop from the soil, allowing the wind to blow it around, creating bare spots in some parts of the field and mounds of mulch in other parts. Moreover, planters could not plant seeds well in those larger mounds of mulch. So mowing wouldn't work, but the Rodale Institute found a system that did—and it was discovered by accident.

On one research plot a cover crop of vetch was planted on the edges of the field. These edges were not used to produce food, but to capture any soil erosion from the middle of the field. When the field was worked with machinery, the tractors would repeatedly drive over this vetch, so many times that the vetch flattened and died. Jeff noticed, and he decided when the field was again planted to also plant in those areas of dead vetch. Not only did corn germinate and reach for the sky, but the mat of mulch created by the vetch prevented weed growth. Eureka!

That wasn't the final answer, though, as there had to be a better way of killing the vetch than running a tractor across the field over and over. Rodale researchers realized they had to invent a new type of farm implement—something like a huge roller mounted to a tractor. But that alone wouldn't do, because if the stems are not crimped, the cover crop will eventually resume its erect posture. A steamroller, like those used in paving roads, is heavy enough to kill the plant but would be slow and would compress the soil. You needed a roller that was not too heavy, not too light, modified to crimp—not cut—the stem of the cover crop just above the ground and lay it flat. No such implement existed, so the Rodale Institute had to invent it.

What resulted was the invention of the roller-crimper, which Jeff Moyer designed with John Brubaker. It is a large roller but with V-shaped ridges and used with rye instead of vetch as the cover crop. The ridges make contact with the rye stem just inches above the ground. As the roller moves forward, these ridges approach the ground and compress the plant stem in the process—just enough to kill the plant and keep it from returning erect, but not enough to sever the stem. The multiple ridges crimp each plant stem about every seven inches. At Rodale the workers place this roller-crimper on the front of the tractor and pull a modified no-till planter behind the tractor, as shown in figure 2.3. Just seconds after the cover crop

FIGURE 2.3 Jeff Moyer, crimping cover crop and planting new crop
Image courtesy of the Rodale Institute

is crimped, becoming mulch, the planter drill parts the mulch just enough to plant a seed.

Think about what this invention accomplishes. It allows a farmer to produce food without tilling the earth and without applying herbicides. Only recently, with the advent of the roller-crimper, was this even imaginable. The organic no-till system does pose some challenges. For instance, it can only be used when there is a long period between the harvesting of one crop and the planting of another, allowing the cover crop of rye to grow. It cannot be used in continuous wheat farming because wheat fields are harvested and planted again a few months later, and that doesn't give the cover crop enough time to grow. Despite these and other difficulties, farmers now have a unique option that ten years ago was almost inconceivable.

The option is becoming increasingly profitable, and universities and even conventional farmers are taking notice. There is an extension agent (someone at a university who helps educate the public, and farmers in particular) in North Carolina who tells his farmers that the only way to plant organic soybeans in the Carolinas is to use the roller-crimper. Dr. Erin Silva of the University of Wisconsin has conducted independent experiments with the organic no-till system, confirming that it works, so that farmers do not have to rely on the word of the institute that invented it. Moyers notes, "We have as many people in the conventional world using the roller-crimper as we do organic people," attesting to the value of Rodale Institute's research.

What was the motivation behind development of the organic, no-till system? Jeff Moyer himself and Rodale Institute, which have a dedication to developing and promoting organic farming, were crucial. Jeff was a young man in the 1970s, a time when there was a back-to-the-land movement among many of the young and an interest in both alternative ideas and natural living. All of this appealed to him, including the concept of organic food, so early in his life he accepted a job at the Rodale Institute, and he has been there ever since. Growing up on a small farm gave him the agricultural background he needed to farm, and the zeitgeist of the 1960s and 1970s made him dissatisfied with the traditional way of doing things and a willingness to consider new paths. Importantly for Moyer came the realization that "we can't keep dumping millions and millions of pesticides into our food system and not expect it to have some negative result. Everything has side effects, unintended consequences. . . . What we do in Oklahoma, and what we do in Iowa, and what we do in California impacts children in Boston. It's in the food."

Moyer and the Rodale Institute have a powerful ally. It isn't university scientists or government organizations. Moyer says it's consumers and their willingness to pay the premiums necessary for farmers to produce organic food. When he was young, organic food was available only in health food stores. Because a government organic standard didn't exist at the time, people didn't really know what the organic label meant. Today there are strict, enforceable standards for anyone wanting to sell organic food, and organic is growing in popularity. Today about 4 percent of all food sales are for organic food,[31] and organic food is sold in most grocery stores.

The idea that healthy soils equal healthy food is gaining credence among the American public and is discussed in unexpected settings. Diamond Dallas Page is a professional wrestler (the fake kind of wrestling) and has an enormous following. In discussing his development of DDP Yoga, designed for athletes with high-impact injuries, he remarked, "Most of the soil in the fields is so depleted of nutrients from the onslaught of pesticides, it's robbed the nutrition from our produce."[32] Joe Rogan, former *The Man Show* host, sports announcer for Ultimate Fighting, and current host of one of the most popular podcasts in existence, devoted one recent episode to food. Rogan points out that food raised from fields that use ma-nure and compost as fertilizer (as opposed to chemical fertilizers) will pro-duce healthier foods.[33] Ideas about chemical use do not exist just among stereotypical foodies, but also among those who body-slam opponents and provide commentary for bare-knuckle fistfights. Consumers like them are creating the demand, and Jeff is trying to make sure there will be a supply.

A consumer buying organic food is doing something rather radical, Jeff asserted to us. The conventional wisdom is that food is food and that food is safe. That is the position of most government agencies and ag-ricultural scientists. Yet Jeff argued that "if we think about the soil as a system of living, biological organisms and we feed those organisms, those organisms feed us. It's kind of exciting. And is it radical? I think it is. People are beginning to look at that radicalism and say, 'You know there's something there that makes sense. We can't ignore it.'" The organic move-ment certainly did not stem from experts exclaiming a need for safer food. It emerged, and continues to gain in popularity, thanks to radical farmers who question the conventional wisdom, and radical consumers willing to do the same.

Amory Starr Gives a Talk

The plow doesn't always harm the soil. It depends on how you use it. Plowing and tilling can take place even while the soil improves, so long as you take care to mimic nature. When a plant has grown and died, it becomes food for the soil, which then creates new plants. To mimic na-ture, then, one must return organic matter to the field after the crop has been harvested. Fergal Anderson is an Irish organic farmer who tills his fields frequently, but he always grows a cover crop to till into the soil, so that he is not just piercing the ground but replenishing its organic matter. Once the ground is tilled, it is quickly covered, perhaps by planting a new crop or by covering it with straw or seaweed. Fergal has no need for insecticides, for he plants multiple crops in the same field and plants var-ious types of flowers to attract beneficial predators, as shown in figure 2.4.

On the Rodale Institute farms Jeff Moyer has shown that tillage doesn't necessarily degrade the soil if you add organic matter. In fact, what this book called his organic no-till system actually does involve some tillage about every five years. Yet before he tills he adds compost to the field so that when he tills, he is adding organic matter. Fergal does the same. Even though their fields involve periodic tillage, the carbon content of their soil

FIGURE 2.4 Fergal Anderson's Leaf and Root farm
Image courtesy of Fergal Anderson

has risen from about 1 percent to about 3 percent (6 percent is about as high as one finds in virgin prairie).

The reason this type of agriculture is radical is that most farms return only a little of what they harvest. Of the many elements and organic matter harvested in crops, most farmers return only nitrogen, phosphorus, and potassium. What about other elements, like calcium? They are mostly being mined from the soil. What about organic matter? It is disappearing from tilled fields, and that is why we are losing so much of that thin layer of the earth's crust that feeds us. We are still producing more food than ever, and at a cheaper price, but the loss of soil and its loss of organic matter must concern us. It is possible that we will come to regret our current system of producing monocultures under industrial agriculture.

That is what Amory Starr tried to explain to a student group called the Collegiate Farm Bureau at Colorado State University (CSU) in 2002, and it wasn't received well. The students screamed at her.

Starr covered organic agriculture in her class, and though CSU is an agricultural college, hers was the only class to do so at that time. Organic was not considered a serious agricultural system by those who taught crop science and other traditional agricultural subjects. The students were more receptive than the professors, though, so many would take a class under Amory—and Amory was not an agricultural scientist, but a sociologist. When a small group of students created an organic educational program and started their own organic garden, there was no one in the agricultural college who knew enough about organic agriculture and wanted to help them, so the students largely had to teach themselves. When it came to choosing a faculty adviser, this group of agricultural students chose Dr. Amory Starr. Again, a sociologist.

As she was increasingly recognized as a faculty member with an alternative perspective on agriculture, a student group called the Collegiate Farm Bureau, consisting largely of students from the CSU agricultural college, invited her to present her views. Amory shared her perspectives, and the students did not like it. They not only disagreed, but were hostile and yelled at her.

If you want to know what Amory said, you don't have to speculate. She writes all of her speeches in advance, and this one is posted on her website. It is an impressive speech, demonstrating expertise in a variety of topics from economics to industrial agriculture to small-scale organic farming in developing countries. The speech was titled "Can Industrial Agriculture Feed the World?" and Amory's answer was no. Her reasons were many, and they will be explored throughout this book, but for now consider her view on the farming technologies. Taking on the idea that the developing world could produce more food by using the same industrial agricultural methods employed in the United States, she discussed the benefits of local plant varieties, raising multiple crops instead of monocultures, relying on plant diversity to control pests and fertilize the soil, and cover crops to protect the soils.

In essence, she was promoting biomimicry—making the same arguments as Ray Archuletta, but years earlier, making criticisms similar to those by famous authors like Michael Pollan, but years earlier, providing the language that would appear years later in countless documentaries. So while some might not consider Amory a food radical now, she certainly was then!

In all likelihood the students were unprepared for Amory's criticisms for two reasons. One, this was 2002, before food became as controversial as it is today. Two, most agricultural students are not exposed to criticisms like these and are instead taught that the technologies Amory rejected are necessary to feed the world.

Why would the students have such an unfriendly reaction to Amory's remarks? One needs to understand the culture of agricultural colleges to understand this. Agricultural colleges began over a century ago to help educate farmers about new technologies, and they continue to conduct research and educational programs regarding pesticides, chemical fertilizers, machinery, and the like. They were specifically designed to transition farmers away from organic agriculture (which at the time was simply agriculture) to industrial agriculture. Classes are designed to prepare students to work in industrial agriculture, whether it be the farmer or the pesticide salesperson. So if industrial agriculture is the wrong way to feed society, the methods of agricultural colleges are called into question. The students enrolled in these colleges tend to align themselves with industrial agriculture, so much so that it becomes a part of their identity. They develop their own culture, their own truths and myths, and, as in every culture, they resent threats to their identity. It becomes a larger issue than simply which agricultural system is best—it becomes "us" versus "them."

In the last few decades an alternative agricultural culture has emerged, one that promotes biomimicry and organic methods instead of industrial techniques. Those championing alternative agriculture differ not just in their views on food, but in many other regards. For example, this new agricultural culture tends to be politically liberal, while the audience at Amory's speech was probably politically conservative. Those who are part of the new culture like getting their hands dirty in the garden, whereas the old culture prefers to stay above the ground, rolling along in large tractors. The new culture enjoys direct transactions with consumer families, while the old culture is about mass production for sale to middlemen. The new culture is more likely to see similarities between the minds of livestock and the minds of pets. The new culture is more urban and eats a more diverse set of foods (think quinoa). Radical ideas in agriculture are not just controversial because they are new, but because they involve culture wars as well.

Katie Michels Is Pro-agroecology, Not Antitechnology

Because they want to return to older, organic practices of producing food, advocates who are part of this alternative culture are sometimes depicted as being antitechnology. A closer look shows this may not be the case. Jeff Moyer doesn't oppose new technologies, he creates new technologies. Katie Michels lived in an intentional community called the Weybridge House at Middlebury College that ate only local, organic food.

An 'intentional community' is a group of residents who design their living area and social customs from the beginning to achieve certain goals. Most intentional communities in the current age are specifically designed to be environmentally friendly. This wasn't because she was against GMOs but because she was "excited about opportunities to just slow down, and connect with local farmers and good food, and with other house residents who shared those values." Katie can't be against GMOs—she is diabetic and requires the insulin produced by genetically modified bacteria! She noted, "I wouldn't say that I so much eat an anti-GMO diet as I eat a pro-community and regenerative, agriculture-based diet."

Amory's speech would probably have been given a standing ovation had it been delivered to Katie Michels's intentional community. Sometimes people like Katie are criticized for being detached from the farm and unaware of how food is produced. This too would be incorrect. Many agricultural students know how to artificially inseminate a cow and operate a $100,000 combine, yet don't know when a radish is ready to harvest or how to keep spinach alive during a Vermont winter. Katie knows, as she was once the comanager at Middlebury's organic farm.

Katie is not alone. There are many student-run organic farms at US universities, and though some are at agricultural colleges like Iowa State, most are at smaller colleges that do not offer traditional agricultural science degrees, yet offer degrees regarding food studies or something akin to agroecology. An example is Warren Wilson College in North Carolina, which maintains a working farm, and though it does not offer agronomy, crop science, or animal science degrees that teach industrial agriculture, it does offer degrees in sustainable agriculture. Middlebury College does not offer agricultural degrees but does offer a food studies major. It turns out that developing this major was a student-led initiative. The organic farm where Katie grew food for her community was also started by students, not the faculty. The organic farm at CSU that Amory advised was also student driven, and not only did the university fail to support it, but once it was established, the university repeatedly tried to get rid of it.

Ray Archuletta taught us that science progresses when new blood replaces the old, and Jimmie Kinder taught us that one must sometimes be seen as a heretic to create change. Katie provided us with a similar lesson by showing us that students are transforming our system of higher education. They see little leadership in their faculty, except for rare individuals like Amory Starr, so they assume leadership themselves.

Young food radicals of today are not just protesting industrial agriculture, they are making deliberate efforts to opt out of it. You could say their love for agroecology is even stronger than their dislike of industrial agriculture. Katie was once in charge of acquiring food for Weybridge House, and this responsibility entailed far more than just buying organic. Residents tried to limit themselves to food raised within one hundred miles, so that they could meet the farmers and verify that they used sustainable practices. One summer Katie was the preservation intern, which meant that she spent the summer canning and freezing foods purchased for consumption during the rest of the year. Residents did this out of a sincere love for good and ethical food, as it did require sacrifices. Though half of the house ate meat, the community served vegetarian meals because local meat was expensive and residents preferred to spend money on foods like local, organic dairy. Dairy was especially prized not just for its nutrition and taste, but because raising animals on pasture works well in Vermont's rolling landscape and doesn't require heavy tillage. Katie and her intentional community wanted to make ethical choices and be in harmony with their environment: "I feel powerless when it comes to addressing some of our larger ecological and social challenges. With food I have more autonomy to pick something positive that I'm passionate about and excited about. For me that means supporting local, organic farmers, folks who are practicing diversified agriculture and taking good care of the land."

Our Bigger Friends with Legs

Bob Benner raised a cow with the intent of eventually eating her. The cow's name was Minnie. It lived on Bob's small farm along with various other livestock. Although the animals there are raised for food, Bob runs the farm like a petting zoo, allowing visitors to pet the animals and hosting birthday parties. It made sense, while Minnie was small and cute, to let it be a source of delight for visitors. Bob planned to eat it when it was older with larger horns. This seemed perfectly natural to Bob and his family, as they had no trouble thinking of the animal as a pet one year but food the next.

Kimberly Sherriton had seen Minnie during a visit, and she did not feel the same. Others agreed with Kimberly, and they started a petition at change.org asking Bob not to slaughter Minnie but to send her to an animal sanctuary. They protested outside his farm with signs that said, "Let Minnie Go!" and "Would you eat your cat or dog?"

This story hit the news and made the rounds on social media, particularly Facebook. Some people mocked the protestors, especially one poster who suggested that they spare Minnie and purchase beef from the grocery store instead. Others were sympathetic, believing that once the farm treated Minnie like a pet, she should continue to be treated as such.

The debate over the destiny of Minnie the Cow mimics the debate over livestock in general. On the one hand, livestock are sentient and intelligent, like our pets. On the other hand, we like the way they taste. How do we reconcile these two facts? Most of us don't bother to reconcile them, and those who do often come to different conclusions.

Food is socially and culturally constructed, particularly so when it comes to the use of animals as meat. Jainists practice strict nonviolence and eat only foods that kill no living thing.[34] Some Native American nations believed hunting was moral because the animal had tacitly consented to be killed.[35] A number of accused heretics during the Middle Ages would profess to eat meat to prove that they abided by the teachings of the Catholic Church, while other Catholics would abstain from meat to display piety.[36] The positions are diverse and contradictions are many across time and place.

If an animal is to be eaten, how should it be treated? Again we find diverse beliefs. Today we raise chickens in crowded, dark houses. So did the ancient Romans.[37] Some women in India breastfeed animals, while wealthy Americans run animal sanctuaries for cattle, pigs, and chickens. Instances of both love and cruelty abound in the same society and for the same animal.

People in most of the world today eat meat, if they can afford it, and so must consider the treatment of animals. Many vegetarians, like the millions of Hindus in India, eat dairy products and eggs and thus must decide how animals that produce those products should be treated. We wish to introduce you to two individuals with contrasting views on this topic.

Cody Carlson Goes Undercover

History provides a long list of once-acceptable behaviors that today seem morally repugnant. This has to make us wonder what beliefs we hold today that our grandchildren will find immoral. The philosopher Patrick Grim has suggested one candidate: the way we treat farm animals. In reflecting on this question he remarks, "Our treatment of animals as food is clearly to our economic advantage, and we go to great lengths to remain ignorant of the process."[38] Indeed, in a survey of one thousand Oklahomans, about one-third admitted that they do not want to know how farm animals are raised. While many of them desire ignorance because they trust the farmer and have more important things to worry about, they say, about one-third of that one-third said they were fearful they would feel guilty if they knew the truth of animal agriculture.[39]

It is the job of activists to confront ignorance, and in his midtwenties Cody Carlson decided he was going to dedicate his life to animal activism. This was not just a change in job or a new charitable activity to perform in his spare time. It required a complete life transformation. He broke up with a girlfriend he adored, quit a promising job, and left New York to make low wages in a difficult job—no one could know where he was or what he was doing. He was going undercover.

Cody became an undercover investigator for the animal protection group Mercy For Animals. Posing as an ordinary guy needing work, he would move close to a farm and apply for a job. Once hired, he would work for several months, all while wearing recording equipment so that he could document how animals were treated and raised. He recorded conditions on a dairy farm, a hog farm, and several egg farms. He recalled that "the full assault on all five senses is really something you just can't be prepared for. When you walk into the battery cage barn and you get hit with that thick ammonia air and you just hear all the . . . two hundred thousand birds flapping, and you see these animals shoulder to shoulder, farther than the eye can see because they just disappear into the haze." The videos show baby birds drowning in a bucket of filthy water, chickens sharing cages with the carcasses of dead birds, and workers throwing and kicking animals. The footage was made into several video exposés that animal rights groups promoted. Readers can watch a short video of his adventures and some of the footage he filmed at www.whatcodysaw.com.

Many people have trouble viewing his undercover footage because the scenes of animal suffering are so disturbing. They reveal three important pieces of information regarding our supply of meat, dairy, and eggs. One is that some of the problems have to do with the actions of a few people. Cody remarked to us that most people working on farms are good people trying to do the right thing, but some of his coworkers clearly had emotional issues that they took out on the animals. Certain employees would "come to work ranting about their personal frustrations and their family life. Very quickly, you start to see them take liberties with the animals: kicking them, torturing little baby pigs in front of the moms, and throwing them around. These were really disturbed people. But the really scary thing to me wasn't just that these people exist, but that they're tolerated in these operations." This "people problem" is more than just these few bad apples. In our interview with Cody he explained that even the kindest worker can't treat all the animals with care because there are just too many animals. Just keeping them fed, reproducing, and growing is exhausting for the few available workers. "When you're surrounded by thousands or even millions of animals, it quickly becomes easy for any one creature to lose her individuality. You get so used to whatever is around you that it becomes normal. It starts to seem normal to you very quickly." Workers get through the day by thinking of the animals as machines, not sentient, independent beings. The people problem thus has idiosyncratic, social, psychological, and systematic components.

The second lesson is that some of what viewers find disturbing is standard livestock production practice. Cody noted, "Everywhere I worked, my managers and coworkers would say, 'This is really cruel, I hate it. But this is how we're told to do it.'" If you take a livestock production class at an agricultural college, you are likely to go on a tour of modern hog production facilities, where sows (pregnant females) are kept in gestation crates (figure 2.5) on a hard concrete floor. These crates are just barely larger than the sow herself. Though she can make a step forward or backward, she doesn't have enough room to turn around. The crates are side by side. When the sow lies down, it is on a hard floor—her feet overflow into the gestation crate next to her. The livestock production class tout the benefits of gestation crates, such as protecting the sows from one another and allowing the farmer to place many animals under one roof. As agricultural students, few of them will consider the animals' welfare. Yet the average person, seeing these crates, would likely consider them akin to torture. So what is taught by universities as the gold standard in pork production is perceived by many people as cruel, and they may not know this is standard practice until they see one of Cody's videos.

The third lesson is the mental separation most people on the farms are willing to make between animals raised for food and animals raised as pets. Cody remembered talking with one of his coworkers at an egg farm, listening to her say what an animal lover she was, showing him pictures of her six rescue dogs. Yet as she talked, behind her stood stacks of cages filled so tightly with birds that none could turn around without bumping into another hen. Her dogs were like children, but those birds were like machines. As Cody said to us, "There's this huge disconnect between the

FIGURE 2.5 Sow in gestation crate
Image taken by authors

animals we care about and the animals we don't." Most of us are like this. We dote on our pets but show little interest in how our meat is produced— but when one of Cody's undercover investigations hits the news, we are forced to face this contradiction: "I think it's fundamental for people to know how their food is produced. Problems with factory farming developed behind closed doors and have not been properly vetted by society. Step one is to get this information out there so we can begin to have a conversation about it."

Working undercover on a farm to document conditions is definitely a radical act. Few people are willing to change their eating habits. Even fewer will give up a girlfriend and promising career to work to uncover animal welfare problems. What experiences can make someone engage in such a difficult and unusual life?

A reader who hasn't met Cody might think in stereotypes and be tempted to imagine him as a sensitive, emotional person who pleads with you to be more empathetic. While he certainly does possess an ability to empathize with any sentient creature, he is tough. Rather than just pulling on your heartstrings, he roots his arguments largely in logic.

One of Cody's first exposures to how farm animals are raised was at a punk rock show. The band Gather had a merchandise table on which they played the video *Meet Your Meat*, presenting images of cruelty on livestock farms and slaughterhouses taken by undercover investigators, narrated by Alec Baldwin and produced by PETA. Cody could not have imagined that this video, which got him thinking about how his food was raised, would eventually lead him to taping an undercover video of his own.

The band Gather was not unusual in its animal advocacy. Animal rights and veganism are consistent themes in punk music and culture,[40] and animal rights information was present in most punk rock shows by the mid-1990s.[41] A 2006 survey conducted by a punk rock publication found that out of a sample of 306 punk fans, 55 percent were vegetarian or vegan.—that percentage for all Americans is only 4 percent.[42] Amid the strong, loud guitars, rebellious hairstyles, and mosh pits, there might be more concern for pigs than at the average American's dinner table!

Researchers who study the link between punk culture and animal rights argue that the link is anarchism. Not the kind of anarchy where there is lawless violence in the streets, but where an individual has absolute freedom. No police officers to stop you from speeding. No government to force you into war. No restrictions against gay marriage. Absolute freedom to use birth control, absolute freedom from all exploitation by government. Scholars have described anarchism as a political system where all forms of domination are opposed, which includes dynamics of racism, sexism, anti-LGBTTQIA, ableism, ageism, sizeism, colonialism, and punitive justice. Adding speciesism (where one species dominates another) is a natural progression, so as the punk rock culture evolved to embrace anarchism, it embraced animal rights as well.[43] "Not everyone interested in punk music is vegetarian by any stretch, but it's definitely a big part of the scene. It fits into the general punk attitude of questioning authority and questioning what you were taught," said Cody. He doesn't identify as an anarchist, but his involvement with punk culture—and the video it led him to at that fateful concert—did have an impression on his future engagement with the food system.

Another influence in Cody's youth was the book *McLibel*, which describes how a pair of UK activists, Helen Steel and David Morris, were sued by McDonald's for distributing a pamphlet critical of the company. A section of this pamphlet had the title "In What Ways Are McDonald's

[Restaurants] Responsible for Torture and Murder?" They describe how chickens and pigs live without freedom of movement, and say that their deaths are "bloody and barbaric."[44] The book exposed Cody to problems in the food system, and it seemed to him that instead of fixing the problems, McDonald's was trying to hide them. Helen and David were members of the London Greenpeace movement, an organization with an environmental focus that sought to protest activities of large corporations like McDonald's.[45]

It took tenacity for Helen and David to stand up to a powerful corporation, especially in 1986 when animal rights and food activism were only nascent movements. Cody admired the sacrifice they were willing to make to improve the world. In further reading, he developed a respect for other activists, like Cesar Chavez and Dolores Huerta, organizing with the United Farm Workers, who spent their lives fighting for the rights of migrant farmworkers. The activists were people who insisted on defending those who could not defend themselves—always through nonviolent means.

The *McLibel* book was particularly pivotal because it began a dinner table conversation that led to Cody's early choice of vegetarianism and later veganism, options both unknown to him at the time. "I've eaten a vegan diet for over fifteen years now. I enjoy it, I feel good, and I know it's the most effective way to withdraw my support for animal cruelty. Veganism means a better food system for farmers, a healthier diet for consumers, and a better world for animals."

It would not be until after college that Cody became an activist. Between reading *McLibel* and graduating from college, he was reading books and attending conferences on animal rights. After graduation he worked for a corporate investigation agency where he performed background research on potential executives. It was a promising job, and he had no desire to leave it. But when he saw a Mercy For Animals investigation on the news, he felt compelled to do something. His firm performed pro bono work and Cody volunteered to donate some of this work time to Mercy For Animals. The group appreciated his offer, but told him what was really needed was undercover investigators.

After careful consideration, Cody agreed to leave his old life behind and became a farmworker with a hidden camera and secret agenda. We mentioned earlier that Cody is a tough guy. We say that because he was able to spend most of his time in a workplace that violated his sense of morality. Maintaining a stoic demeanor, he watched people harm animals that he cared for. On an egg farm he observed some hens who had prolapsed. Their uterus had been expelled from their bodies, getting tangled in the wire cages. Cody asked a coworker if they were supposed to provide veterinary care for the animals, at which point another employee accused him of being an undercover investigator. From that point on, he knew he could help animals only if no one was watching. The days were long, often beginning at 5:00 a.m., entailing strenuous physical labor inside foul-smelling livestock facilities. After a full day's work he went home and watched all the footage and added an entry to his log. This was his life for two years: working in an environment he considered cruel, so that he could better expose the cruelty.

Cody's defense of his activism was succinct and logical. "We're in an era where people understand that animals are very complex creatures who are not just sentient, but capable of feeling pain, have rich emotional lives, and have family and community structures. Their lives matter in a way very similar to the way that our lives matter. But at the same time that we've learned so much about how complex animals are, we've also developed new technologies that threaten animals on an unprecedented scale." Most of us would never treat our pets like farm animals are treated, yet farm animals are equally sentient, so why do we condone the current poor treatment of farm animals? For those who agree that pets and farm animals are equally sentient, the logic is hard to refute but easy to ignore—all you have to do is not think about it. That is where Cody comes in: he captured this footage to *make* you think about it. "Reasonable people may disagree about whether it's okay to eat meat," he said, "but almost no one would defend the way we treat these animals today."

Since leaving the world of undercover investigating Cody has completed law school and now works as a lawyer for Mercy For Animals. Animal advocacy is still his passion, but his efforts are in the open. Today he engages in policy-oriented approaches to improve conditions for animals on factory farms, including banning battery cages for egg-laying hens, gestation crates for mother pigs, and the like.

There is a decent chance readers have seen Cody on television before if they watch *The Daily Show*. On June 11, 2013, the episode "Blowing the Whistle on Whistleblowers" featured a segment with Cody as a guest. A popular farcical news show, especially among a young and well-educated audience, the show was receiving around 2.5 million views every night when Cody's segment aired.[46] It not only gave Cody and animal advocacy groups an enormous platform to project their message, but demonstrated how threatening to livestock industry groups are undercover investigators like Cody.

The story concerned the "ag-gag" laws being passed in various states, making it illegal for farmworkers to record video or audio. For example, when Cody applied for a job on an egg farm, he was asked if he had ever been associated with an animal rights group. Of course, he falsely answered no, but under a law enacted months after this investigation, this false information could have sent him to jail. Some laws require investigators to turn over footage of cruelty immediately, forcing undercover investigators like Cody to blow their cover before they are able to document a broader pattern of abuse. The laws can even make it illegal to take pictures inside a farm without the owner's consent. There are currently four states with ag-gag laws specifically aimed at silencing undercover investigations and employee whistleblowers, and the Humane Society of the United States claims to have helped defeat more than thirty efforts to put such laws in place.[47] The livestock industry seeks such laws to deter people like Cody. At the same time, by pushing the bills, the industry is admitting that consumers would not like what they would see if the films became public.

Cody offered a telling story highlighting a key conflict he saw while undercover and illustrating his purpose in animal welfare work. At one hog farm there was a room of seven thousand sows in gestation crates, all packed so tightly they could not turn around. One sow in particular started getting attention from the workers. They named her Buttercup, and they would bring her treats and pet her. "They talked about Buttercup like she was their pet dog. The more I thought about it, I realized that they were channeling their empathy into this one individual. That let them forget about the other 6,999."

Cody sees such lines as immoral and illogical, and his objective is to do as much good for all farm animals as he can. To him, every sow is Buttercup. "I don't think that we have a very radical outlook, the groups that I work with. These are mainstream values, and we're just applying them in a way they haven't been applied before. Most people I know love animals." To further animal welfare efforts, instead of giving one animal special treatment and ignoring all the others, Cody had to refrain from acting on behalf of a few animals to benefit all the rest. What he saw—and filmed—was with the intent to share it with the world, hopefully preventing that same cruelty from happening thousands of times in the future.

Trent Loos Defends the Livestock Industry

Undercover investigators may be radical critics of the livestock industry, but Trent Loos is a radical defender. His industry needs one. When farmers and ranchers defend their practices, their arguments are often considered insincere. Critics argue that because agricultural producers make money from their activities, they are speaking not out of a sense of ethics but rather out of self-interest.

This is a mistake. Farmers and ranchers have a deep, personal attachment to their vocation, so deep that few of them even consider it a profession. A profession is something people do on the weekdays, to earn money for recreation. For people who raise crops and care for livestock, it is their occupation *and* recreation. Most importantly, they consider it a life calling. When a critic makes accusations of unethical food production, it is like accusing a priest of worshiping a false god. The accusation strikes at everything dear to ranchers.

In fairness, it is difficult for those without an agricultural background to see this sincerity—but being authentic and sincere is where Trent Loos excels. If you fly much, there is a decent chance you have seen him. He wears a black cowboy hat, an old-style Western vest, and a bandana around his neck, and sports a quintessential cowboy mustache. This attire is chosen both because it feels comfortable to him and because he is eager for you to identify him as a rancher and to strike up a conversation. You see, ranching is his first calling, but educating the public about agriculture is his second.

Trent is every bit the rancher he appears. It is in his genes. In 1832 a German immigrant with the last name Loos struck ground on a farm in Illinois, and that land has remained in his family ever since, still being farmed by Trent's father. Trent currently raises purebred cattle with his wife (a fifth-generation rancher) and three daughters in Nebraska. There was never any doubt about what he wanted to do with his life. If you could ranch, why would you want to do anything else? Toward the end of the 1990s Trent realized life beckoned him elsewhere. Fortunately for him, his wife and kids are able to run the ranch, giving Trent the time needed to become agriculture's most ardent advocate.

Trent foresaw the rise of the "foodie" culture (note: the term is not used as an insult) and the problems farmers might encounter when those without an agricultural background—"people who talk about agriculture but really don't have dirty hands, have never actually been there and done that"—criticized production methods. In the era of the Lewinsky scandal, the Columbine High School shooting, and fears about the Y2K computer virus, the animal rights movement was still emerging. It was years before Florida citizens would cast votes on the use of gestation crates in swine production and more than a decade before *Portlandia* made a splash with its humorous depiction of two hipsters ordering humanely raised chickens, where Fred Armisen asks the waiter whether a chicken had the opportunity to "pal around" with other chickens.

Most farmers did not see a threat in the late 1990s, but Trent did. He sought to wake up agricultural producers while also making personal connections with urban consumers. So in 1999 he entered a South Dakota radio station and said, "My name is Trent Loos, sixth-generation United States farmer, and I want my own radio show." He couldn't introduce himself as a talk show host with experience, because he had none. Nor could he provide a resume showing his past work in public relations, communications, entertainment, or journalism. The station manager first laughed but, realizing Trent was serious, heard him out and gave it some thought. Three months later they were producing the radio show titled *Loos Tales*. It still airs today on over one hundred radio stations and is being streamed across the world. Its tag line is, "Dedicated to exploring the interesting people and places of rural America."

It is a short program—only a few minutes—and is as authentic as Trent himself. The shows are often recorded on the road and at rural events, like livestock shows. The rural life is expressed not only in the activities that take place but the values that are expressed and the people behind them. You might get to hear from a scientist in the food industry, a teenager in a livestock competition, an elderly female farmer, or anyone interesting he encounters in his travels. A few years later he started an hourlong show called *Rural Route* that had equal appeal. "I want *Rural Route* to be more about bringing the factions of America together so that we all understand each other's values, and culture, and beliefs on how we go forward. I work hard at bringing people on there that I don't agree with. Having that respectful discussion where we can make everybody think about things maybe in a way they'd never thought about them before." Hosting two radio shows is indeed unusual for a rancher, but that is not what makes him a radical agricultural advocate.

What distinguishes Trent is his willingness to personally engage with agriculture's critics and to confront them face-to-face when he believes they are being dishonest. He doesn't just wait until he happens to cross paths with them—Trent goes to them. Consider his interactions with Robert F. (Bobby) Kennedy Jr., an attorney and activist, the son of the assassinated Robert F. Kennedy, and the nephew of President John F. Kennedy. Kennedy began an environmental organization to protect surface waters from pollution and associated hog farms with water pollution—an argument that he advances in speeches all across the country. Given his affiliations with America's "Camelot," his comments gained much attention, including Trent's.

It is well known that Kennedy said in 2002 that "hog producers are a greater threat to the U.S. than Osama Bin Laden," but it is less known that he was telling audiences that farmers were losing their humanity. It is one thing to disagree with how farmers operate, but something very different to suggest they are becoming evil. Trent was aghast and angered, not because Kennedy had insulted the industry that feeds Trent's family, but because he had derided people Trent loved and admired. So Trent hit the road, following Kennedy to his speeches, and recording them so he could rebut them. Once he confronted Kennedy in a restroom: "I said, 'I'm here to tell you, sir, if you continue to lie about my industry, I'm going to be there to hold you accountable to your lies.' That really fostered something inside of me that people are going to continue to talk about my business—and my business is taking care of the God-given natural resources and converting them into the essentials of life for mankind: food, fiber, pharmaceuticals, and fuel. Unless someone is there to hold them accountable, they will take these selective portrayals of the truth and make them sound like fact." This wasn't an undercover operation, as Trent wore his normal ranching attire and was clear about his position.

Kennedy sometimes introduced Trent to his crowds as his "shadow": "He actually started introducing me to the crowd, and had me stand up and people would boo. And you know he would say, 'This is Trent Loos. He represents the evils of agriculture—that's why he wears a black hat.' And they didn't really have any clue who I was or what I was doing other than what he said. But it created some opportunity for dialogue."

A key component of Trent's advocacy is that he carefully listens to agriculture's critics, even going to animal rights conferences to hear their arguments. People from food industries sometimes do this, but they usually go incognito. Not Trent. His black hat and vest make him stand out in the crowd, and in a roomful of vegans and animal right activists, his nametag proudly says, "Trent Loos, Sixth Generation Livestock Farmer." He learned the arguments of animal rights activists so well that once, before he was well known in livestock circles, he impersonated an animal rights activist in a debate. So convincing was he that people thought he really was such an activist, and many farmers were upset with him for his views.

Not only does Trent listen to his critics, but his major objective as an agricultural advocate is to get people to listen to each other. He pursues this goal because he wants people to become more independent thinkers, not simply to adopt the views of one's peers without investigating for one-self. "I'm trying to help people think about everything in life, particularly the big picture, and to not accept things at face value. I tell my listeners to go find out for yourself. So from that standpoint, if that's radical, so be it, but I don't consider it radical."

Trent was advocating on behalf of agriculture when few others thought it necessary. "I've tried to live in the trenches. I wanted to understand why people think the way they think. And I think far too often, those of us that have been—like myself—in an industry for six generations, we never stop and ask ourselves why we do what we do. We just accept those things as progress without actually stopping and asking ourselves why we do that. And it's very simple. We do it to produce more with less. We do it to improve the life of the plant or the animal so that we can be more efficient with the finite amount of resources that we have. And that led me to every endeavor that I can find to try to connect the dots between food producers and food consumers."

One of Trent's greatest frustrations is the failure of agriculture to acknowledge the groups organizing to challenge it. Eventually, partially thanks to people like Trent, farmers and ranchers did listen. Now it is considered the solemn duty of farmers and agribusinesses to advocate on behalf of modern agriculture, so important that some universities teach classes on agricultural advocacy, and you won't be surprised to learn that the list of guest speakers sometimes includes Trent Loos. Today there are all sorts of institutions attempting to improve communication between agriculture and its critics, like *The Food Dialogues*, a site created by the U.S. Farmers and Ranchers Alliance. You can consider these institutions to be Trent's children—his legacy. Yet they typically only provide web content or perhaps host a conference. Trent travels in person to interact with his critics, and that is what makes his form of advocacy both effective and radical.

When it comes to views on livestock agriculture Trent may be on the opposite side of the spectrum from Cody Carlson (the undercover animal rights investigator described previously), but they share a number of personality traits. Both are a pleasure to interview and seem to be kind, respectful people. Both are brave, and it does take boldness to repeatedly enter the lairs of your greatest critics. Both are willing to make personal sacrifices toward a greater goal. Finally, although they are both passionate in their roles, in conversation they are reflective and philosophical. They just express very different philosophies on the role of livestock in the world.

Cody argued against livestock production because few people would allow their pets to be treated in the manner of livestock, recognizing that pets often achieve an almost human status. What Trent argued is that raising animals—pets or livestock—to the status of humans actually demeans humans. "I began to sense that the animal rights community in particular was gaining a foothold, and it was parallel to people's misconstrued view of their own pet. And I started focusing on how people were considering themselves to be mother and father of their pets, how we treated horses as much more like a family member than a property, much more than livestock. I saw this as a danger not to agriculture, but a danger to the future of the human race. In the hierarchy that God put forth—I now believe that much of what I'm dealing with is an anti-Christian movement as much as attack on agriculture—human beings are atop the food chain because we have the cranial potential to reason and make decisions that allow us to be sustainable in the future." One of the authors once attended his talks (and Trent is a talented speaker) where Trent joked about that some pet owners are giving their dogs neuticals: fake testicles for castrated dogs, so that the dogs do not miss their natural testicles (this is a real thing, by the way). Trent is making humor, but he is also making a point: that our views toward animals have become warped—and this poses dangers for the human race.

Animals were created to serve humans, Trent believes, and though animals should be treated humanely, we should not forget that they exist to serve human ends. "Now I don't abuse animals. I don't egregiously do things to inflict pain. But I believe they were put on this earth to improve the planet and improve human health. And I believe it is my job to provide the utmost respect, including a quick and timely death for these animals because only in death can another thing live." This is a core value expressed frequently in his advocacy, and just as Ray Archuletta stressed the need to understand *why* we protect the soil, Trent believes that people need to understand *why* we use modern technologies if people are going to accept them. When explaining why we need GMOs, gestation crates for sows, cages for chickens, and antibiotics in agriculture, the "why" is not profits or convenience but agriculture's noble aim to be efficient with the resources that we have so that we can feed as many people as possible. He doesn't believe livestock production is a regrettable need, but a moral obligation. There is one phrase that every one of Trent's fans knows by heart: "Everything lives, everything dies, and death with a purpose gives full meaning to life."

The assertion that we need livestock and technology like GMOs to feed the world is not a unique argument. It is remarked so frequently by the food industry that it has become something of a cliché. Yet it comes across differently when Trent says it. With his authenticity and unique form of advocacy, there is no doubt that he believes it. If you conducted a debate between Cody and a public relations person from Smithfield Foods (a corporation controlling about one-quarter of all US pork),[48] Cody is going to be favored because people will assume that the person from Smithfield cares only about corporate profits. A debate between Cody and Trent, however, is a fair debate, because they both put their personal convictions foremost. No one will mistake Trent for a corporation.

If such a debate were held, you would notice a difference between Trent and Cody: their depiction of what livestock need. Cody would say that livestock need the amenities we provide to pets and other emotional, sentient beings for a satisfactory life. This would include ample space to move around, comfortable resting places, the ability to express natural behaviors, and food and healthcare. Trent's depiction is much simpler. As he states in his book *The Best of Trent*, "Farm animals need only three things: protection from predators, protection from Mother Nature and an adequate supply of food and water on a daily basis."[49]

Trent has no problem with gestation crates, as they meet all three criteria. He isn't saying that a pig can't be made happier by treating it as a pet, he is only saying what they *need*. He concentrates on needs instead of wants because he believes that animals were put on earth to be useful to humans. Giving livestock anything more than what they need requires more resources, and that reduces our ability to serve humanity. This is why Trent was so riled when Kennedy suggested farmers had lost their humanity. "It has to be humans. It has to be the value of human life. At the end of the day whether you believe in one style of food production or you believe in another one, we should all believe in improving human lives." In Trent's view, it is elevating pets and livestock to the status of humans that threatens humanity.

Taber Ward Brings the Farm to the City

In the 1970s the secretary of agriculture, Earl Butz, became known for urging farmers to "get big or get out." It isn't that he disliked small farmers, but believed that only large farms would be able to operate profitably. He simply saw a trend that had been developing for centuries and assumed it would continue. In 1900 the average farm size in the United States was about 150 acres and there were around six million farms. By 1970 only around three million farms remained, but their average size had grown to around 400 acres. Secretary Butz was right about his prediction. The average farm size has continued to rise as the number of farms has steadily fallen.[50]

One reason for this trend has to do with technology. Most new agricultural technologies can lower the cost of production, but only on large farms. Consider the milking technology used on today's dairy farms. Using the old-fashioned method of milking by hand, one person can milk a single cow in ten to fifteen minutes. A single milking machine can milk multiple cows simultaneously in only about 5 minutes. This is a substantial efficiency gain. If a farm has hundreds of cows, it can afford the technology, allowing it to produce milk at a lower per gallon cost. Milking machines are expensive, likely too expensive for a farm with only a few cows.

Secretary Butz was right, but only in regards to farms producing commodities that will enter the mainstream food system. A one-hundred-acre farm raising corn and marketing corn in the same way as a five-thousand-acre farm is guaranteed to lose money. Small farms can still survive, but they have to employ a different business model. Some bypass the mainstream food system and sell directly to the consumer, making use of the local farmers' market, local food cooperative, community-supported agriculture (CSA, where households purchase a share of the farms' overall harvest in advance), and by combining ag-production with ag-tourism. They produce a differentiated product, like organic produce or heirloom wheat varieties. Most smaller farms are able to operate because they have established close relations with their customers and the local community, and because they provide more than just food—they sell an experience, a more tangible connection between the farm and the fork.

That is certainly the case with Taber Ward, founder and manager of Mountain Flower Goat Dairy. Taber first became interested in agriculture in college, where she worked with a Montreal organization similar to Meals on Wheels. As she pursued her anthropology major, she would work on small farms during the summer. One of these farms had goats, and she developed an affinity for the animal—especially one goat named Doodle. The more she worked on these small farms and the more she learned about how large livestock farms operated, the more disenchanted she became with the conventional food system. The videos from undercover investigators like Cody Carlson shocked her, making her want to avoid the mainstream food system whenever possible.

At the same time she developed an interest in protecting farmland, and when she moved to California after college she worked with the Sonoma Land Trust to help preserve "scenic, natural, agricultural, and open land" in Sonoma County. A chasm was growing between the places where food was grown and the places where people lived. This made it easy for people to abdicate responsibility for how animals are treated, and as a result, she felt large farms were able to exploit animals in order to sell cheap meat. People like Cody Carlson were trying to bring the farm to the city through undercover videos. Taber had a different idea: why not literally bring the farm—a humane farm with an alternative structure—to the city?

Taber moved to Boulder, Colorado, so that she could attend law school and specialize in food systems and agriculture. Right down the road from where she lived were the last twenty-five acres of farmland in the city limits. Access to land is tough for small farmers, and most rent rather than own. "My friend said, when I was walking by this piece of property dreaming about goats, 'Why don't you go ask the landowners? . . . You're not going to lose anything by asking.'" Taber approached the landowner and struck a deal to rent the land so that she could start Mountain Flower Goat Dairy. With only thirty-two goats on twenty-five acres, and continuing controversies and fluctuating regulations about raw versus pasteurized milk, she couldn't expect the goat milk to deliver enough revenues to make it a profitable operation. Taber established the farm as a nonprofit organization and learned to provide other services in addition to goat milk. "I am a zealot for small farmers making it. If raw milk is a stepping stone, and there's ways to do it safely, and if we can help provide those ways, let's do raw milk. It can be a very safe product. For me, it's really about getting small farmers to market in innovative ways, and not creating a lot of barriers around that. I don't really care if it's raw or pasteurized, to be honest, but I care about surviving at the farm." The farm has become an educational institution as well as a community fixture, using a strategy of being part farm, part agri-tourism. "Personally, it's a way for me to feel like

I can affect food policy, but also really understand the issues because I'm living the issue. It makes me more effective."

Mountain Flower Goat Dairy, in addition to selling raw goat milk, hosts summer day camps for kids, field trips for schools, cheese-making workshops, tours, and birthday parties. There are official visiting hours, and being a nonprofit means there are volunteers, a board of directors, and the like. No one has to worry about how the animals are treated when the visitors go away. At any time of day one can go to the farm's web page and watch a live video feed of the goat barn. Figure 2.6 shows a few of Taber's goats.

The farm even has goat yoga. Yes, goat yoga is a thing! Though it began only in 2016 in Oregon, videos of people doing yoga alongside baby goats went viral on social media, and the idea spread around the country, eventually becoming a featured activity at Mountain Flower Dairy as well.[51] Goats love to climb, on anything, and as participants stretch in the tabletop position, the goats jump on their back, sometimes jumping from one back to another. Goat yoga has become such a craze that an Arizona farmer made an April Fool's Day video where she explained her new exercise project: goat CrossFit.[52]

Goat yoga aside, the dairy is not a petting zoo. Taber's passion is to bring agriculture to urban areas and help people make a personal,

FIGURE 2.6 Goats grazing at Mountain Flower Goat Dairy
Image courtesy of Taber Ward

healthy connection to food. In high school Taber knew women who had eating disorders, and she had personally seen the toll that an unhealthy relationship with food can have on a person. "If you've never even been able to know what it feels like to be around food in a healthy situation, the farm is a place to connect with food, and connect with agriculture. It's not about a body project, it's about connecting with the earth, connecting with our food in a nonscary, nonthreatening way." Food is not just a biological need, but a form of connection, and it was partly this desire to approach food differently that led her to work on a variety of small farms—but only small farms. When she sees large livestock operations housing thousands of animals in cramped cages, and vast expanses of cropland where tractor tires work the soil but human hands do not, Taber sees something almost as disturbing as the eating disorders she witnessed in her youth.

Rather than feel depressed at the current food system, Taber is trying to fix it. "The meaning of farming for me is looking around, and thinking—what in the world sucks for me? And for me, the food system really sucked and it sucked for a lot of people. Farming was a way to be on the ground making change in that thing that I really cared about, and I wanted to be part of that community, and to be embodied in my work. It's great to get out there and talk to people. And I needed to be much more embodied in my work than the legal practice would ever give me." Yet Taber's law degree and practice give her unique insights into existing regulations and how they can both support and hinder small-farm production. "We talked about local food and local food systems, and food education, and farmers' markets, but really the regulations around this stuff are not keeping up with the demand, the supply, or actual practice, which is always a problem between practice and policy."

By preserving this farmland and operating a real dairy in an urban area, she has brought the farm to the people, and in the process helped them make a healthy connection to food. Almost every day she gets an email from someone wanting to volunteer, tour the farm, or enroll children in a summer camp. Many of the kids even come from the rural areas around Boulder, which surprised Taber at first, until they told her that most farms don't have visiting hours and tours. For these country kids to learn about farming, they had to come to the city! For Taber it is about "disturbing the system—which is what I want to do. I hope to do that. Disturbing law and policy. A lot of people are doing what I do. I learned from a lot of farmers that are paving the way."

Brave New Farm

James Underwood, Master of Robots

In a short story about farmworkers published in *The Sun*, Alison Luterman writes, "Strawberries were too delicate to be picked by machine. The perfectly ripe ones bruised at even too heavy a human touch. It hit her then that every strawberry she had ever eaten—every piece of fruit—had been picked by callused human hands."[53] That was twenty years ago, and things have changed. Machines can now pick strawberries. The Spanish company Agrobot has commercialized a machine that uses an artificial vision system to determine where the berries are located on the plant and assess if they are ripe. If they are, the machine picks the fruit without damaging it.[54] It is a new system used on few farms to date, but in ten years, perhaps many of the strawberries you eat will never be touched by a human. How clean. How *radical*.

But it's radical only to one outside the industry of agricultural mechanization. The delicate French grapes used to make the finest wines are sometimes harvested by a machine with gentle, fiberglass fingers,[55] while other machines are designed to milk cows without the need of human presence.[56] Slaughterhouses (though they prefer to be called meatpackers) are developing machines to butcher animals.[57] An indoor Japanese farm uses robots to perform every task of lettuce production, from planting to harvesting—this isn't just a small experiment, but a real farm that produces thirty thousand heads of lettuce every day.[58] Today we are debating the merits of driverless cars, but there are already over two hundred thousand self-driving tractors working fields.[59]

Machinery replacing human and animal labor on the farm is nothing new. The first combines appeared in the mid-nineteenth century, running on steam engines and pulled by mules. Once a field of grain was ripe and ready for reaping, the farmer could take one machine back and forth across a field, separating the seed from the plant.[60] Early machines operated on brute force. A century after the combine appeared, Basil Savage designed a machine to harvest pecans by violently shaking the tree until its nuts fall—again, using brute force.[61]

What makes the new machines in development innovative is the lack of brute force. The combine severs and thrashes; the pecan harvester clasps and shakes. The old machines can only pound and punch whatever the farmer places in front of them. The new machines can see, even think. They are keen, precise, careful, and pacific. The people designing these robots may have more impact on the food system than anyone in their generation. We should get to know one of them.

James Underwood is a researcher at the Australian Centre for Field Robotics at the University of Sydney in Australia. His job is to teach robots to see, think, act, and report. In 2013 his work using robots to herd cattle received considerable attention. The BBC played a video of James's robot "Shrimp" herding a group of dairy cows, as shown in figure 2.7. The cows reacted calmly to the robot, and Shrimp performed well. If you just glanced at the headline and didn't read the article well you would think that Shrimp was herding the cows all by itself. In reality it was being controlled remotely by James.[62] These were the first exploratory steps on the road to building a robot that can herd cows while the farmer is busy doing something else.

Robotic potential involves far more than saving farmers a short walk and a few minutes. Perhaps the robot can slowly move about the herd at night, noticing when a cow goes into labor and notifying the farmer's smartphone. The possibilities are many, and so are the benefits.

Another robot rolls among trees in an orchard, as in figure 2.8, using sophisticated cameras and lasers to recognize the fruit in the tree and calculate how much fruit each tree is yielding. It can do so with high

FIGURE 2.7 Shrimp agbot, a herdsman
Image courtesy of James Underwood

FIGURE 2.8 Shrimp agbot rolls among the fruit trees
Image courtesy of James Underwood

accuracy. It then returns a map to the farmer showing the amount of fruit being produced at various places in the orchard, allowing the farmer to identify problems. In one case it recognized that some places in the orchard had a surprisingly low amount of fruit. Once alerted to this fact, the farmer surmised that it was due to insufficient pollination. So he planted more pollination trees in those areas in order to achieve a higher and more uniform production.[63] By using the "agbots" as our better eyes and smarter mind, we can harvest more fruit from every acre, reducing pressure on land, and allowing more fruit for every dollar spent on fossil fuels, thus reducing our carbon footprint. It might even reduce the use of synthetic pesticides and allow for a more efficient form of organic fruit production.

Our favorite is an agbot named Ladybird, named so because it looks like a ladybug. "We iterated towards that," said James. "The covers are functional in that they provide a shadow so that when we look down we get the best kind of quality imagery. We're not drowned out by the sunlight. Then they're functional in the second way, which is the solar power—a significant percentage of the power budget is provided by solar. We have a third aspect, which is that the design all comes together to make it look like a ladybug, also referred to as a ladybird, which farmers consider a helpful insect. It's a predatory insect that eats other pests that spoil the crops. It is a nice combination of form and function."

The Ladybird, shown in figure 2.9, is like a farmworker that never tires, always moving about a field looking for weeds. The solar panels on its roof and its batteries allow it to work throughout the day and night, and its keener eyes allow it to distinguish weeds from crops. Anyone interested in raising vegetables with less herbicides and less tillage should be a fan of Ladybird. It can identify weeds and deliver a precise jet of herbicides to that weed and nothing else, whereas most farmers today have to spray an entire field. The cute little Ladybird can thus achieve the same amount of weed protection with 40 percent less herbicides.[64]

Just think of all the other possibilities agbots like Ladybird can provide. Instead of killing the weeds with a herbicide, perhaps it could be designed to kill the weed manually, like a human pulling weeds. Then one could raise vegetables with even less tillage and herbicide. Or instead of identifying weeds, it could spot pests, like aphids, and then deliver a small amount of insecticide right onto the aphid instead of the whole field. This would allow farmers to raise vegetables using even less insecticides than organic producers (note: organic farmers can use organic pesticides).

FIGURE 2.9 The Ladybird, tending fields
Image courtesy of James Underwood

Perhaps the agbot's sensors could detect soil moisture levels, allowing it to communicate with irrigation equipment and turn on the water pumps. We already have handheld sensors that can scan a plant's leaves to determine if it needs more nitrogen, so there is no reason such sensors couldn't be installed on the Ladybird. Maybe these sensors could also detect other nutrient problems, like insufficient iron. Maybe the agbot could communicate with a farmer's smartphone, telling the farmer when it's time to harvest, or allowing the farmer to view live video of the field. Feral pigs are a big problem in our state of Oklahoma, so maybe Ladybird could watch for them and when they arrive emit a sound that will frighten them. All of these may be realities in the coming decades, thanks to technology radicals like James Underwood. Given these possibilities, people like James will have a transformative impact on our food system, benefiting people, animals, and the environment all at the same time.

Robots in agriculture will eliminate some jobs, but they will also create new jobs. For over a century the modern world has seen technologies create and destroy jobs at roughly the same rate, so that (not counting the Great Depression) the unemployment rate has remained about the same. Just as few regret that the automobile destroyed the horse industry, future generations may not lament how agbots changed the way we farm.

It might be surprising, then, to learn that James did not begin these adventures out of an interest in food and has virtually no agricultural background. From a young age he was programming his own computer games, and he loved math and science. He was building things, but what he was building was a game inside a computer, projected onto a screen. It wasn't until his undergraduate studies in mechatronic engineering that he built something substantial he could touch. Here he was using computer programs to manipulate physical objects, and he loved it so much that he continued his education by getting a PhD in robotics. It just so happens that this work led him to applications like mining, defense, and agriculture.

As time passed, opportunities in agriculture arose, and his interest in food and farming grew with it. Working on a team with other engineers and farmers has given him a profound respect for the challenges farmers face and the ingenuity they display in overcoming them. "Agriculture, to me, has been the most fascinating area to apply this stuff to. It's a combination of the way that natural systems work, the biology of the trees and the crops, and so on. The way that interacts with high-tech stuff like sensors and robots to me is a fascinating combination, and it's one that

I think creates the best sort of challenges, where the state of the art is up to at the moment in terms of the technology. My deep core interest is in this area of engineering, robotics and sensing technology, but the application area of agriculture is just a brilliant match for all of that." The more he learned about food, the more interest he took in understanding where his own food comes from. This gave him that personal knowledge Ray Archuletta and Taber Ward spoke of and gives his own research a more profound personal meaning. His passion wasn't originally to revolutionize farming, but to revolutionize robots—but now he is passionately doing both. "When I was a kid I used to program my own computer games. Now I'm programming robots to herd cattle and control weeds."

James thought we would be disappointed to learn that he didn't have an agricultural background. He was wrong. His case is particularly inspiring because it shows that you don't need an agricultural background to improve the food system. Producing and distributing food is a highly sophisticated business, and only a minority of the people involved could even manage a garden. For each dollar spent on food, only about $0.16 goes back to the farm, which means most of the money is spent on food processing and distribution. Moreover, of the $0.16 given to the farm, a substantial amount of that money is paid to input suppliers for things like fertilizers and tractors.[65] Though we do need people who know how to raise plants and care for livestock, we need even more people with other skills. James is one of these other people.

Improving our food supply, then, requires more than improving our understanding of the art of farming; we need technological innovation and a better understanding of science in our citizenry.

Providing tasty fruit will require molecular biologists and botanists. Affordable bread calls for engineers who design efficient harvesting equipment, and safe bread requires designers and microbiologists who can design a bakery that minimizes exposure to air and eliminates contamination. We need architects like Bob Moje who design school cafeterias to encourage healthy eating, marine biologists like Dominique Barnes to protect our oceans by inventing shrimp substitutes, and marketing specialists like Marc Oshima who can get lettuce grown indoors into mainstream grocery stores. Regardless of your background, your skills, your interests, there is a way for you to improve the food system.

To better understand the role a tech guy like James plays in agriculture, let's take a more precise look at his work. At the Australian Center for Field Robotics James is part of a team. He stresses his research is a team effort, and they design robots of all sizes for any industry that can use them, from agriculture to aerospace. The center is mostly funded by industry groups, and though some of the work leads to commercialized products sold by these companies, the team is also engaged in general robotics research whose benefits are shared by all the companies (as well as consumers). For example, Ladybird is designed for general research and could result in numerous different versions of agbots sold by different companies. "I see our role in research as getting to the point of almost de-risking some of the ideas, getting to a point where we scientifically demonstrate that certain ideas actually do work, in practice. . . . Then, obviously, it comes down to commercial entities to take on the business side of it, develop that technology."

The agbots built at the Center for Field Robotics are designed to work efficiently on the farm, but also to make for efficient research. They are overdesigned for their task, on purpose, to evaluate what other tasks they might be able to perform. Let us return to the adorable little Ladybird, with its arm that sprays a herbicide to kill weeds. To perform this job the arm needs only two degrees of freedom: up, down, left, and right. Imagine you are holding a hose to spray water. To hit a spot on the ground you can simply hold your arm straight, and move your wrist up, down, left, and right until the water hits its intended spot. However, because you can bend down, bend your elbow, and move your arm, you have more than two degrees of freedom, allowing you to bend down and spray underneath a car if you needed to.

Though the Ladybird arm only needs two degrees of freedom, it actually has six degrees, allowing experimentation with other uses for the arm. For example, Ladybird can use the arm to yank out a weed underneath a vegetable plant, using joints akin to elbows and wrists. In addition to being scientists conducting controlled experiments, researchers are engineers, tinkering, modifying, and exploring.

If James does not have an agricultural background, how does he know what ideas to explore? Remember James is on a team, and this team consists of agronomists and farmers. These farmers are innovators of their own, radical farmers like Jimmy Kinder and Jeff Moyer, who can give James ideas, tell him about the problems they face, help him understand how a farm works, and brainstorm about the various ways agbots can contribute. (Again, we see that technological innovation involves radical farmers who are willing to imagine different ways of farming.)

One of James's specialties is algorithms, which is a set of rules to be used in calculations or computer programs for problem-solving. In most cases it is a computer program. When Ladybird is programmed to spray herbicide on individual weeds, it has to be able to distinguish between a weed and the crop. How does it do this? It relies on an algorithm, similar to those that perform fingerprint or facial recognition.

One reason his research center serves so many different industries is that algorithms designed for one application are often useful in another. Remember Shrimp, the agbot remotely controlled by James to herd cattle? After James conducted the herding demonstration, he used the video Shrimp recorded to run various algorithms to determine if it was possible for Shrimp to automatically detect and track individual cows as they moved about. James was once involved in the creation of an original algorithm used in security surveillance to track the motion of individuals in a scene. If a person grabbed a lady's pocketbook and ran, this algorithm would be able to track the thief's movement in the video, as well as the victim's. It turned out, James discovered, that this algorithm could be successfully used by Shrimp to track the motion of cattle. If Shrimp ever herds cattle on its own, without a remote driver, it might owe this achievement to research algorithms from a completely different application. It might sound strange, because trees don't move, but this same algorithm was even successfully applied to identifying different trees in an orchard.

Many decisions are made in the design of an agbot but one of the most important ones is which algorithms it will use, and this can require considerable experimentation. Though they are computer codes, the number of commands is large and complex. It is impossible to know which algorithms will work best just by looking at the code, so they have to be tested.

Algorithms are not solving well-defined math problems, but problems in a changing environment, and algorithms are designed to help computers learn as they work—they must search for answers, not just calculate them. The manner in which they search are algorithms themselves, so there are algorithms within algorithms. Think of the last time you misplaced your keys in your house. There are different ways to search. You could try to recall your latest movements and backtrack accordingly. You could think of the three most frequent places you put your keys and look there. Just walking around the house and looking around is also an option. Which search method works best? Only experience can make that distinction, and so it is with algorithms.

You can think of James as a math teacher and the agbots as young students. Sometimes students are taught to memorize multiplication tables, and, likewise, sometimes James installs computer files on an agbot. Much of the time, though, teachers are helping students learn how to solve problems for themselves. For instance, different ways exist for students to solve division problems. Most of us were taught one particular routine we call long division—well, that is an algorithm. Moreover, there are different ways of performing long division—different algorithms within algorithms, and students can differ on which method they prefer.

In the same way, James is teaching agbots how to solve problems, but he does so by loading different algorithms into the agbots' computers and then testing how well each performs. He is a teacher of machines, though his style of teaching entails modifying computer code. Sometimes James will write one of these algorithms himself, but more often he will find an existing one and test it. Some of these are freely available to the public, while others must be purchased from the private sector. The algorithms might work well as they are, or James might have to modify the code.

As algorithm is piled upon algorithm in the same machine, and as that machine learns by experience and modifies those algorithms itself, we have artificial intelligence. This is not the future, but the present, and when you combine artificial intelligence with sophisticated sensors and a robotic body, there is almost no limit to what agbots can do. Self-driving tractors are not new, but the latest versions do not even have a place for a driver or passenger. They can spot an obstacle in the field and decide for themselves how to avoid it.[66] The innovations are even making forays into mainstream agriculture. A Japanese farmer is using cameras and an artificial intelligence system developed by Google to identify cucumbers and sort them by color, shape, and size.[67]

When it comes to robotics, the hardware is already available to do most anything. The lenses and cameras already work remarkably well, as does the mechanistic body that moves the agbot and the robotic arms. Basic robotics is simple and cheap enough now that a few farmers have been able to design their own self-driving machines.[68] The real challenge is getting the robots to think well. Evolution had billions of years to design the human mind. The computer age is less than a century old, yet James is young and his agbots can already perform some key agricultural tasks. "I don't think of any of it as radical really. When you're doing it day to day and you're seeing all the incremental steps that you're taking, it doesn't feel like you're necessarily suddenly doing something very different. If we fast forward twenty years from now, and we're looking at what [farms] look like, and we compare that to today—there'll be a radical shift in how those farms are working. It depends on the timescale and maybe it also depends on the degree to which you're involved day to day. One way in which it is not radical is that . . . we're not advocating completely changing the way everything is grown, or done. Growers already have hundreds of years of history built up in the knowledge of the best practices."

This computer whiz from Australia probably wouldn't be considered a "foodie"—he doesn't write a blog about food, doesn't garden, and doesn't wax philosophical about his diet—but he is part of a team that may very well lead to tastier, more abundant food produced in a more environmentally sustainable manner. Though not a radical himself, the ideas his team pursues certainly are.

Radical mutations

Nature is remarkable in her ability to be both redundant and creative. She can take a single microorganism, plant, or animal, and, using a byzantine barrage of miniscule tools (e.g., DNA, RNA, ribosomes), create billions of copies. What results are sheets of uniform algae, blankets of wildflowers, armies of ants, and 7.5 billion humans. Then, randomly, from this seemingly infinite repetition, an organism undergoes a genetic mutation that makes it a little different from its peers, like the 35 percent of humans with the ability to digest milk as adults.[69] Or this difference might propel the individual to be the founder of a new species or organism. It was nature's genetic mutations that took a single species and from it created both the whale and the hippopotamus.

Put nature and humans together and this creative redundancy is magnified. Consider the 350-plus breeds of dogs that exist today, most of which became a distinct breed through selective breeding by humans only in the last two hundred years.[70] Take cabbage, cauliflower, kale, and Brussels sprouts, all of which are different "foods" but are really the same species of plant. You can still find their wild ancestor growing on the cliffs of the English Channel, known as wild mustard, wild cabbage, or (scientifically), *Brassica oleracea*. As humans selected seeds for certain plants with terminal buds, they acquired (or did they *create?*) the cabbage variety. As they selected for stems and flowers, they got broccoli, and selecting for tightly clustered flowers produced the cauliflower.[71]

Creating cauliflower and Brussels sprouts from the same plant took a keen eye, as plant breeders noticed small differences in the appearances of plants. It also took patience, as they sowed seeds from those plants with desirable traits and waited to watch the progeny grow—then select and plant again, and again, and again. Developing these alternative varieties of *Brassica oleracea* was a considerable investment, as segregating certain plants away from others to control their breeding required resources that could have been used elsewhere. The most famous example of such dedicated cultivation is the Roman emperor Diocletian. After his abdication, the empire erupted into a civil war. When leaders urged him to return to politics and settle the disputes, he replied that he could not leave his cabbages.[72]

This investment would not always be fruitful, because significantly altering the genetic makeup of organisms is not easy. True, by selective breeding some genetic changes are easily made. The most famous example is the taming of captive, wild fox by Russian scientists. By selecting and breeding only the most docile and gregarious offspring of each generation, within forty years they had a fox that behaved very much like a dog.[73] Still, it was a fox. It was not like wild cabbage transformed into Brussels sprouts.

Transforming an organism's genetics is a slow process because every species has a tendency to "regress" toward its average. King Frederick William I of Prussia once tried to establish a military unit consisting of especially tall soldiers. He thought this would be best accomplished by forcing tall men and women to marry, but this did not always produce tall offspring. Often they were shorter than both their parents, and the slowness at which tall offspring could be produced led the king to acquire his tall soldiers by kidnapping instead.[74] Francis Galton later collected data showing that children of tall parents tend to be shorter than their parents, and the children of shorter parents tend to be taller than their parents. A similar phenomenon was observed with the diameter of seed. He termed this behavior "regression towards the mean" in that the appearance of offspring did not just depend on the appearance of their parents, but also the population at large.[75]

This regression toward the mean makes improving plant genetics difficult. Just as the Prussian king could not create an increasingly tall army of soldiers by marrying off tall people, a plant breeder cannot just breed two wild cabbages with close-clustered flowers and expect them to turn into cauliflower during a lifetime. Nor can you continually breed cattle with particularly short horns and expect to acquire polled (hornless) cattle. This isn't to say you can't make some progress altering plants or animals from breeding, but Galton's reversion to the mean is so powerful that it makes this progress particularly slow.

To revolutionize plant and animal genetics quickly, we need more than just small alterations in plant genetics: we need genetic mutations. That wild cabbage morphed into broccoli and cauliflower due to naturally occurring genetic mutations and careful plant breeding that permanently altered different wild cabbage plants. Humans did not create these genetic mutations, but they did notice them when they occurred and, by deliberately planting the seeds of those plants, preserved those genetic traits. It was nature's creativity that produced mutations, but humans aided in replicating those mutations in crop after crop. Most all of the domesticated plants we rely on for food emerged from a genetic mutation in a formerly wild plant.

Humans are renowned opportunists. Naturally occurring genetic mutations are rare. Any one gene has only a 0.00055 percent chance of mutating in any one generation.[76] When mutations occur and are beneficial to humans, we preserve them for future generations. It was because of our inability to create mutations in the first place that agricultural progress was slow in past centuries.

Some might see it as a radical act for humans to stand in nature's place and create genetic mutations of their own, but today, that is considered a standard of crop breeding. An organism's DNA is akin to written instructions on how an organism should be built (scientists even use letters to describe the structure of DNA). It is like a manuscript, and waiting on natural genetic mutations is like waiting for a medieval monk to make a small error while transcribing a holy text. It will happen, giving us slightly different versions of the same story (like different versions of the *brassica* plant), but it is slow. Once DNA was finally understood, scientists set about investigating how they could induce mutations themselves.

First, scientists zapped plants with radiation to induce mutations, and what resulted were many of today's standard food plants, including Ruby Red grapefruit and the wheat used to make the highest-quality pasta.[77] Here in Oklahoma we have a popular variety of wheat that is resistant to a particular brand of herbicide, allowing farmers to spray a field and kill almost every plant except the wheat. This wheat is resistant to the herbicide because of a genetic mutation induced by exposing the plant to harsh chemicals. Inducing mutations through radiation and chemicals is a bit like taking written instructions and randomly scrambling some of the letters: turning "roses are red" to "rosse are red." It changes things, but is imprecise. It may sound unnatural, and it is (that's the point, nature is too slow), but the public exhibited little concern over the new plants produced with this method.

Passive approval was not given to transgenic crops, produced when scientists learned to remove a gene from one organism and insert it into the DNA of a different organism, creating what we now refer to as GMOs (genetically modified organisms). This would be like cutting an excerpt of words from one set of instructions and inserting it into another: turning "roses are red" to "roses are red hope springs eternal." To most scientists this was hardly different than radiation-induced mutations, but activists disagreed. To some it was like a speech given by Franklin Roosevelt that had been modified by inserting a phrase uttered by Big Bird. Even if the overall speech was improved, to some it just didn't seem right. Moreover, the new transgenic crops seemed to be designed only for farmers, reducing their need to plow or spray certain insecticides. Some consumers felt that they were exposed to a new type of food that provided them no direct benefit, with uncertain risks.

So for decades the controversy persisted. The process of inserting genes from one organism into another continues to be used and continues to be opposed. Though the GMO controversy remains intense, it is perhaps a bit outdated. It was the removal of genes from one organism and its insertion into another (one example being the integration of arctic fish genes into tomato DNA to enhance frost tolerance) that gave rise to "frankenfood" fears, but through scientific advancements this exchange of genes between organisms is no longer necessary. The GMOs of the past seemed to benefit farmers only, but the new GMOs promise to benefit consumers directly. Genetically engineered food of the future has more advocates and offers more benefits for the average person, and we have food radicals like Dr. Dan Voytas to thank.

Dan Voytas, a Radical Plant Breeder

A professor at the University of Minnesota and the chief science officer at the biotechnology firm Calyxt, Dan (on the right in figure 2.10) is "editing" the genes of plants to create healthier foods. With this process, a soybean variety has undergone gene editing and now has higher amounts of oleic acid. As a result, the oil does not have to be hydrogenated and therefore

FIGURE 2.10 Dr. Dan Voytas (right), editing plant genomes
Image courtesy of Calyxt

contains no trans fats in the final product. Trans fats are unhealthy, so much so that the US Food and Drug Administration has declared them unsafe for consumption.[78]

A new soybean variety without trans fats is an enormous accomplishment. Other plants can produce vegetable oil free of trans fats, but soybeans are an ideal crop. They have a relatively short growing season, can be easily adapted to different regions, are a terrific crop to rotate with corn (as they do not suffer from the same pests), and are a legume, meaning they do not need the nitrogen fertilizer known to create greenhouse gas emissions and pollute surface waters.

The DNA of this new bean was indeed changed, but not by inserting genes from some other organism—meaning that this new soybean is *not* a genetically modified organism. Dan created not just this particular soybean, but also something much grander. He invented the gene-editing tool that made it possible in the first place. Not just improving crops like wheat, soybeans, potatoes, and canola, he has revolutionized science itself.

The tool he developed is called TALEN, which stands for "transcription activator-like effector nucleases." If we think in terms of our comparison of DNA to written instructions, we can say that TALEN allows scientists like Dan to remove any letter they wish and add whatever letters they desire.

They can turn "roses are red" to "roses," or "roses are red, violets are blue," or "roses smell nice," or anything else. Such gene-editing is much like the editing of this book. We delete what we want and add what we want, with deliberate precision. Tools like TALEN eliminate the major obstacles to better plant breeding. Before we did not know how to custom-design an organism's genome. Now doing so is just a matter of time and money.

We wish we could explain how TALEN works, but, not being biologists, it is beyond our reach. We feel much like Dan's father when Dan was studying biology at Harvard. When people would ask how his "Harvard son" was doing, he would "pull out a little piece of paper from his wallet and read, 'He's working on the extracellular proteins from fungal plant pathogens.' And then he'd fold it, and put it back in his wallet."

Dan's father probably understood more than he let on, and he was certainly proud of his son. From an early age Dan and his father would garden together. The father was the son of Slovakian immigrants and one of ten children in a family who produced much of their own food by gardening, hunting, and fishing. In their garden, Dan's father would pass down to him the time-tested ways of breeding and caring for plants that had supported his family for so long. There was nothing radical in this garden, but it did encourage Dan's atypical interest in plants. He would sell tomato plants to neighbors and was one of the few young boys with subscriptions to horticultural magazines. In addition to growing his own plants, Dan learned how to identify wild edible plants: "I was really interested in medicinal herbs and the like. I was fascinated by the notion that all of these wild plants were making compounds that had some sort of medicinal benefit. There was a period there where I was quite avid . . . more of a botanist than a biologist. But it was all motivated by interest in essentially medicinal plants."

Dan had to leave his Minnesota garden behind in the ninth grade when his family moved to New Hampshire, but he maintained his love of botany. Though most subjects interested him, it was biology he liked best, especially when it came to plants. In high school he competed in a state science competition where he presented a paper regarding how pH, temperature, and light impact the growth of petunias.

Although Dan has the quiet, introverted nature stereotypical of a scientist, when seeking new ways to learn more about plants, he is outgoing. To learn as much as he could, he wanted to attend the best school he could. He had the audacity to apply to Harvard and was accepted. His mother didn't believe he was accepted until he showed her the letter, for she thought it beyond the reach of her middle-class kid.

Had he attended an agricultural school, Dan would have majored in horticulture, but no such major existed at Harvard. There was biology, though, so that is what he studied. Over time he grew frustrated because he was not learning enough about plants. As an undergraduate he convinced a professor to let him take a graduate-level plant taxonomy class. This is the extroverted, adventurous side of Dan. How many undergraduates would dare think about taking a graduate level class at Harvard? Yet that is what he did, while also taking his undergraduate course load in organic chemistry and biochemistry.

The big picture of life itself "clicked" with Dan. He could see how the microscopic mechanisms at the cellular level operated to create the differences in the tomatoes he sold to neighbors and the petunias he once used in a high school science competition. At their smallest levels he could see that all plants were made of the same materials, and the instructions on how different plants should be built were made of the same nucleotides, but differences in the order of the various nucleotides led to vastly different species. The same materials produce the nutritious corn plant, the majestic Sequoia tree, and the beautiful but foul-smelling corpse flower. This was the early 1980s, when the biotechnology revolution was in its infancy:

> What I really connected with was being present as the genetic blueprint was unfolding and coming up with new ways to manipulate it. That became my new passion. We were in the reading phase of genetic information at that time, determining genome sequences, figuring out what the genetic blueprint looks like. Gene editing, which I'm engaged in now, is the beginning of the writing phase. We now manipulate genetic information. And then someday we'll synthesize whole genomes on spec, I'm sure. But the gene editing was a transition from reading to writing—to reading, editing, and writing. What really made me passionate about my work was to be surrounded and in the middle of a time when so much was being learned so fast about the basic information of life.

The air was filled with a nascent optimism that by understanding and manipulating the genome scientists could benefit the world in ways previously deemed impossible. Being a part of this revolution became Dan's passion.

He stayed at Harvard for his PhD in genetics, where he studied transposable elements, which are "pieces of DNA that can move around and when they move they create mutations." Transposable elements are commonly referred to as "jumping genes." Scientists think it was one of these jumping genes cleverly named Hopscotch that leaped into one particular part of the teosinte plant's DNA, giving it bigger seeds. Thanks to this mutation and others, the teosinte would eventually become what we refer to as corn or maize.[79] Dan wanted to learn more about these jumping genes, but they were too reticent to jump in the plants he studied to generate much data.

As in his undergraduate years, when he needed to learn more, this introverted scientist did not hesitate to ask others to work with him. He found a researcher at Johns Hopkins working with baker's yeast who had great success making genes jump, and asked to join his team as a postdoctoral student. It turned out he was accepted for the postdoc and offered an assistant professor position at Iowa State University (ISU) on the same day. ISU allowed him to postpone his arrival by one year so that he could study these jumping genes. For the first time he was not working with plants, but his objective was to learn from the yeast so that he could develop new ways to study plants.

What he eventually learned was how to edit a plant's DNA, using the tools of plants' enemies: harmful bacteria. A bacterium called *Xanthomonas* has a sophisticated way of attacking plants. When it invades, it secretes proteins into the plant cells that bind onto certain parts of the plant DNA in a way that encourages the plants to create certain proteins that helps the bacteria infect the plant. Much as a cold causes you to sneeze, enabling the bacteria or virus to infect other people, the *Xanthomonas* causes the plant to sow the seeds of its own destruction by manipulating the plant's DNA. The key element of these proteins is that they are able to recognize specific portions of DNA and bind to them.

You might remember that a virus infects a bacterium by injecting its own DNA into the bacterial cell, forcing the cell to replicate the virus's DNA so that the virus can reproduce. Well, this is against the bacterium's interest, so the bacterium protects itself by producing restriction enzymes that can detect foreign DNA and destroy it. For example, the bacterium *Flavobacterium okeanokoites* produces a restriction enzyme called FokI. The key element of these restriction enzymes is that they can cut specific parts of DNA.

Dan's contribution was to discover how to combine the proteins produced by the *Xanthomonas* bacteria with the FokI enzyme produced by the *Flavobacterium okeanokoites* to remove any portion of an organism's DNA. Scientists have long known how to cut and repair certain parts of DNA, but only a subset of all possible parts of DNA. Dan's method, eventually named TALEN, can remove *any* part of a DNA strand the researcher wishes. Once the DNA is cut at the desired spot, methods already existed to replace that strand with different DNA, but much of the time a desired trait can be acquired simply by removing certain genes.[80] In cases where DNA is added, this "different" strand of DNA does not have to come from a different organism. It can be taken from a different part of the same plant's DNA or even created synthetically in the lab. For the first time, the genome of an organism could be altered in whatever way the scientist wishes, without it being deemed a GMO.

Consider the healthier soybean oil made possible by TALEN. There were already soybean varieties that produced this healthier oil, but they were produced by other companies that modified the DNA by inserting foreign DNA into the soybean genome, making it an official GMO. Though the oil is healthier, its GMO status may deter some consumers from using it. Dan was able to produce the same type of plant not by adding DNA, but simply by inactivating certain already existing genes.

How's the public going to perceive a gene-edited plant relative to a plant that has foreign DNA in its genome? And how many edits can you make before it becomes a GMO? What is a GMO? How do you define it? I've spent a lot of time, mostly in my university hat, talking to a lot of different regulatory bodies about the technology, how it works, and what's coming down the pipeline. I think there's a collective sense that this is very powerful, very valuable, technology. And at the same time we want to regulate it so that the public, the environment is safe—the food supply is safe. I've been very impressed with the thoughtfulness that's gone behind it by regulatory authorities. There's still a lot of decisions to be made.

Lest you think gene inactivating is as unnatural as adding DNA to a genome, know that your cells are inactivating various genes as you read these words—it is a natural process more than a billion years old and the basis of evolution.[81] Harnessing this natural process makes it possible for production of a healthier soybean oil without it being a GMO, increasing the likelihood that consumers will be willing to use it and experience associated health benefits.

Do not think this genetic breakthrough only altered the crops we grow. There is a darling little human girl named Layla who developed an aggressive leukemia at the age of three months, a disease that in the past would almost certainly have been fatal. Then came Dan's TALEN, which was used to genetically alter Layla's immune cells so that they could seek the leukemia cells and destroy them. TALEN was also used to inactivate the genes that reject white blood cells of donors, so that little Layla could be given the healthy and numerous white blood cells of others. "I love basic research. I love discovery for the sake of learning how life works. That is extraordinarily rewarding. To invent something like a TALEN and then wow, the chairman of my company pulled me aside to tell me about a couple compassionate use cases where the technology was used and infants were completely cured of leukemia. You know? When the chairman pulls me aside and says, 'I have to tell you as inventor of the TALEN technology what was just accomplished.' That takes your breath away."

As of this writing, both Layla and another infant who received the treatment are still living and thriving due to the innovative gene-editing therapy.[82] Dr. Dan Voytas had set out to design improved crops, and in addition he helped save human life. This testifies to the many benefits from general scientific research, benefits that are hard to predict as the research is being conducted. TALEN is just one of many advanced genetic engineering techniques being used today that make genetic alterations not classified as producing a GMO. Some readers may have heard of the new "CRISPR" technology for gene editing (another acronym meaningless to most of us). The way CRISPR has been covered by media makes it sound as if gene editing like that described above was impossible until CRISPR, but TALEN does the same thing and was discovered first. "It's become a verb. Like 'let's CRISPR it.' There's not that many people using TALEN anymore. It's CRISPR for the academic scientist. It is cheaper and easier to perform. Not that much cheaper, not that much easier, but enough to motivate you to use it." Today much of Dan's editing work at the University of Missouri is conducted using CRISPR. In fact, what Dan finds especially fascinating about this area of biology is that there is more than one way of editing genes.

Conventional breeding of plants is now being aided by technology. Even the old method of breeding two particular plants requires advanced science. Scientists are identifying the specific genes in plants that lead to desirable foods, like genes that give lettuce a longer shelf life,[83] genes that allow soybeans to grow in salty soils (the more a soil is irrigated the saltier it becomes),[84] genes that produce a better-tasting tomato,[85] and genes that make rice seed stay dormant during a flood.[86] These are genes already present in some plants, but instead of waiting for seeds to grow into plants to determine if they have those genes, scientists can simply sequence the DNA of the seed to determine if the genes are present. If they are, those seeds can be grown and used in a breeding program. Breeders are still altering the genetic makeup of crops using old-fashioned methods, but are able to select which crops to breed much faster.

Some breeders are even using robots to aid the process, like drones that fly over experimental wheat lines, using an infrared light and algorithms to determine which wheat plants are most robust against heat stress. These drones have taken what used to be a daylong activity for a person and turned it into a ten-minute exercise for a robot.[87]

Then there is epigenetics. We all know that you can change your DNA, but you can also change which parts of your DNA are expressed (if a gene is not expressed it is like the gene doesn't exist). The role of DNA is to determine what types of proteins the body should produce, but an organism has the ability to "cover" a portion of its DNA such that the protein it was meant to produce will not be produced. Whether a gene is expressed or not partly depends on the experiences of that organism throughout its life, acting as a "memory" for a plant to pass to its offspring. For example, the plant *Arabidopsis* will produce faster-germinating seeds if that plant was exposed to warmer conditions in the early part of its life—before the seed was formed.[88] It is almost as if the parent is telling its child, "The weather is warmer now, so go ahead and germinate." Crop scientists may soon begin influencing which genes are expressed by how its parents are managed, allowing us to alter plants without changing their DNA.

What the reader may not know about radicals like Dr. Voytas is that their job requires more than just biological brilliance. It requires entrepreneurship. "Part of running a research laboratory at the university demands a degree of entrepreneurism. You have to go out and seek funding, whether it's the federal government, or private foundation, or private companies. If you're entrepreneurial, if you're passionate about your work—you seek other opportunities." It takes a considerable amount of money to run genetic experiments. Scientists have to secure funding from either private or public sources, and usually do a little of both, and the public and private realms are not as separate in the university as some may think.

Antibiotechnology advocates frequently complain about the close connections between the world's premier biotech scientists and corporations, but this is a relationship that exists for a reason. Recently the National Academies of Sciences was criticized because many members of its panel on Sciences, Engineering, and Medicine profit from biotechnology ventures. This is a panel the government relies upon for developing effective regulations. It would be difficult to find scientists who understand the most advanced tools in molecular biology that are not involved in biotechnology firms.

Most universities have a technology transfer office designed to help researchers acquire patents and to secure money from private sources for technology development. The first time Dan plunged into the private sector was when he decided his jumping gene work could be used to add genes to plants. He was at Iowa State University at the time, which has a technology transfer program funded in part by John Pappajohn—an insurance entrepreneur and venture capitalist (and no, not the pizza guy). This office allows scientists to present their ideas to potential investors. It is akin to the show *Shark Tank*, but less sensationalized and without the commercial breaks.

Dan and a colleague had developed a way to use jumping genes to add DNA to plants, and when Dan participated in ISU's version of *Shark Tank* it was Pappajohn himself who gave him the money to acquire intellectual property (think patents) and start a company. The biologist with little business experience, aside from his time selling tomatoes as a kid, now had his own company called Phytodyne. Between 1999 and 2004 he was on partial leave from the university, using the seed money he had been given to try to develop new plant varieties.

What is important is that Dan did not just "jump ship" from the university when he thought he could make more money in the private sector. Iowa State University deliberately established a research system to *encourage* people like Dan to enter the private sector when they are able to secure funding. Universities know that society benefits when research is funded by both public and private sources. Governments have limited funds, and universities do not have the expertise to develop products for market. Life-enhancing products do indeed require basic research funded by governments, but basic scientific research best impacts people's lives when utilized by the private sector. Thus, patents owned by universities have the most value when they can by licensed to private companies.

Any new company attempting to develop new products based on recent proprietary technology must anticipate three things. First, a high likelihood of failure. Second, the firm will probably need to pivot at some point, when initial ideas are not fruitful and new strategies must be formed. Third, since many proprietary technologies must be used with technologies owned by others, the firm is going to have to navigate the byzantine world of patents and be able to develop harmonious relationships with other firms.

Each of these three events occurred with Phytodyne. Dan's method of adding genes did not work as well as he hoped. This meant he had to pivot, and when he did he began using a new gene-editing technique called zinc finger nucleases instead of his own patented process. The change in editing process required using a technology patented by another company that proved difficult to work with. The frustrating thing for Dan was that although he was able to do the actual work—his plant genes were being edited, and improved crops seemed promising—patents and struggles over profits prohibited him from bringing products to the market. Phytodyne ceased to exist in 2004. This was not just a disappointment for Dan and his private investors: the State of Iowa had committed millions to the company, with the anticipation that its success would bring jobs and prosperity to the state.[89]

As Phytodyne closed its doors, Dan reopened the door to his Iowa State University office, pledging he would never start a new company again and would instead focus on academic research, some of which involved developing gene-editing tools that people could use without infringing on the patent rights of others. His eagerness to collaborate with others to advance science and the public interest gained him a favorable reputation. Teamwork in genetic engineering is a difficult process. One must cooperate with others and share ideas, but at the same time the potential profits from patenting a good concept mean that people might steal your ideas and try to make them their intellectual property. "Sometimes your best friends end up scooping you. I train graduate students and postdoctoral fellows. So I try to keep them focused on an area that I think has great potential and that has so far been overlooked. They can have a head start before someone else jumps on that bandwagon. Sometimes we can make an important advance before the other groups, and sometimes we just have to acquiesce and say okay, we lost this battle, but look what's been learned and how can we take that knowledge and go one step further."

Dan's collaborative reputation paid off in his early career when a colleague suggested he try a different tool for gene editing (specifically, a different tool for "binding" onto the specific portion of DNA). After investing so much time in the zinc finger process, he was hesitant. Upon moving to the University of Minnesota, he decided to give this new idea a try. With some refinements, what emerged was the now-famous TALEN technology discussed earlier—the tool that created the healthier soybean oil and saved Layla's life.[90]

Dan's story reveals the contradictory nature of intellectual property in radical biology. It takes a large amount of money to conduct gene-editing research, and patents give investors the financial incentive to fund the research. Pappajohn is unlikely to fund Dan's research if some other company can profit from his discoveries, and there aren't enough public sources of funding to cover all the research that needs to be done. Unless governments and philanthropists are willing to increase their funding, intellectual property is essential to intellectual progress.

Yet, as we have seen with Dan's Phytodyne venture, patents can hinder progress also. Companies can be so eager to profit from their intellectual property that they discourage others from making investments that they would need to license that property. The company may be difficult to work with, and it is not always clear whether a process violates an existing patent—it must be decided in court. This makes companies reticent to venture into an area where patents already exist, even if that company believes it does not violate any patents. Somewhere between 40 percent and 90 percent of patents are never used by anyone. They exist for self-defense and for exploiting others.[91]

This is why Elon Musk in 2014 announced that his electric car company (Tesla) would no longer enforce the patents that it holds. Musk saw that the patents were hindering the development of the electric car industry in general, preventing the invention of new technologies that might benefit Tesla. His company would not prosper unless the electric car industry prospered, and one thing holding this industry back were the patents Tesla held.[92]

Just as the robotics engineer James Underwood needs industry connections to know what type of applications have value for people, so do geneticists like Dan. His work at the University of Minnesota concerned how to edit genes, not which type of engineered crops would do the most good. At the same time, a company called Cellectis was considering expanding its engineering to the agricultural world and approached Dan about collaborating. The company was not using TALEN, and so Dan suggested it, and he referred the company's representatives to the university's technology transfer office. They saw the value in TALEN, bid to use it, and talked Dan into venturing once again into the private sector to help run a new company that would be called Calyxt (a subsidiary of Cellectis). In addition to their soybean, Calyxt is using TALEN to remove genes from wheat that make it susceptible to a mildew and edit potato genes so that they produce less neurotoxins when cooked.

Dan's story illustrates the complex world of biotech discovery in agriculture. On the one hand, genetic research is a public good and governments invest money in the research, expecting it to benefit society overall. On the other hand, private companies are investing money as well, and their goal is to make profits. So Dan is supervising graduate students and leading science into a new world while he is also the chief science officer at Calyxt. While it is a potential conflict of interest, the engagement with both organizations can also be interpreted as a synergy. The university had to establish a conflict-of-interest committee to oversee his work, and so long as Dan and this committee behave ethically (all indications are that they have), this represents the best of both worlds. This system affords the opportunity for scientists both to nurture the general scientific knowledge that makes genetic engineering more effective and to develop products that will impact people's lives. "We wanted biotechnology 2.0. It is super powerful. We wanted people to adopt it, and it seemed like the first products should be those that benefit the consumer and the food supply." In the private-public partnership in a university, students can earn advanced degrees under the best scientists while consumers directly benefit from the scientists' work. "Gene editing is going to be ubiquitous in agriculture. It's going to be an integral part of the food supply. It's been fun to be at the early stages of the game, and to contribute to technology that's made it possible. How about an 'accidental radical?' Some things were deliberate and some things were fortuitous."

Consider also some of the similarities between a university and a corporation. Both benefit from the advancement of general knowledge but both also own patents for their discoveries and protect them with armies of lawyers. Both benefit from having the world's best scientists, but those scientists only thrive if they are also entrepreneurs. "Running a research lab at a university demands a degree of entrepreneurship," Dan commented.

"Universities have improved their methods of technology transfer. They teach faculty about the patent process, help them meet potential investors, and aid them in securing space for creating start-up companies."

Do not think this relationship between university researchers and businesses is a new phenomenon, though. Roughly half of the nitrogen in your body originated in a fertilizer-manufacturing plant,[93] the same plants that help feed roughly half of the world's population today.[94] This nitrogen was created using a process discovered by the university scientist Fritz Haber in 1908, but he did not know how to commercialize it or produce it on a large scale. To do that he needed the help of the corporation BASF. It was Haber's university itself that encouraged this partnership and made it possible, resulting in what is arguably the greatest agricultural discovery of all time.[95] One day, perhaps that trophy will go to gene editing.

Evan Ellison, Continuing the Genetic Revolution

A farm kid named Evan Ellison gave Dr. Dan Voytas a call. Evan was majoring in biotechnology at North Dakota State University and wanted to be part of Dan's team. Coming from a corn and soybean farm, he knew the significant changes that genetic engineering had provided to agriculture in the last few decades, but also the challenges remaining. He wanted to help continue the genetic revolution.

Evan (figure 2.11) had seen a documentary on Norman Borlaug when he was about sixteen. Borlaug used innovative technologies to develop several new crop varieties in the mid-twentieth century adapted for developing countries—crops that have fed many more people than was otherwise possible. Some speculate he has saved more human lives than any other person.[96] Borlaug's life impressed upon Evan the potential contribution of science to humankind, and the impact one dedicated plant breeder can make. Although more interested in mathematics, he majored in biotechnology because of its direct contribution to humans, and he figured that if Norman Borlaug were alive today, he would still be breeding plants—but would be using gene editing. As Evan read about gene editing, one name kept surfacing: Dan Voytas. So he gave Dan a call and explained, "I am a farm kid. I may or may not want to return to the farm, but the farm is where my roots are. I want to improve agriculture." Today, Evan is a PhD student in Dan's lab.

Born in 1994, Evan doesn't recall ever not planting a GMO corn or soybean, but his father and grandfather remember what the pre-GMO days

FIGURE 2.11 Evan Ellison (left) with his brother and father
Image courtesy of the Evan Ellison

were like. The seeds they plant today are transgenic, meaning a strand of DNA from a bacterium was inserted in the plant's DNA. This makes the crops resistant to herbicides, allowing herbicide to be sprayed right on top of the crop, killing the weeds but not the crop itself.

Before transgenic crops, Evan's family mainly controlled weeds through plowing. Before a field was planted, it would be plowed until no living material could be seen. Then, while the plant was growing, they would plow the dirt between the rows of crops (that type of plowing is called cultivating). All summer they would plow constantly. Today they simply spray the field three times (sometimes less, sometimes more, depending on conditions) and achieve the same amount of weed control. Corn and soybean farming today requires much, much less work than before and reduces soil erosion by minimizing disturbance of the topsoil. While firms like Calyxt are working hard to use biotechnology to deliver direct benefits to consumers, farmers like Evan's family have directly benefited for decades.

Transgenic corn and soybeans may have saved the Ellison family a lot of work in the last two decades, but Evan knows plant breeders cannot become complacent. Though young, he has personally experienced weeds evolving to resist the herbicides (it is rare for a person to personally witness evolution). "I guess something that I've noticed in my lifetime is that the weed pressure has increased in my memory. There are more and more herbicide-resistant weeds. It is definitely manageable, but it is a conscious thing you have to think about." Genetic modification gave Evan's family a brief advantage over the weeds, but nature always adjusts, so technology must also, and so his farm has adopted many new technologies in Evan's lifetime.

They have tractors that drive themselves, forming perfectly straight rows. Precision agriculture is used to plant more seeds per row in productive parts of the field, and less in others. The specific herbicides they use must be strategically adjusted, and they haven't had to plow a field in the last ten years. Modern farms regularly hire consultants to study the farm and make recommendations. "I think it boosts your innovation and your ingenuity a little bit. We have a good agronomist that helps us out with that. It is important also to spray the right mixes, [with] more tilling and more conscious decisions about when we till. The big thing we have really boosted in the past four or five years is our precision planting, trying to be smarter about how much seed we plant, what kinds of seed we plant, how we can cover the field appropriately to drown out weed pressure that way. And then that even goes on to spraying and your spray rates in the field." Every aspect of farming must be scrutinized with experience and science, and every aspect must be updated to take advantage of new technologies— technologies like gene editing.

Though he knows genetic engineering is controversial, Evan largely stays out of the GMO debate. "I think all too often it is just two sides shouting at each other, unwilling to listen to the other side." To the farming community in his area and the scientists he works with, gene editing is a proven technology and a best hope for feeding a growing population. "Basic gene editing is safer than traditional breeding. It is pretty incredible. You can knock out a gene, which is the same thing you can do in traditional breeding, but you can do it in one-tenth of the time."

Ironically, Evan embraces genetic engineering for the same reason some oppose it. With so many farmers adopting similar seed from a few companies, some fear we are losing plant diversity in agriculture. They fear the conformity in plant genetics places much of our food supply in jeopardy, should those crops prove vulnerable to large-scale pest infestations— like the fungus that ushered in the Irish Potato Famine. Later in the book we will meet two members of a group of Iowa State University students, Hannah Dankbar and Rivka Fidel, who opposed a GMO banana partly because the problem the banana was meant to address is best accomplished (the students believed) through crop diversification.

Yet Evan is looking to genetic engineering to increase plant diversity. Most farmers in his region of west central Minnesota grow only corn and soybeans, though some others raise crops like sugar beets, wheat, peas, beans, or sunflowers. He would like to see new crops being introduced, crops that could not be profitably grown in Minnesota until its genes were edited. This would provide farmers with better financial security, as they can rely on this new crop when corn and soybean prices are low. It would be good for the environment and the soil, as being able to plant a new crop in a field traditionally grown in soybeans and corn will reduce pest pressure, minimizing pesticide applications and plowing. Moreover, it would enhance food security for everyone, should corn and soybeans become too difficult to raise. "What can we get out of plants that help boost your immune system or give you anticancer fighting compounds or things like that? I think we are going to see more of that in fields and farms all over the place. I would like to see more diversity in some of the crops. If we are able to figure out a way to incorporate an alternative crop that has good yield and bring higher prices . . . farmers would be a fan of that."

Gene editing makes it easier to plant different varieties of the same crop in different regions of the world. "I wouldn't consider myself a radical person personality wise, but certainly with what we are doing and working on here, it is pretty out there. It is the latest and greatest stuff. Some may say that is radical. I think that is important . . . to push the boundaries a little bit of what people think." The Irish saw their entire potato crop rot due to a blight in the 1840s, and this was partly because the potatoes they planted were basically clones. Gene editing makes it easier to use plants that are nearly clones, but genetically tweaked to suit specific regions. So we discover that different groups of people may have a similar vision for the future of food, but radically different notions of making it a reality. The nice thing about pursuing the same goal through different means is that it increases the odds that one of them will work.

Marc Oshima Farms Vertically in the Shade

What could be more radical than farming without the sun? Sure, it is not difficult to grow a few plants indoors, and a unique plant, the bird's nest orchid doesn't even need sunlight. Yet to raise large amounts of food at a low cost in the absence of the sun seems impossible. It isn't impossible—but it is radical. And it isn't just the absence of the sun that makes this type of farming so interesting, but the intensity with which it is managed.

While breeders tinker with plant genes to make the plant better suited for their environment (like soybeans tolerant to salty soils), indoor farmers design the environment to match the plant's needs. This may sound absurdly expensive, but it introduces a number of cost-saving efficiencies and produces a high-quality product. The food from these farms can easily compete with food grown using traditional outdoor methods.

To picture one of these indoor farms, first imagine a library with stacks and stacks of books that rise from the floor to the ceiling. The ceiling is so high that one would need a ladder to reach the highest shelves, twenty feet off the ground. Now replace each shelf with a row of leafy greens and herbs on the bottom and LED lights on the top, emitting shades of blue and pink. The plants do not grow on soil. The seeds are imbedded in a fabric, and as the roots dangle below, they are fed by a mist of water containing plant nutrients (see figures 2.12, 2.13, and 2.14). The temperature is constant, as is the humidity.

No farm is more sanitary. The workers dress like surgeons, with face masks and sterilized clothing to ensure they bring no pathogens in from the outside. The building is pressurized, such that as you leave the building, the higher pressure inside tries to escape. You feel a gust of wind

FIGURE 2.12 Inside an AeroFarms Facility
Image courtesy of AeroFarms

FIGURE 2.13 A bird's-eye-view of AeroFarms' Vertical Farming System

Image courtesy of AeroFarms

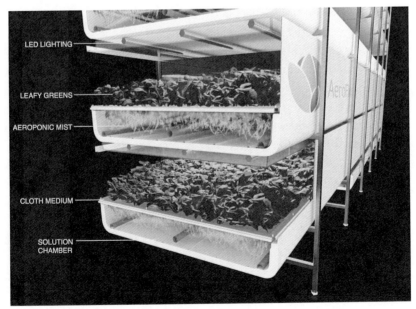

FIGURE 2.14 Growing plants without soil

Image courtesy of AeroFarms

at your back, pushing you out. That is the point: this pushing keeps plant pathogens from entering the building.

Building such a farm is obviously expensive, but the advantages make it economically feasible. LED lights save money by providing plants only the part of the light spectrum they need for growth. Feeding plants with a mist saves money on both water and fertilizer. Using pressurization to keep pests at bay means that not a dime need be spent on pesticides. This is not a greenhouse, so production can take place in any facility, allowing farms to repurpose almost any building (even a nightclub) into a farm.

The quality of the product cannot be exceeded by any traditional farm. Any one of the indoor farms may have close to three hundred different types of plants, and each type can be delivered the precise light spectrum it needs for maximum nutrition and flavor. With no bugs or fungus to damage the plant, the arugula looks too perfect to be real. One bite will remove any skepticism. While most farmers can grow crops only during the right seasons, an indoor farm can grow the same crop year-round, allowing consumer access to the same delicious lettuce during the dog days of summer or a winter of discontent.

Such a system is referred to as vertical farming, and AeroFarms is its leader. Many video tours are available online, but less information is accessible about some of the people behind the company. Let's meet one of AeroFarms' cofounders: Marc Oshima.[97]

Marc is a testament to the idea that success comes from marrying established business principles with out-of-the-box (or out-of-the-sun) thinking. Food is a business. It is one thing to identify a new way of producing food, but a very different thing to do so in the context of a sustainable business model. A theme of Marc's life has been understanding how food systems can differ and how those differences can be sustained—a medley of flux and permanence. "I've been fortunate to have exposure. It starts with the cultural aspect. I'm half German, half Japanese. Food has always been a window into different countries, different cultures. It's been an opportunity to be able to appreciate what food does in terms of celebrating, in rituals, and norms. Food can really bring people together in sharable moments." Being half German and half Japanese, he has witnessed the stark differences between food cultures, differences preserved by each culture through centuries of tradition. From this, Marc appreciates the fact that our poor eating habits can change for the better, and under the right conditions those changes can persevere.

Raised in the United States, Marc earned an undergraduate degree in East Asian studies, providing him another window into the malleability and permanence of culture. "It was about making that connection with my heritage and my background. It's been important for me to always have a different perspective, a global agenda, if you will, that is not just myopic about what's happening immediately here in the US. I think that's been very seminal when I think about the work that I've done on an international basis as well." His business education includes an MBA from Columbia and much experience in the corporate world. While earning an MBA, one learns about standard business practices and also about industry disruption—how firms capitalize on a new technology to offer consumers something other firms can't. "My career has been focused on . . . disrupting the traditional norms."

In the corporate world Marc developed an expertise in marketing, learning how to understand consumers, communicate with them, and establish a brand presence. He honed his craft working at a variety of nonfood companies like Arbitron (a ratings company purchased by Nielson), MTV, L'Oréal, and an online beauty retailer, but also food industries like Kraft.

The path that took Marc to AeroFarms really stems from a friendship and a desire to solve social problems through business. Marc was part of the US national fencing team, which traveled the world representing the United States in tournaments (he also fenced at Columbia as an undergraduate and became the 1991 NCAA champion in men's épée). Also on the national team was David Rosenberg. The two became close friends partly because of their time traveling together and partly because of their shared values.

For two decades they wanted to work together. During that time David was developing an interest in environmental issues, while Marc was involved with food security concerns. When he was the head of marketing for a regional supermarket chain in the Northeast, Marc began helping the Food Bank for New York City, where he used his marketing expertise to raise awareness and money, eventually becoming a member of its marketing advisory board, a position he would hold for over ten years. While helping the food bank in its mission, he became aware of the food security issues facing the nation. Upon learning that one out of four children in New York City faces hunger every day, he felt he had to play a role in transforming the food system. The system was broken. Simply maximizing the food bank's efforts, while necessary, was not going to fix it.

A focus on indoor growing systems resulted from a desire to address water issues. Through his work with the World Economic Forum and the Global Water Security Task Force, David learned that most of the fresh water used by humans goes to agriculture, and most of the water pollution comes from agriculture. If you want to improve the way we use water, David realized, you need to focus on farming. He reached out to Marc, who was in charge of marketing for Citarella Markets, a top US specialty food retailer, to learn more about locally grown produce. Marc had witnessed a change in consumer food preferences, watching the development of a much keener interest in how food is grown. He knew that if they could develop a more transparent, sustainable food production method, consumers would respond with enthusiasm.

Suspecting that they could identify a business opportunity to rectify both environmental and food security problems, Marc and David started a company called Just Greens and spent six months studying how food might be produced locally indoors. This period was akin to the stories of entrepreneurs starting a successful corporation in their garage. Imagine having a family and deciding to devote half a year to research and planning. They generated no income in the process, with no safety net should the planning come to naught. One can imagine the anxiety. Marc countered that this process was actually energizing, and the stress they experienced was a healthy stress. His business experience had taught him that the moment healthy stress becomes anxiety, it is time to reevaluate. That never happened. They were entirely self-funded at this time, but Marc remarked that they were fortunate to have supportive families. Moreover, Marc said they were confident that these months of research would reap rewards somewhere: if not this endeavor, then the next one.

During these months of writing business plans, they learned about a unique, patented system by Ed Harwood, a former Cornell professor who spent the early part of his career developing technologies for use on dairy farms. Harwood's company was called Aero Farm, and not only was its technology unique but it seemed scalable, meaning it could be efficiently installed in small and very large buildings alike.

Scalability doesn't just refer to the technical aspects of the farm, though. It also includes the business model itself. Are there enough consumers to purchase the product if more vertical farms are built? Are there enough food retailers interested in vertical farm produce to justify expanding? Is the business concept sufficiently enticing to investors to raise the capital needed to expand? These are questions a scientist concentrating on the technology is not prepared, or doesn't have time, to answer.

Experienced business people like Marc Oshima make their living answering these questions, and that's why people like Marc are so essential to transforming the food system. The three began talking, meeting, and suggesting collaborations, eventually agreeing to change "Aero Farm" to "AeroFarms" with David as the CEO, Ed as the chief science officer, and Marc as the chief marketing officer—and all of them as cofounders.[98]

It is easy to underestimate the marketing component of the company. When the *New York Times* recorded a 360-degree video of an AeroFarms facility,[99] the journalists marveled at the farming system, not the marketing plan. If the system really works well, then it shouldn't be difficult to sell the product, right? Not exactly. For AeroFarms to grow, it needed investors. Building one of these farms costs tens of millions of dollars. For a farm with this price tag to be profitable, it must produce—and sell—large amounts of produce. One has to show the investors that these markets exist, that the product can be sold. Marc's many years in food marketing taught him what kinds of foods will sell well, and how those foods should be marketed. The brand must gain recognition and respect. Marc recognized that people are increasingly concerned with how their food is produced. "There's a few reasons why we focus on short-stemmed greens and herbs. One is nutrition. How we can bring a better product to the marketplace and have an impact? The other aspect is where do we see the ping-points in the industry? California is called the 'salad bowl' because it had the right climate to be able to grow; 95 percent of our leafy greens are coming from there. It's become a very large-scale, commercialized, centralized production. All that has to travel throughout the United States. We can take that exact same seed and grow it. It might take thirty or forty-five days out in the field. We can grow it in twelve to sixteen days. Thirty harvests a year we can achieve versus two to three out in the field. . . . This way of growing has over seventy-five times greater productivity per square foot than the traditional field farm, uses 95 percent less water, and uses zero pesticide."

If he is going to sell lettuce that looks like it has never been touched by a bug, Marc needs consumers to understand the process and to specifically understand that it was never sprayed with an insecticide. "From day one in launching AeroFarms, our vision has been to build responsible farms all over the world and fundamentally transform agriculture. Technology is an enabler, but you need a fundamental business plan, and my background has been in building brands and companies and understanding the right economic model. Our entire business is driven by marketing insights into what products to grow, what marketing channels to use, what price to charge, and how to develop the right brand to connect with consumers."

An indoor farm like those run by AeroFarms needs not only marketing specialists, but many other specialists as well. AeroFarms employs plant scientists, plant physiologists, mechanical engineers, electrical engineers, and the like. No one person can understand, much less manage, the entire AeroFarms system. AeroFarms is currently doing work on four different continents to address challenges facing the contemporary food system. "Our mission is, how do we transform agriculture and how do we have a better approach to what we're doing? We are radically changing the mindset around how we think about our food, our food system. We're really trying to champion an overall dialogue about how to create a better system. That's where I think we're most excited. How do we get everybody else on board?"

Consider the fact that every time they harvest a plant, they are collecting over thirty thousand observations of data, and they must explore those data to optimize the amount and type of light, fertilizer, and water used, as well as the temperature of the building. Moreover, there will not be just one combination of inputs that is best, because these inputs can be adjusted to create plants that taste different. AeroFarms can create a "recipe" for a basil or a lettuce, spelled out not in ingredients or cooking instructions but in the growing environment.

In this vertical farm, to be a chef requires the help of engineers, data scientists, and specializations of many flavors—including marketing. Everyone brings a strategic asset to the table.

Dominique Barns Invents a New Shrimp

One of the authors once overheard a conversation between two friends. One of them lamented that his niece was majoring in marine biology. "What is she going to do with a marine biology degree?" he asked, implying the major held few job opportunities. The next day we interviewed a food radical named Dominique Barnes, a marine biodiversity and conservation graduate, who took her degree and became the cofounder and CEO of New Wave Foods. It takes all kinds of backgrounds. Dominique may one day be referred to as a savior of the marine ecosystem.

Though she grew up in Las Vegas, Dominique always had a love for marine life. After graduating from the University of Nevada, Las Vegas, with a psychology degree (the marine biology degree came later) she worked as a guide on whale-watching boats, in various capacities at a zoo, and several aquariums. One of her favorite jobs was being a shark biologist at the Golden Nugget in Las Vegas. "I was so excited to be diving every day, and learning more about these animals. All the maintenance, all the upkeep, from diving to preparing the food, feeding them, taking water samples, testing the water, maintaining life support equipment. I was more than just a diver and a biologist. I was also a plumber and their chef and all those great things."

For two years she thought she was living the dream, but then "I really started to think about it. Well no, I'm taking care of a small drop of water in the middle of the desert. Our globe is mostly ocean and there's just so much going on out there that needs to be addressed." She applied for and was accepted in the interdisciplinary marine biodiversity and conservation program at the Scripps Institute for Oceanography.

Though excited to be studying the subject she loved, the first semester was rather depressing. "I went there and was so excited! Learning more, diving in deeper, going to broaden my horizon and skills in this space. I think the first quarter I was in a complete depression because all we learned about was climate change, and the things that are devastating for oceans: overfishing, poor fisheries management, and sea level rise. It was like, wow, so many things are changing so quickly and it feels like there's nothing we can do."

Politicians were debating whether climate change was real rather than taking action. No one owns the ocean, no one country controls it, and the seafood market is enormous. It is difficult for the private or public sector to moderate seafood harvests to ensure a sustainable catch. Something had to change.

Dominique became exposed to the idea of social entrepreneurship, where positive social change occurs through an innovation in the private sector. Dominique saw innovators propose various uses of algae for solving social problems, and she enrolled in a social entrepreneurship program at the University of California, San Diego.

In the past the corporate world held little allure for Dominique. It seemed to be more about greed than social justice. Yet she was warming to the idea that one can earn money and serve the greater good at the same time. In cases where public policy was not responding to problems, entrepreneurship seemed an effective solution.

As she learned more about social entrepreneurship, she was also learning about algae and was becoming quite enamored with it. Until her class in phycology, she was unaware of its pervasiveness in nature and consumer products—even food. "I took a phycology class, which is the study of algae, and that was around the same time that I learned more about business and entrepreneurship as a strong tool. I was learning about algae . . . it's not a plant, it's not an animal, it's this amazing part of the world that I think is really underappreciated. I learned more about how now people are looking at it for biofuel alternatives, food alternatives. It's actually very present in our food already. Go and buy toothpaste, or go and buy ice cream, and you'll find algae products." We are told that fish is healthy because of its omega-3 fatty acids, but those acids largely come from the algae the fish eat. If you take fish oil supplements, there is a good chance that some of the fish oil comes directly from algae farms like the one shown in figure 2.15. People have been eating seaweed (an algae) for centuries (probably millennia), and the antioxidant supplement astaxanthin is produced from algae.

FIGURE 2.15 Yes, Algae farms are a thing!
CSIRO [CC BY 3.0 (http://creativecommons.org/licenses/by/3.0)], via Wikimedia Commons

While Dominique was figuring out how to use entrepreneurship to create change, a materials engineer named Michelle Wolf was interested in creating artificial shark fin in the lab so that shark fin soup could be made without having to harvest sharks. She was interested in talking with an expert on sharks, so a friend introduced her to Dominique.

It turned out that Dominique was not the kind of expert Michelle was looking for, because she wanted information about the molecular structure of the shark fin, which was not part of Dominique's training. However, Michelle ultimately received something much better. Their shared interest in protecting marine life sparked a conversation that eventually led to a start-up called New Wave Foods, with Dominique as the cofounder and CEO and Michelle as the cofounder and chief technology officer. They would eventually pivot from artificial shark fins to artificial shrimp, made from plant proteins, algae, and other ingredients.

One of the greatest gifts humans could bestow the oceans is to stop harvesting so much shrimp. Catching wild shrimp requires casting large nets that drag the ocean floor, thus trapping nearly everything in its path: shark, snapper, grouper, and turtles, among other sea life. "You can't line fish shrimp. You really do have to use a net. Unfortunately, that results in a large by-catch ratio. Even if you have turtle excluders—exclusion devices where if a turtle got stuck in the net, it could escape—you're still going to have a higher ratio of dead animals that you're not going to eat, just throw away, to the one pound of shrimp." The practice also results in damage to the ocean floor and harm to the ecosystem. Even if nets caught only wild shrimp, harvest occurs to excess, leading to declining populations. Overfishing and climate change are so damaging to shrimp populations around Maine that a complete moratorium on shrimping was enacted in 2014.[100] Additionally, shrimping practices remain one area in which human slavery continues to be perpetuated in the food supply, where humans are kidnapped and forced to work on shrimping vessels without pay.[101] Shrimp can be farmed but must be fed fishmeal made from wild fish—wild fish that are already harvested at or beyond their maximum sustainable level.[102] For these and other reasons, shrimp lovers must either accept the damage their consumption entails or replace it with a more ethical product. Most people are choosing the former, but if an artificial shrimp that tastes just like the real thing could be invented, they might choose the latter. It was this perfect shrimp substitute that Dominique and Michelle sought to invent.

At first all they had was a shared passion and a vision, no money or lab space to begin experimenting. Lucky for them, there are investors eager to help such ambitious visionaries. IndieBio is a biotech accelerator that specializes in identifying talented people with creative ideas to provide access to existing networks, give them funding and lab space to get started, and offer training in how to turn their vision into a real company. As an accelerator that specializes in biotechnology, IndieBio provided Dominique and Michelle with access to other scientists for technical help. The two applied to IndieBio, were accepted, and only a year after graduating with her graduate degree in marine biodiversity and conservation, Dominique was the CEO of a start-up with solid investors.

Let us pause for a moment and note the similarities in the origin stories of New Wave Foods and AeroFarms. Both began with a friendship between two people who wanted to improve the world through entrepreneurship. Both sought a sustainable business model by first disrupting the food industry (New Wave Foods' motto is Disrupting Seafood, Not Oceans), and both demonstrate the positive role that the financial industry can play in food. "We are focused on a food system that has been harming marine life for a long time, so we want to disrupt that system to make it better. That was the idea behind the slogan Disrupting Seafood, Not Oceans."

After the 2008 financial crisis and the Occupy Wall Street protests, it is tempting to associate finance with bad disruptions ("disruption" is a term loved by the "tech" industry). The term "disruption" is "used to think about systems that have been in place for a long time that are themselves destructive. You want to disrupt that system to make it better. That was the idea behind using Disrupting Seafood, Not Oceans, because the seafood supply chain, broadly, is a broken system. It has resulted in so many of the challenges—overfishing, by-catch ratios, and derelict fishing gear. Disrupt this system that is broken. Build it to be better."

It is difficult to disrupt the food system for the better without private funding. So if the reader is a finance major wanting to also be a food radical, your industry is just as essential as visionaries like Don Voytas, Marc Oshima, and Dominique Barnes.

Also note that one service IndieBio provided New Wave Foods was a branding and media expert—marketing, much like Marc Oshima's contribution to AeroFarms. "Being at IndieBio, we were introduced to countless people, from investors to other entrepreneurs. It almost sounds like a joke, but three rabbis walked in to IndieBio, and the next thing that we know, our product is kosher. We weren't thinking about markets, and who this would appeal to. When these rabbis came into IndieBio, they were actually looking to further understand the intersection of Jewish kosher law and the new technology in food." Up until then she hadn't really thought about marketing the product, but now she was able to develop specific targeted markets. So if the reader is a marketing major, you, too are important to revolutionizing the food industry!

It remains to be seen whether New Wave Foods can help heal the oceans, but it is off to an auspicious beginning. "I think you can call this a radical disruptive idea." More investors have backed the venture, and the artificial shrimp is now being served at Google headquarters (more on how New Wave Foods made that connection in a later section). A reporter for *Business Insider* remarked, "The texture was almost perfect. The lab-made shrimp had that springiness and mixture of crunch and chew that you'd expect from the real thing. I could see myself replacing real shrimp with this in some situations."[103] It has a look (see figure 2.16), feel, smell, and nutrient profile similar to real shrimp and can be eaten by some people who have shellfish allergies. For the first time in a very long time, the animal rights activist Cody Carlson we met earlier will with a clean conscience be able to savor the taste of shrimp if he so chooses.

FIGURE 2.16 Dominique's more ethical shrimp
Image courtesy of New Wave Foods

We are betting that the reader will one day be eating New Wave Foods shrimp and loving it. "Hopefully, it means that we're moving that needle on the demand for seafood from our oceans, or even farmed. Really starting to shift how we get food to feed ourselves. It's just so inefficient and we can't feed this growing population the way that we're doing it now. We have to think about change. Hopefully, what we're doing helps towards that change, but also inspires other people to think about food differently. How do we get that food, and what does that look like moving forward into the future?"

Perhaps the most important element of their success is the friendship between Dominique and Michelle. In the process of designing their product there were successes and failures along the way. Imagine yourself in Dominique's place, given large sums of money to develop an acceptable synthetic shrimp in a relatively short period of time with little indication as to whether it can be done. There were times when Michelle would become pessimistic, and Dominique would have to be the optimist to keep the team going. Other days they would switch roles. Each could read the other, and each knew what it took to keep the duo persevering.

During one particular long day of work Dominique recalled what it was like when she was employed in a structured corporation. She had to take the Myers-Briggs personality test (it tests people's personality types, like extroversion versus introversion). It turned out that Michelle had taken the test also. When they looked up their scores, it turned out they were the perfect compatibility.

If you are going to be a food radical and employ "radical disruption," it is best not to go it alone. You will be trying to revolutionize a food system that is resistant to change. There are days when you will feel that change is impossible, and without a Dominique or Michelle for encouragement you might throw in the towel too soon. "Sometimes your passion leads you on a path that you didn't anticipate, but can be more exciting than what you thought it would be." It is one thing to be a food radical, but another to be one that creates meaningful change, and to be the latter requires support from others—both professional and personal.

Liz Specht, the Utilitarian

There is a Buddhist ritual in China where live fish are purchased from markets and then released back into the wild. The belief is that this act of altruism has a karmic reflex, healing illness and enriching the lives of all sentient creatures. Of course, not all Chinese are Buddhists. Many love the taste of fish. Fishermen have begun gathering around the release location with nets to catch the liberated fish and return them to the dinner plate. Arguments and even brawls have taken place at the sites, with Buddhists often wading into the water to cut the fishermen's nets.[104]

This is emblematic of the struggle between those who choose to eat animals and those who do not. The conflict persists because one side is not able to convince the other that the ethical satisfaction of giving up meat is worth the culinary sacrifice. Our current age, however, points to a solution that has never been available before: *good* meat alternatives that reflect the experience of eating products produced by animals. The Chinese have had substitutes like tofu and gluten for centuries, but these items are in texture and taste different from animal meat. What if these options were as delicious as the real thing? We might then have a world where the Buddhists can release the fish in peace, because the fisherman are at home eating synthetic fish instead. (Of course, if no one is buying fish to eat, there might not be any fish to release.)

That is certainly the world Dominique Barnes at New Wave Foods is seeking to create. How realistic is it? Tyson Foods, a processor of one out of every five pounds of meat eaten in the United States,[105] certainly seems to think the market for synthetic meat is profitable. In 2016 Tyson purchased a 5 percent stake in Beyond Meat, a company currently selling burger (and other meat) substitutes made only from plant protein. In Tyson's announcement of the purchase, one of its senior vice presidents remarked, "The quality of the Beyond Burger is amazing." There are many other firms in addition to Beyond Meat and New Wave Foods trying to knock meat out of the market.

Impossible Foods has made plant proteins taste more like beef by adding "plant blood." The soybean plant makes heme (a molecule in blood responsible for part of its taste when cooked). Impossible Foods took the part of soybean DNA that produces heme and inserted it into the DNA of a yeast. The modified yeast produces large amounts of heme, which can be added to plant-based proteins to make them taste more like meat.[106] In this sense, companies are working to reconstruct the constituents of meat, just without the animal.

Other firms are literally making real meat, not from plant or algae proteins, but from live animal cells. It isn't "the cow" or "the pig" itself that produces meat, but certain cells within the organism. Scientists have learned to take these cells, grow them in the lab, and have them produce meat—and it's working.[107] At least one company is developing a synthetic leather from a similar cell process.

Dairy is not immune to these synthetic innovations. Alternatives like soymilk and almond milk are now common in grocery stores, with 29 percent of households purchasing plant-based milk at least once a year.[108] The dairy industry (the *real* dairy industry) is pushing for bills that would prohibit these alternatives from being called "milk,"[109] just like they fought against margarine decades ago.[110] Like meat, the dairy industry is threatened by entrepreneurs who want to make actual milk without the cow. By inserting just the right cattle genes into yeast cells, those cells can be used to make a liquid that is very close if not identical to real milk.[111]

Why all the interest in getting rid of the cow, pig, chicken, and shrimp? Are people becoming more vegetarian or vegan? It isn't clear. Gallup Polls asked Americans about being vegetarian in 1999, 2001, and 2012. The percent of vegetarians was 5–6 percent in each year.[112] However, there seems to be more interest in reducing meat consumption. Some schools and even the Norwegian military have adopted meatless Mondays.[113] Every year new celebrities announce they are vegan, from Beyoncé to Bill Clinton. Former president Barack Obama has even said that to help mitigate global warming we need to eat less meat and "produce protein in a more efficient way."[114]

Although there are some instances when food from livestock can be climate friendly, when produced using conventional methods, meals produced from animal-based products have a higher carbon footprint than vegetarian or vegan diets.[115] This realization has made not only animal rights activists, but environmentalists, interested in reducing meat, dairy, and egg production and consumption. Most activists have given up trying to convince us to adopt a more ethical diet, though. The developed world just isn't interested, and as the developing world gets richer, people there too want meat. To protect animals and the climate, many have concluded that the only way to wean us from meat is to replace it with something just as tasty.

We need social entrepreneurs like Dominique Barnes working together to develop meat alternatives sooner rather than later. Dominique is working in the private sector, developing patented processes. You can't expect companies like Impossible Foods and Beyond Beef to freely trade information to speed up the development process—they are competitors, both trying to patent the best meat alternative. This isn't because they care more about profits than the environment, but because they were given large sums of money from investors to develop meat alternatives, and those investors did so expecting to be paid back. They will not see a return unless the firm's production process is patented and successful in the marketplace.

If alternatives to meat are a key strategy for mitigating climate change, helping these organizations is one of the best things a philanthropist could do. It would be nice if there was a scientist, an organization, who was there to simply help these companies succeed—someone to help the helpers—simply for the greater good, not asking anything in return, so that these entrepreneurs had someone they could trust to move their ideas forward. Such a scientist and such an organization does exist. Her name is Liz Specht, and she works for the Good Food Institute.

Liz Specht grew up with an engineer for a father who loved to perform science projects with his children, allowing her to see the wonders of science from an early age. She enjoyed all of her classes, was particularly good at math and science, and naturally had an interest in animals and ecology. Both the big picture of how humans interact with the environment and the microscopic picture of how animal cells develop sparked her interest. At first she was just naturally interested in science. It was a summer program for gifted students that instilled a moral imperative to use science for the greater good.

Three weeks out of every summer, for four summers, Liz attended Duke University's Talent Identification Program. She relished every moment. It was an unusual opportunity to be around other students equally interested in learning, where subjects were taught not to prepare them for a test, but to inspire them. Part of the camp involved ethics and technology, where students were exposed to different moral philosophies. One of these was utilitarianism, originating with Jeremy Bentham (1748–1832) and popularized more recently in arguments about animal rights by philosopher Peter Singer. The concept emphasizes that the preferred action is that which results in the greatest amount of happiness for the greatest number of people. It focuses on the consequences of an action (as opposed to the intentions) and treats each person equally. This philosophy more than any other reduces moral dilemmas to a math problem, with actions on the left-hand side and total human happiness on the right-hand side. It seemed logical, pragmatic, productive, and therefore appealing to Liz. So at the age of thirteen Liz announced to her parents that she had become a utilitarian.

This didn't just mean that she wanted to lead an ethical life. It meant she wanted to concentrate on actions that would have large, positive impacts on many people or many animals. She thought about becoming a veterinarian. While personally tending to a few individual animals seemed a noble life, she preferred to use science and technology that would benefit hundreds, thousands, millions . . . perhaps billions of animals.

Of course, at the age of thirteen she didn't exactly know how to do that, but she knew it would require much learning. After graduating from high school she went to Johns Hopkins University, where she majored in chemical engineering and began working as a research assistant in her sophomore year. "It was predominantly a computational lab. The graduate student I was working with was particularly looking at the folding of proteins. It had potential applications for biomedical implants that you want to interface with proteins in the body. I did not do the computational side of the research, but the wet lab validation of those predictions." Our utilitarian was becoming a scientist.

She was also learning that fixing problems requires more than clever engineering. "I was very interested in the ways that society uses technology, and realizing that all the research in the world—and all the tech development—doesn't matter if you can't convince people to use it in the right way. This realization that science is not happening in a vacuum really came about through some travel I did while I was an undergrad." After her junior year of college Liz was accepted into a summer program called Engineers for a Sustainable World (ESW). ESW sent her to India to address water and sanitation issues in low-income communities. What surprised her was that there were already many easy solutions to existing problems. Chlorine droplets and water purifiers are two examples, but they were not widely used because they were not already embedded in the community culture. "You get there and you realize there's all these other kinds of cultural and societal factors. It's not just a straight translation. We have the technological fix, now we just implement it. There's all of this background research. How do you gain trust within the community? How do you position this product as something that's desirable? How do you increase adoption rates of a new technology, doing it in a sensitive way so that you're not a bunch of white people rushing into the community and telling them how to drink their water."

Readers may have recently seen that India is encouraging its citizens to use toilets but is making slow progress because so many are accustomed to defecating in the open.[116] The country adopted mobile phones quickly, so quickly that 88 percent of Indian households have a mobile phone,[117] yet half a billion Indians practice open defecation.[118] This is the type of cultural resistance to easy solutions Liz witnessed, and it impressed upon her the importance of gaining community trust and understanding culture in helping find workable solutions. This experience would come in handy later, when Liz joined a movement to help Americans forgo their meat and replace it with "fake meat."

During college, Liz was mostly a vegetarian. "My concerns were not animal welfare related. They were stemming from what I like to think of as my engineering disdain for inefficiency. The thought of eating a meal that required potentially ten times as many resources as a plant-based meal seemed inappropriate to me." A meat-based meal requires more resources to produce than a plant-based meal. Being a vegetarian most of the time just seemed a prudent way to live a responsible life. This wasn't a dominant theme in her life at the time, though, as she still had much more science to learn before she could determine how she would change the world. Liz was still a student learning the essence of life and searching for her destiny.

For her graduate work Liz attended the University of California at San Diego, in a bioengineering program that employed a more interdisciplinary approach than if she continued studying chemical engineering. Here, like our friend Dominique Barnes, she was surprised to discover a fascination with algae, and ultimately conducted her dissertation on developing new tools to genetically engineer algae. Though she enjoyed the laboratory work, the world of teaching and advocacy still called to her, and she taught at various academic summer camps, similar to those that inspired her so much as a child, and even taught some high school classes. "For the classes that were long enough, I would always have students come up with their own genetically modified organism that solved some type of problem in the world. Then they had to go out and actually find what gene they would put in, why they think it would work. Who needs to approve this at the regulatory level? What kind of backlash or concerns might you get from the public? How would you address those? I tried to make it pretty well rounded in that they definitely got the hands-on science, but we were also thinking a little bit more broadly on the implications of this type of research." Liz was becoming a scientist and a teacher, and her utilitarian perspective remained.

By the time she was finishing her doctoral program Liz was unsure of her next move. Though she still loved science, the academic life did not seem very appealing. Science professors are planners, managers, entrepreneurs, and administrators more than most people think. They must apply for grants, chart creative new ideas, and manage many people, many labs, and large amounts of money. This type of job did not call to Liz personally. She took a postdoctoral position where she engineered bacteria to help diagnose human disease, "doing a lot of what is called tool development. That's been kind of a recurring theme to me that I find really fascinating, developing a technology that then enables other people, other researchers, to develop other tools that actually are applied." She also began studying animal agriculture in great detail. After watching online lectures, reading books by Peter Singer and Howard Lyman, and studying other sources on livestock production, Liz came to the firm conclusion that animals were not only an inefficient source of food, but their use was inhumane and unethical on a variety of fronts. "I was doing this really cool research project during the day, but then at night I would just come home and read all of this information about animal agriculture and factory farming. It really started to feel like a significant disconnect from my day job versus what I was starting to become consumed by and really passionate about." After eating mostly vegetarian food for ten years, Liz was now a vegan and felt a calling to confront the problems she saw in livestock agriculture.

Liz also realized that although society was engaging in a number of pro-environmental behaviors, like switching lightbulbs and driving hybrid cars, the topic of meat production seemed taboo, even though plant-rich diets have been ranked as the fourth best way to combat global climate change (out of one hundred considered).[119] Sure, there had always been groups encouraging people to go vegan or consume less meat, but they seemed to convince few. What do you do if you believe people need to eliminate meat, dairy, and eggs from their diets for a more humane and sustainable society, but they are unwilling to make that change?

Liz wanted to do something to help wean the modern world from livestock, so she applied for a job as a director of education at Mercy for Animals (the organization for which our food radical Cody Carlson performed undercover investigations). Given her extensive experience teaching, not to mention her vast scientific knowledge, she was qualified for the position. It would entail leaving unused all the advanced chemistry and biology she had acquired over the years. Mercy For Animals could not hire her because she was unable to start soon enough, but knew the perfect organization for combining her scientific achievements, her experience as an educator, and her desire to reduce livestock production. She needed to talk to Bruce Freedrich at the Good Food Institute. When she checked out the organization, she noticed they had an opening for a senior scientist. "It was like a lightbulb moment. I started reading about the potential of food technology to change the set of options that are available to consumers, to make this less of an offensive battle, or psychological battle, or fighting against cultural currents, get the options out there and then let's use technology to make this easy . . . eventually." It seemed her entire life had prepared her for that moment. For many years she had been a utilitarian in the sense that she wanted to have the greatest impact on as many people and animals as possible. However, only until then did she know how to go about doing it. Of course, she got the job. "I am a scientific consultant for people who are interested in starting companies in this space. We have a lot of entrepreneurs who come to us who are passionate about increasing food options and animal product alternatives. They're not really sure where to start."

The Good Food Institute (GFI) began with the recognition that investors and entrepreneurs were showing great interest in developing substitutes for meat, dairy, and eggs (hereafter, let's just say "meat"), but there was little coordination in their efforts. Believing that successful substitutes would be good for animals, the environment, and society, philanthropists provided the money to help the industry develop. "I think it really cool that technology allows us to rewrite the rules of what we eat. Science has given us new options generations prior didn't have." You can think of GFI as being a free consultant. Remember the story of how the materials engineer Michelle Wolf was looking for someone interested in helping to develop a seafood substitute, leading her to our food radical Dominique Barnes and resulting in New Wave Foods? Well, if Michelle had not found Dominique, she could have contacted the GFI. GFI would gladly have helped her understand what type of cofounder she should be looking for and develop contacts toward that endeavor.

Recall also that Dominique and Michelle were able to acquire funding and scientific assistance from the accelerator IndieBio. If they didn't have IndieBio, they would have been able to contact GFI for help as well. For scientific questions about what has been attempted in making synthetic shrimp, and what ideas are unexplored by others—or any questions of a scientific nature—Liz is there to help. If innovators need help contacting potential investors or want information on accelerators receptive to startups in the meat substitute business, the GFI will happily provide that information also. Should they want someone to look at their business proposal for constructive criticism, GFI is there for that too.

The GFI also exists to chart a course for the meat substitute industry, by collecting information on progress made thus far and obstacles remaining. For example, Liz remarks that there are already great egg substitutes for baking but not for scrambled eggs. "Pretty much all of the plant-based meats that are out there are either wheat-based, soy-based, or very recently pea-protein based. There are whole other fields of plant-based proteins that are unexplored for their suitability for plant-based meats, which is a little dismaying. We've constrained ourselves to this little corner of the possibilities from a food science perspective. It's exciting because of all the opportunities—mapping out the opportunities and then asking, what are the technological risks, barriers, or obstacles for any of these?"

Moreover, almost all proteins are currently extracted through extrusion, and this tends to produce a product whose texture does not have the "fibrous" mouth feel of meat (the texture is more like beans than steak).[120] "We've got one technology recently out of Europe that's two cylinders that spin within each other, and they're producing that shear force in one direction to give you those fibers that have the mouth feel of meat fibers. This technology has been demonstrated on a small scale, but no one's using this at production scale to make plant-based meats that are sold on the market. That's just one example of a new processing technology that—even with the same ingredients we're using—could give you improved food properties in terms of texture and moisture, and all those flavor retentions, fat retention." (See figure 2.17.) Any new or existing firm wanting to explore these other methods need only ask for help from GFI in its role as "a nucleating or connecting organization."

The information available through Liz and GFI is useful for social entrepreneurs wanting to enter the market but not sure what the market currently looks like or the unexplored realms. The GFI also works to avoid redundancy. With so much competition between different companies, each relying on proprietary processes, it is unlikely that one company will share information about its success and failures with another. So that a new firm doesn't waste investors' money on a process already shown to fail by another firm, Liz and the GFI provide such information.

While each individual company is focused on ensuring its individual success, Liz is working to make sure the meat substitute industry as a whole succeeds, and the GFI does this by not just lending a helping hand but by being a leader. "I actually don't see it as in conflict, or resisting, or

FIGURE 2.17　Using a Couette Cell to make a meat-like texture from plant proteins
Image courtesy of The Good Food Institute

disrupting. Everyone in the start-up phase really loves the word 'disrupting.' I don't like that term so much, because to me it's more of a revolution, it's like an evolution. We're innovating ourselves away from the least beneficial practices of the way we get our food, rather than ditching the whole system altogether."

In a previous section on Dan Voytas we saw how the government and universities partner with the private sector to promote biotechnology because it provides benefits to the public. The story of Liz Specht and GFI demonstrates that philanthropists (who fund the GFI) see public benefits in promoting vegan foods. They are also partnering with private firms for the sake of the greater good.

There need not always be a bright line between investing and philanthropy though. Working at the GFI brought Liz into a different world, where for the first time she was working with private investors. She was pleasantly surprised to learn that investors were not just interested in the highest rate of return for their investment, but are specifically interested in funding companies that align with their ideals about the social good and environmental sustainability. "There's certainly a lot of interest in letting these start-ups figure out what works and what doesn't. These big and established food companies are watching the writing on the wall with interest, not with fear or trepidation. They see that the landscape is changing in terms of what consumers are looking for and the considerations we have about our food choices. They want to be a part of it. I think they're watching what happens on the innovation side in this space and letting the risk pan out in these start-ups before getting involved."

Most of us go through phases that as a teenager we grow out of. Liz has remained the utilitarian she became at the age of thirteen. "Just from like a geeky, tech perspective, one thing that I find really cool is that we can completely rewrite the set of rules that you use to govern what things you eat and what things you don't eat." If she can help meat substitutes thrive in the supermarket, she believes she will indeed be doing "the greatest good for the greatest number." Yet at the same time it is a risky venture. Had she stuck with her early plans of becoming a veterinarian there is no doubt she could have helped some animals. Instead, she is rolling the dice and hoping her scientific expertise can help the billions of livestock in the world and the earth's ecosystem—but there is no guarantee the meat substitute industry will make a large dent in the livestock industry. Liz is optimistic though. She's betting it all, and she's certainly not bluffing.

3

The Forum

FOOD IS HIGHLY political. Readers do not need two university professors to tell them that. That message is painted across a mirror of society we call comedy. When writers of the film *The Dictator* sought to poke fun at those on the political left, they crafted a character named Zoey, who runs a grocery store described as a "free earth collective . . . a vegan, feminist, non-profit cooperative within an antiracist, antioppressive framework for people of all or no genders . . . a pure democracy" with an organic farm on its roof and a wellness center in its basement.[1]

In this section we see that Zoey is not quite the caricature the film suggests. Today's radical food movements are led by creative thinkers and targets of racism; they are speaking out for environmental and social justice, and they seek to achieve this by establishing a more democratic social system. Food becomes a central issue in these movements because its absence causes so much pain. Structural racism is manifest in the food deserts of the United States, where gas stations serve as grocery stores. Oppression is magnified in developing countries by an entire nation's inability to control its own food supply. Simply being able to vote in a representative democracy is insufficient for correcting injustice. We will meet people experimenting with new, radical forms of democracy, with food as a central part of their organizing strategies.

The movements we address will seem out of the ordinary but are occurring across the world. We will encounter an armed insurrection in Mexico that established a quasi-independent region seeking not only food justice, but gender equality. That movement will inspire peasants across the world to insist on their rights and dignity. We illustrate how this inspired a young Irishman to return to his green island and seek food sovereignty for a developed nation, and an African American woman to insist on food sovereignty in Oakland, California.

Laugh at the Zoey character if you like, but by the end of this chapter the reader will realize she is real, sophisticated, and determined. Indeed, the reader will find that there are many nonradicals who sympathize with her on some issues, and that it is those who laugh the loudest at her who may be the most naive.

Karissa Lewis versus the US Food System

Karissa Lewis grew up in a "food desert." This is not merely a phrase describing an area with poor access to food, but a technical term used by researchers and government agencies to understand patterns of food insecurity. The exact definition varies across regions, but for Oakland a food desert is defined as an area where more than 20 percent of the population is below the poverty threshold and 33 percent live more than a mile from a supermarket.[2] Food deserts are areas where there may be convenience stores for acquiring junk food but few places to buy healthy foods. Snickers bars and alcohol are just around the corner, whereas fresh fruits and vegetables might be miles away.

Karissa's childhood was filled with difficulties caused by an oppressive economic system that seemed intentionally designed to keep her community in continual stress. "When we were growing up, we were low income. A few times in my life as children, we were homeless. McDonald's and Burger King were our go-to places to eat. We were the family that would go in and sit down like it was a regular restaurant."

Years later, as her husband returned from an eight-year prison sentence in 2008, he returned not from an institution designed to punish wrong, but one calibrated to hinder minorities—an institution designed in a representative democracy where politicians often preserve power by gerrymandering voting districts to dilute the influence of an African American vote,[3] where companies are less likely to respond to a job applications containing an African American name,[4] and where a car is less likely to stop for an African American (as opposed to a white person) in the crosswalk.[5] Upon his return he had difficulty finding a job because of his incarceration. For Karissa, the oppression felt intentional and never seemed to end—and this includes the failure of the US food system to provide her community with adequate amounts of healthy food.

Around 2010 Karissa drove some of her family from California to their home on a reservation in South Dakota. "They were giving me a history lesson. I was raised black; I wasn't raised indigenous. I wasn't engaged in indigenous culture or indigenous history. This history lesson my mother was giving me was really profound and taught me a lot about the way white supremacy has not only impacted the black community but had also decimated the indigenous communities of this continent. She told stories of colonizers riding on trains through the plains and just shooting buffalo. Not because they were going eat it, but because they wanted to take away the indigenous folks' means of self-sufficiency and self-determination." It was a cruel and deliberate choice with lasting implications.

Our readers may not have heard this story in school, but this is no exaggerated tale. President Grant saw the elimination of the buffalo as solving what was called "the Indian problem," and one US army colonel remarked, "Every buffalo dead is an Indian gone."[6] Perhaps many readers will lament this story and feel thankful that those cruel days are gone, but what Karissa saw in that story was similar to modern life in Oakland, California. "When I returned from that trip, I decided that I wasn't going to engage in a capitalist system. I stopped everything and started to engage more in learning about the land."

Her periods of homelessness as a child, her husband's incarceration, and his difficulty finding a job once out. The lack of food in her community. Karissa sees this much like the killing of the buffalo in the eighteenth century: the intended outcome of deliberate actions designed to oppress minorities.

By the time she took that drive to South Dakota, Karissa had already begun to fight back. The election of Barack Obama to the US presidency two years earlier inspired her, instilling a genuine feeling that change was possible. As they searched for a place her husband could work, her sister suggested considering the Center for Third World Organizing, a racial justice organization "dedicated to building a social justice movement led by people of color." "Someone recommended that he participate in a training program. Organizing is one of the only career paths that sees your experience of being incarcerated as a plus, because you have intimate knowledge and access to a system that folks are engaging to change and to abolish."

So Karissa and her husband attended a weekend program hosted by the center and designed to train people to be activists. This became a life-changing event for both of them. "I had never been in a room of a group of people of color who all believed that we were the answer to building power, that our collective work could impact systems that were destroying our communities." For the first time she was surrounded by people who genuinely believe that *they*—not rich philanthropists, not politicians— were the solution. Their engagement could correct the food insecurity in their communities by taking control of the food system—by relying on themselves, to the greatest extent possible in an urban area, for food production and distribution. They could not continue depending on assistance from "snow-capped" organizations, where the organizations' board of directors are all white but the people they are servicing are of color, as it reinforces the "white savior" complex and discourages African American communities from directly participating in solutions.[7] The center is "really helping folks see that our collective power is going to change systems. I believe that we need to be teaching people how to grow food and we need to be providing healthy foods. But folks need to be building power so that we can change systems. Because as long as these systems continue to operate in the manner which they are, it's going to be detrimental to black and brown communities."

It is the recentering of the food system to focus on the "aspirations and needs of those who produce, distribute and consume foods" that shapes the basis of fair food access and effective food sovereignty. Karissa's remarks might seem odd to people who are not familiar with the language used in organizations like the Center for Third World Organizing and in food sovereignty movements.

> When you're able to do a full analysis of the entire spectrum of consumption and production, you see that the entire chain is being exploited. It creates the conditions in which, if you're really engaged in creating a sovereign food system or a self-determined food system, you have to engage in all of the points of intervention. We can fix the consumption piece, but if folks who are harvesting or producing our food are still being exploited, it doesn't solve our problem. We're eating organic food, and that solves some of the impacts of inorganic foods and processed foods in our bodies, but that doesn't create a sustainable food system. Being able to engage all of those layers, I think, is paramount to a sovereign food system and a sustainable food system.

She frequently mentions her desire to opt out of the capitalist food system that has failed Oakland. Karissa's agenda does not include an abolition of property, a centrally planned economy, the elimination of money, or an absence of markets. Her definition of "capitalism" is quite different from the ones used by economists or those invoked in mainstream policy debates.

Capitalism to Karissa is more like a system where the privileged wealthy use their money to influence policy, widen income inequality, entrench class systems, and maintain obstacles that prevent equality. (Karissa didn't use this word, but others in the movement have simply referred to it as fascism.[8] Academics would probably use the world "neoliberalism.") When you dig deep into her narrative, what you find is that she is not espousing replacing capitalism with some type of socialism or communism, but with more democracy, not a representative democracy where change only occurs through votes and lobbying, but a system where an individual is more than just a worker from nine to five, an occasional voter, and otherwise a consumer.

Karissa specifically refers to herself as an international twenty-first-century socialist, a system where people have control of their labor in the food system and the economy more broadly. "I think new systems have to operate through a lens in which all of us are valued, to operate in a way that honors the wisdom of elders and young folks. New systems have to be based in a frame that is not exploiting. So all of our systems—our economic system, our food system—they're all deeply exploiting to specifically communities of color across the globe. I'm not interested in a shared economy if it's operating from a capitalist one because capitalism in its very nature is exploitive. A new system has to be able to push back against that." She is building a system where individuals interact with their community members under an assumption of equality, and social decisions are made through collective consent, not votes. "I see my work as being direct action to the state. I'm not interested in getting a slice of the America pie because I think it is poison. It's been disastrous for people of my community, so I'm interested in building a new system for the sake of black liberation."

How does a brave, determined person like Karissa counter the mainstream food system which she believes has failed her? First, she farms, even referring to herself as a "black radical farmer." She cofounded Full Harvest Urban Farm in East Oakland. Approximately half an acre, it hosts chickens, ducks, goats, rabbits, bees, a pig, an orchard, and a wide variety of vegetables.[9] It is located in a compound containing six families and ten to fifteen people,[10] and its Facebook page describes it as being "Black led and Black centered." As part of its effort to detach itself from the capitalist economy, the farm uses energy generated from solar panels donated by the Green Panthers. The idea of the garden being black-led may sound hostile to whites, but is due to the fact that the community experienced problems when sympathetic white persons established urban gardens in the name of food justice. The presence of whites increased police patrols, as the police wanted to make sure the white people were safe. Those patrols were seen as a threat and caused local residents to become less involved.[11]

The farm's purpose isn't just to grow food, but for education and community enhancement. It has an outdoor classroom, a stage, and a few yurts.[12] The purpose of urban farming is more expansive, more political, than just growing food. Karissa describes her urban farm as being powerful *because* she is black. Black Americans were forced to farm generations ago, and now she is reclaiming their past. The farming is "in our bones," she says in an interview with Movement Generation.

The educational components of the farm extend beyond food, and Karissa described it as a place where formerly incarcerated people of color can come to learn how to navigate the world that has removed the bars but not the oppression. Her husband said the farm goes against "... the senseless war on drugs ... we know what [the war on drugs] was put into place to do: to lock people that look like me up." Karissa sees the farm as a direct challenge to "the state" by providing the people it has deemed illegitimate with the tools to flourish. "It's really rewarding to be able to learn and build with folks who oftentimes are seen as throwaways ... who oftentimes are seen as not valuable to develop. It's healing. To be able to literally feed myself and my community is healing. To also push back against power is healing. To reclaim power is ... deeply healing."

Other farms in the area operate in a similar spirit, like the West Oakland Farms, where formerly incarcerated persons are given partial ownership and work in the garden,[13] while others concentrate on working with youth. The idea of urban gardening as a partial solution to food injustice has attracted much interest, so much so that the University of California has hired an extension agent to advise small urban farms. For example, an agent can help the communities test the soil to ensure it does not contain dangerous amounts of heavy metals prevalent in urban areas due to industrial development.[14] Students attending Oakland University may become a part of its organic farm, and this farm is integrated into its organic farming and permaculture classes.[15]

Oakland is not the only place where the urban agriculture movement is growing. Browse the internet and you will find similar urban food movements in seemingly every city, many pressing the same arguments we heard from Karissa. As an example, the lyrics of a rap song produced by North Minneapolis nonprofit Appetite For Change Inc, called "Grow Food," includes the commentary, "See in my hood, there ain't really much to eat / Popeye's on the corner, McDonald's right across the street / All this talk about guns and the drugs pretty serious / But look at what they feeding y'all, that's what's really killin' us."[16]

There is even an organization called Black Urban Growers (BUGS), which hosted a conference of black urban farmers. Karissa mentioned this conference as helping her connect with similar farmers from other cities, giving her an appreciation for the fact that she is part of a national, not just a West Oakland, movement.

Of course, urban agriculture is not just a people-of-color movement. We have already met Marc Oshima, who is building the most expensive urban farms yet, and "hipsters" are raising so many chickens in cities that animal shelters are sometimes overwhelmed with abandoned chickens when they no longer lay eggs, or when the hen turns out to be a rooster.[17] When some raise a chicken, they might do so for fun and food, but Karissa is pursuing something much deeper: basic human rights.

As a speaker at the University of California at Berkeley, Karissa argued that "state-sanctioned brutality" also encompasses lack of access to health food—poor access to safe water (think Flint, Michigan), gentrification, and failing school systems, among others. After all, both bullets and unhealthy food harm the body. The movement that Karissa Lewis joined and now helps lead is not just about acquiring better food, but what she sees as basic social justice and human rights. "I see my work as being deeply radical. I see my work as being a direct action to the state. I see my work as being revolutionary and radical in that I recognize that the systems are operating exactly as they are intended to work. They were built on the genocide of indigenous people and the oppression of black and brown people."

Karissa is more than a farmer. She is the program director for People's Grocery, a nonprofit farm and food supplier located in the food desert of West Oakland. It is dedicated to providing healthy food to the neighborhood that the mainstream food and political system has ignored. "We have not as a movement done a good enough job of a few things: one, meeting folks where they are. We're really trying but oftentimes the food justice worlds and organizations were asking folks to go from eating McDonald's to quinoa, right? There's no understanding of the impact of food stories and how our food legacies and food histories impact how we show up in the world. Being able to meet folks where they are, I think, is an important piece. Then, folks are traumatized, some facing addiction. The work that we're able to do is just hitting [the tip of] the iceberg. I think it's important for us to have a broad, front-facing movement."

This isn't just a different type of grocery store. Like Karissa's farm, People's Grocery does more than provide food. For people who have eaten out of convenience stores and fast-food restaurants most of their lives, they offer cooking classes. Its urban agriculture activities include three community gardens and a two-acre farm. Part of the food supply program resembles community-supported agriculture (CSA), in that residents are provided prepackaged bags containing a share of the farms' production,[18] but the grocery also sells food obtained from distributors, and because it is given large discounts from the distributors, it can sell the food at low prices to Oakland residents.[19] The program is intimately connected with a nearby low-income housing development, where the grocery helps administer a garden and nursery and provides a weekly program titled "Flavas of the Garden," with activities intended to encourage self-sufficiency and healthy eating (which might include cooking, art, yoga, and the like). It also offers a six-month Food Warriors program to engage youth in food sovereignty and self-determination.

Although it is tempting to think that organic food is the domain of the wealthy white elite, Karissa and her community are strongly pro-organic. The production of healthy, organic food has benefits for everyone. In their videos and narratives they associate pesticides with unsafe, unhealthy foods, and their farms are managed using organic methods (regardless of whether they are certified as such). The aversion to pesticides is part choice, but, one suspects, part practicality too. It would be dangerous to spray pesticides in an urban area, and their gardens are managed as a polyculture containing many different types of plants. Applying pesticides to one type of plant without some residues moving to other plants is difficult. Furthermore, they want children to be able to visit the gardens, snap off a green by hand, and eat it immediately. If pesticides were used, they might not be able to allow any visitors around the plants.

Karissa is indeed a food radical, helping to pioneer a new food system for her community, but she is also reconnecting with activists of a previous generation, like Fannie Lou Hamer (1917–1977). Hamer was a famous civil rights activist from Mississippi, whose contributions to the 1960s civil rights reforms are many. In addition to helping African Americans vote in large numbers, she encouraged them to return to the land and seek economic independence through farming. We have seen how Karissa sees the US food system as a deliberate attempt to deny healthy food to her community—so did Hamer. The state of Mississippi would prevent public assistance from reaching African Americans, limiting their access to healthy food and healthcare in order to preserve white supremacy, induce African Americans to migrate north, and reduce birth rates of those African Americans remaining. Hamer was one among many who were warned that if she did not withdraw her voter registration application, she would be fired from her job and evicted. She did not comply and suffered both consequences. Denial of access to food was also used to limit minority voting. An interviewer for *The Progressive* magazine in 1968 summarized his conversation with Hamer: "Down in Mississippi they are killing Negroes of all ages, on the installment plan, through starvation. If you are a Negro and voter, if you persist in dreams of Black power to win some measure of freedom in White controlled counties, you go hungry."

Thus Hamer believed African Americans had to become self-sufficient in food in order to mobilize political power. Otherwise, food would be leverage for their oppressors. So Hamer founded the Freedom Farms Cooperative in 1969, with over six hundred acres owned and managed cooperatively by the members, consisting of various cash crops, community gardens, community kitchens, and the like. Like Karissa's farm and People's Grocery, it was operated as a nonprofit institution and acted not only as a farm but as a place of education, selling the food produced to those who could pay full price but offering a steep discount to those who could not.

Like Karissa, Hamer gladly accepted the help of, and offered assistance to, people of other ethnicities, for food is used as a weapon against the oppressed of every color. In the mining towns of Appalachia, the mining companies would not only fire those agitating for better labor conditions, but would destroy their gardens and kill their livestock, as the better the miners could feed themselves, the stronger they could be in labor struggles.[20]

Nevertheless, Hamer believed fervently that her movement could only succeed if the leadership were black. The project lasted only a few years, finding itself insolvent after donations and grants dried up.[21] Her project may have lived a short life, but her spirit thrives in people like Karissa and other people Karissa mentions, like Dara Cooper from the National Black

Food and Justice Alliance, Malik Yakani of the Detroit Food Securities Network, and Leah Penniman at the Soul Fire Farm. "There is a wealth of brilliant black folks who are fighting every day for the liberation of black folks in this country, even broader when we talk globally. I feel grateful and want to recognize the shoulders on which I stand. I am living in the legacy of my ancestors. It is because of them that I am able to do this work. Without that legacy I wouldn't be here." The legacy lives today in Karissa, her farm, and People's Grocery.

Amory Starr Names the Enemy

Karissa Lewis is currently the executive director for the Center for Third World Organizing, the organization that originally inspired her to become politically active. Chances are the name of that organization sounds strange to many readers. Why would Karissa, who lives in the United States and is working to improve the lives of minorities in the United States, be affiliated with an organization with "Third World" in its name?

The reason is that Karissa and others like her believe that they have been colonized in a way similar to Africa and Latin America. In a *Huffington Post* piece, she once remarked, "The United States was founded through the plunder and pillage of Indigenous people and their lands and on the backs of Black bodies."[22] Indigenous people of Africa and Latin America might say the same thing about the Europeans who settled the lands of their ancestors.

As minorities seek equal rights, they have two paths. One is to integrate themselves with the mainstream society, seeking equality through the same social institutions that have oppressed them, and begin mimicking the same people who have oppressed them—in a sense, to accept colonization of one's person and culture. Another is to seek equality by raising their own culture and institutions to the same level as that of the oppressors—if achieved, this lends dignity to one's person and culture. For centuries European settlers in the United States tried to eliminate some Native Americans and force European culture upon others. Some did integrate into settler culture, adopting English names, converting to Christianity, and breeding with settlers, such that today there are many Americans who appear white but actually have Native American lineages. Other Native Americans took the other path of promoting their culture, giving rise to the 567 sovereign Native American nations within the United States.[23]

We met Amory Starr in an earlier chapter about farming. When she was completing her master's degree in city planning at the Massachusetts Institute of Technology, she met many students of color interested in something called indigenous planning. They had taken a number of city-planning courses in order to help them empower their communities, but felt that they were only taught how to colonize their communities. This did not seem appropriate, so they challenged the Department of Urban Planning to revamp its curriculum to be more respectful to communities of color.

Becoming an activist, Amory joined this group for a few years. Observing her scholarly skills, the group suggested she contribute to the cause in academia by studying and writing about the topic. So she attended classes in the Department of Sociology at the University of California at Santa Barbara. Amory wanted to research the relevance of Indigenous people's movements in the Third World (like the Zapatista movement in Mexico) to poor communities in the United States. She especially wanted to explore the indigenous movements' interest in food independence.

The problem was that this was 1992, before food was the topic of interest it is today. Today some sociologists study food issues exclusively and tend to have a more comprehensive perspective on food systems than agricultural departments, but in 1992 food was considered irrelevant to sociology. Her sociology department was at that time focused on the hot topics of gender and sexuality, and Amory's interest in food was received as strange and irrelevant.

Amory would have to get used to this response, for as we will see, she was ahead of her time in regards to food on multiple fronts. In fact, if Amory had begun her career ten years later and pursued the same ideas, she probably wouldn't be considered as much a radical.

With coauthor John Rodgers, she published an article in 1995 describing economic development in the Third World, how economic development had not helped people as much as economists predicted, and how corporations were gaining an increasingly powerful hold over the world.[24] From their studies they came to the conclusion that indigenous people, people of color in the United States, and many others were being harmed by the rise of corporate hegemony over national governments. Amory was excited that such diverse movements were all "naming" the same enemy. This unification became the subject of Amory's doctoral dissertation, and the book based on this research is titled *Naming the Enemy: Anti-corporate Movements Confront Globalization*. In her work Amory predicted the rise of the antiglobalization (or, in her words, "alterglobalization") movement.

With a fellow sociologist, Tony Samara, Amory was exploring linkages between Marxism and indigenous development, and they noticed that many of their students from poor and minority communities were interested in what they were doing but were intimidated by the economics (most people are!). Their solution was to teach a political economy course focused on food. People are not intimidated by food, so teaching economics through food issues seemed like an idea worth exploring.

Tony and Amory were excited about the idea and so were many students, but the university was not. The university refused to pay them to teach the course, so they taught it for free. The university wouldn't even provide them a classroom, so they held classes at the couple's residence. At the first class meeting twenty people arrived, most them hungry, so Tony and Amory fed them and began a tradition of cooking and enjoying a meal together during every class. They created a radical new course, even though Amory and Tony were still doctoral students taking classes of their own and working on their dissertations.

We don't have to speculate about what was taught because Amory keeps the syllabus, now two decades old, posted on her website. It reflects her personality as a scholar-activist. The readings describe the failures of industrial agriculture and the benefits of agroecology, the dangers of biotechnology in the hands of corporations, the damages of globalization and alternative trading schemes, and the like. While some professors at our agricultural college would say her sources are biased, Amory notes that that students at CSU's agricultural college were assigned textbooks written by pesticide companies.

Students were also asked to intern on farms, took trips to the farmers market, and then went back to Tony and Amory's kitchen to learn how to cook the food (we will see later in the book that Amory became a chef). Students were eating vegetables they never knew existed and not only learning how to cook them, but how to grow them. Eventually the students did all the cooking. Amory was preparing them to participate in a food system outside the mainstream. About half the students were people of color, and many came from other departments because there was no other course like this anywhere in the university.

Again, Amory had to do all this for free because food wasn't in vogue at the time, and she was ahead of her time. Now there are sociology positions that deal specifically with food, and classes that deal specifically with the sociology of food. Amory wasn't as "boring" as her department thought— she was prescient.

After obtaining her PhD and negotiating a job offer at the sociology department at Colorado State University (CSU), she stipulated that she would take the job so long as she could teach her Political Economy of Food course as part of her job. Administrators were not enthusiastic about the idea, but not against it either, so they agreed with ambivalence. Though Amory left CSU after five years, the department now has two food courses on the books.

Earlier in the book we described some of Amory's time at CSU, and how, though it is an agricultural school, she was (at that point in time) the only person students could learn from about organic agriculture. Yet even though she was the lone organic-ag proponent at CSU, and even though she appears in this book more than any other food radical, food was not Amory's priority at that time—that belonged to the alterglobalization movement.

Some readers may remember the alterglobalization protests that took place at the end of 1999. Most Americans had difficulty understanding exactly what the protests were about. The World Trade Organization (WTO) met in Seattle to discuss new rules governing how countries trade with one another, knowing that a protest was planned but unaware of its scale. Tens of thousands of protestors showed up to impede the talks and draw as much attention as possible. They marched in the streets with signs hoisted like battle standards. Their main objective was to prevent the WTO talks from occurring, so they tried to block trade delegates from entering the building where the talks would occur.

The protestors, according to Seattle police reports,[25] purchased all the lighter fluid in a nearby store . . . broke into an abandoned building . . . sprayed graffiti on buildings . . . threw rocks at police officers . . . set up equipment and chained themselves together to make it difficult for police officers to remove them from the streets . . . donned gas masks to protect themselves from tear gas . . . stole security fencing and erected it in the street . . . constructed barricades in the streets like a performance of *Les Miserables* . . . locked down at least fourteen intersections . . .

For so many protestors from different regions and political affiliations, even a military general would admire their ability to coordinate. Rangers on bikes would ride ahead of protestors, using radios to alert them to police movements. Although the news often focused on protestors throwing rocks and breaking windows, most of the protestors would deter violence through actions like chanting, "No violence . . . no violence." Part of the organization was spontaneous, but part was planned. Months before the

WTO some protestors were going through training, some in boot-camp environments, some practicing at actual locations in other regions.

Media coverage separated the protestors into two camps. One consisted of nonviolent protestors who simply stood their ground despite tear gas and pepper spray, peacefully blocking the movement of trade delegates. They were so successful that the Secret Service decided the secretary of state, Madeleine Albright, should remain in her hotel.

The other group was the "anarchists," including the group Black Bloc, who dressed in black suits and masks and during the protests damaged the property of multinational corporate retailers like Starbucks and Old Navy. The two groups were not working in tandem—most of the peaceful protestors resented the Black Bloc, urging them to remove their masks and either protest peacefully or leave. Once the Black Bloc arrived, so did the National Guard.

Joining the protestors were various trade unions and United Farm Workers from California. Given this medley of environmentalists, anarchists, worker groups, and the like, there was bound to be some disagreements. For example, one group attempted to remove the American flag and destroy it, but union workers stopped them and replaced the flag at the top of the pole.[26] Despite their differences, the protestors remained largely united and very effective, because they coalesced around a common cause of stopping the spread of globalization.

Throughout the four days of protests there were some victories by the police, many victories by the protestors. Sometimes the protestors were out of line, and sometimes it was the police. Sometimes the protestors were pacific, sometimes it was the police. The talks were not shut down, but they were certainly stymied, and for the first time the ordinary citizen realized the opposition to globalization was much stronger than thought. The Third World delegates, who finally refused to agree to the conditions proposed by the rich countries at the meetings, causing the ministerial to fail, credited the protesters outside for encouraging them to dissent.

Amory Starr was there amid the protestors. One of her students approached her shortly before the WTO talks were to begin and said, "Dr. Starr., we have to go to Seattle." At first she declined, noting her three classes, after which the late John Long insisted, "Dr. Starr, we *need* to go protest the WTO in Seattle." She realized he was right, so she reserved some vans and headed northwest with twenty-two CSU students.

Although the goal of the protests was to interfere with WTO talks, watching news footage of the protests makes it clear that the real enemy was not just the WTO but the multinational corporations in whose interest this set of international rules was written. It was only a year earlier when Amory published her dissertation, titled *Naming the Enemy: Anti-corporate Movements Confront Globalization*, and if she published her dissertation the year before the protests, then she was aware of the movements' rise many years earlier. While many Americans were surprised to see so much dissent against corporations—especially seeing that many of our favorite toys are produced by corporations, from cars to video games to computers—it was no surprise to Amory. She started tracing it years earlier.

Now for a confession. One of the authors (Bailey) is an economist, and economics can be described as the study of trade. During the Seattle protests he thought the protestors were crazy. The major lesson of economics is that trade makes (most) everyone wealthier. This is a lesson resulting from rigorous economic theory, simple logic, and empirical evidence. Watching the protests, he thought that they were against all forms of trade. To Bailey, this was incredibly naive.

It was only after interviewing Amory and reading her writings that he better understood the alterglobalization movement, and he realized that it was he who was being naive. Amory understands economics well and is not at all against trade between countries, it turns out. She notes it has always occurred in history and, when done right, is beneficial to most. Trade does indeed help everyone when it is voluntary and occurs between free people, but Amory argues that because international trade abides by WTO rules and because those rules are designed to benefit corporations, the trade we see should not be thought of as voluntary. Instead of making people wealthier, the trade that occurs destroys democracy and small businesses, like most farms.

Amory is an activist but also a nimble scholar, able to juggle multiple subjects and scientific fields at once and explain them so that anyone can understand. Studying her writings and speeches makes it clear that she opposes the WTO because it has become an institution by which multinational corporations profit by subverting the democratic institutions of all countries. This is difficult to see unless you understand how the WTO operates. It was established to help facilitate fair trade between countries and to do so by initiating an international rule of law superseding national regulations, including protection of domestic economic sectors and producers.

To understand the WTO, consider how the US Constitution prevents any state from impeding trade with another state through the Commerce

Clause. The government of South Carolina cannot stop imports of peaches from Georgia simply to protect South Carolina peach producers. Nor can Georgia stop imports of cars made in South Carolina simply to protect its car manufacturing industry. If Georgia peaches or South Carolina cars were found to be unsafe, then yes, the states could prohibit imports, but only under such conditions. Who decides what is a reasonable barrier to trade? Federal courts, of course.

Note that this Commerce Clause limits the democracy of both states, making their democracies subservient to the federal democracy. Suppose that 90 percent of South Carolina voters wanted to ban all peaches from Georgia because Georgia allowed the use of a specific pesticide that was banned in South Carolina due to health concerns. Further, suppose that federal courts decided that the pesticide has been determined by "science" to be safe, and so forced South Carolina to accept Georgia peaches and enact no labeling procedure that allows consumers to determine which peaches came from Georgia. If you agree with what the court deems to be "science," then perhaps you believe this court ruling is good because it forces the state to act rationally and prevents safety from being an excuse to ban Georgia peaches, when what the state really wants to do (you suspect) is protect South Carolina peach farmers.

Even if you believe this, one must admit that the courts have limited democracy in South Carolina. Moreover, what if you were one of the South Carolinians who believed that Georgia pesticide was unsafe? How would you feel, then?

In many ways the WTO is like that federal court. It is designed to make rulings on whether trade restrictions between its member countries are reasonable. From Amory's point of view, this is dangerous because it limits the democracy of those member countries, and because WTO court rulings are heavily influenced by multinational corporations. That is why both the WTO and corporations were the named enemy during the Seattle protests (and years earlier, in Amory's writings).

Consider two popular examples. The French government once banned imports of US beef because US producers use growth hormones in cattle production, something that French residents fear is dangerous. When the United States took France to court at the WTO, claiming the ban was a barrier to free trade, the WTO ruled in favor of the United States. As US beef began entering France again, French voters sought a labeling law that would allow them to distinguish US beef, but the WTO ruled such labeling was also a barrier to free trade. In both instances, France had three choices it could (1) retain its import ban / labeling law but compensate US cattle producers for the harm caused, (2) remove the import ban/labeling law, or (3) withdraw from the WTO. France chose the second option, but either of the first two options required it to ignore the democratic desires of its citizens and instead follow the dictates of a world court.[27]

If you go to any animal science department in the United States, its scientists will tell you that hormone use in cattle production is perfectly safe. Indeed, the difference between the amount of hormone residues present in beef with and without the hormone treatments is miniscule compared to the amount of hormone in a tablespoon of cabbage.[28] However, what if you are one of the French voters who believes such scientists are often overconfident and you fear this use of hormones? Many French may remember the mad cow scare, where a cattle feed ingredient (rendered sheep carcasses) once deemed completely safe by scientists was later thought to cause a disease that turns the brains of humans who eat the beef into mush. Does France have the right to ban hormone-treated cattle even if the scientists consulted by the World Trade Organization believe it to be an unfounded fear? Amory and her fellow alterglobalization protestors believe the answer is yes.

Artisan cooking oil, made and sold locally, was once a thriving business in India. It was done on a small scale, largely by women working alone. The oil often was not packaged, because people would bring in their own oilseeds and containers, paying the person to press the oils into the containers they had brought. However, pressured by the WTO to conform to its Sanitary and Phytosanitary Guidelines, the Indian government passed a law requiring all cooking oil to be packaged. The artisan oil pressers could not afford packaging equipment, and so in one stroke this local business was made illegal. This market was then captured by multinational corporations that could easily afford packaging. Amory notes this is eerily similar to textile laws in colonial India. The British forbade Indians from making their own cloth, forcing them to purchase British cloth instead. India had broken free of colonization by the British, only to feel colonized by corporations.[29]

It is rare for such a talented scholar to be such an enthusiastic activist, and combining the two can make for a difficult life because it is such a rare combination. Activists are ahead of their time. They have to be, because they are trying to steer society toward a path different from the accustomed one. It rarely pays to be ahead of your time in the social sciences, because it is hard for your peers to understand you. Usually such people are casually ignored, and by the time others realize you were right, you have already left the academy because you didn't fit in. That is the case for Amory. When she was writing her dissertation and predicting the alterglobalization movement, her committee members (the professors who determine whether your dissertation passes or fails) never really understood her interest in the topic (though it wasn't because of her writing . . . she is an excellent writer).

Those professors let her complete the dissertation, but once she was a professor, she faced another version of the problem. It was OK to write about social justice, but not to do anything about it. When Amory worked with student activists, she was held responsible for their activism.

Amory is no doubt a radical. She has referred to herself as an anarchist,[30] when most of us do not even know what it is. Google her name and you can find a picture of her wearing a T-shirt that says "Fuck Corporations" on the front. She was even considered a radical among the radicals of her Santa Barbara sociology department. However, a number of her views are shared by people far less radical, because while Amory has called for radical changes, the food system has already undergone a radical transformation.

Bill Bullard Isn't Radical, but the Food System Is

On March 17, 2017, the Brazilian police raided a number of meatpacking companies, the result of a two-year investigation into bribery of its health inspectors. The meatpackers (companies that slaughter live animals and process the meat) had bribed both inspectors and politicians to ignore health code violations, including exporting salmonella-contaminated meat and processing rotten meat.[31] The US Department of Agriculture (USDA) announced that none of the unsafe beef reached the United States;[32] however, the inspectors may have taken bribes before the police even began their investigation. This Brazilian fiasco naturally makes us question the safety of all beef imports.

Globalization has stretched the supply lines connecting beef producers and beef consumers, such that the beef in our hamburgers could come from almost anywhere. Do we feel as comfortable with beef from a developing country as we do with beef raised in the United States? Consider how globalization impacted the United Kingdom, where one day consumers learned that the ground beef sold in some major supermarkets contained large amounts of horsemeat. France had the same problem, and investigations revealed that the horsemeat originated in Romania; it was bought by a Dutch trader, who sold it to a Cypriot trader, who sold it to a French company. The supply of beef has become so complex, so stretched, so easily corrupted, that consumers now doubt whether their beef actually came from a cow![33]

After reading this, some American consumers may feel more comfortable purchasing beef that was raised and processed in the United States. They can only do that if there is a label indicating country of origin. Around 87 percent of consumers say in surveys they want such a label,[34] and 40 percent of shoppers say they look for country-of-origin labeling when buying fresh meat.[35] Many farmers and politicians also want such a label, and a mandatory label law began to take shape in 2002, with the final law coming into effect in 2009. In that same year Mexico and Canada filed a complaint with the WTO claiming the law unfairly discriminated against imported cattle.[36] Canada and Mexico argued that the WTO agreements "harmonized" food safety regulations for all member nations, making all beef equally safe, regardless of country of origin.

The label implicitly suggests that US beef is safer, making the label law an unfair trade practice, neighboring countries argued. The WTO ruled in favor of Canada and Mexico. After subsequent WTO court battles, the United States was given the choice between eliminating the law or paying Canada and Mexico over a billion dollars in compensation if it wanted to remain a member of the WTO. It chose the former, and as of 2015, the law no longer exists, but companies can voluntarily provide such a label.[37]

A US law favored by citizens and passed democratically was struck down by a WTO court. Is the United States a sovereign democratic body or not? Some might argue that the US has democratically chosen to belong to the WTO, and that choice restricts other choices, just like voluntarily joining a weight loss organization restricts one's eating options. Others would argue that if a country has little power over how its food products are labeled, the WTO rules should be rewritten.

Bill Bullard had worked hard to get country-of-origin labeling (COOL) passed and so was saddened when it was removed. Most of Bill's life has been spent tending cattle or helping ranchers. After working on a relative's ranch during high school and renting one after graduation, he purchased a South Dakota ranch in 1980. Cattle prices were relatively high at that point but soon started falling, and just four years later cattle were worth only half as much.[38] "Soon after the purchase, in fact immediately after, we saw cattle prices collapse. I sold calves the year before I bought the ranch for about $1.20 per pound. And the year that I bought the ranch, those same calves brought $0.65 a pound. Lending policies were changed, and there was no longer that public effort to put cattle producers on the land. It was now purely an economic situation of collecting on the loans. We got caught in the economic squeeze in the early eighties, which was a time when literally hundreds of thousands of farmers and ranchers were forced to exit the industry."

It wasn't just ranchers that were hurt in the early eighties, but live-stock and crop producers of all kinds, resulting in the worst farm crisis since the Great Depression.[39] Farmers across the United States had to take loans to buy the inputs needed to plant next year's crop—so many loans that farm debt in 1984 was double what it was in 1978.[40] "It was alarming that those who were producing the food . . . the sustenance for the entire population, were caught in this cost-price squeeze where they could not sell the raw product—in my case, cattle—for a price that even covered cost of production. I thought there was a tremendous imbalance between the price paid to the producer versus the price that consumers were paying in the retail market." When economic conditions did not improve sufficiently for the farmers to repay those loans, many lost their farms and ranches.

Bill Bullard was among those who lost their ranch. He faced the choice of trying to keep the ranch by declaring bankruptcy, or allowing it to be repossessed by the previous owner, and going to college. He chose the latter, studying political science and business administration. "I could be part of the solution to the problems that I had witnessed firsthand. I witnessed neighbors who had been in the business for many years, who were good stockmen, good ranchers, forced to leave their ranches simply because the market price would not return to them their cost of produc-tion." If you read news stories about the 1980s farm crisis, it is portrayed as a consequence of external factors: low crop and livestock prices caused by a surplus of production, high interest rates caused by the Federal Reserve's need to fight inflation, a ban on exports to Russia, and the like.

However, Bill saw the crisis as something the US government could influence, if it really wanted to. What especially bothered Bill was the fact that most of the ranchers he saw losing their land were superb at their job. If even the best of ranchers could no longer make enough money to stay in business, doesn't that suggest something is wrong with the food system?

There was another event occurring in the early 1980s that Bill credits for the crisis: increasing market power by meatpackers. The neoliberal philosophy of the Reagan administration, which in the past was limited by antitrust regulation, allowed more companies to grow larger through mergers and acquisitions, so much so that the 1980s were referred to as "merger mania." In 1978 the biggest four packers controlled about 30 percent of the market for steers and heifers. By 1994 that number was 82 percent.[41] The fewer the beef packers, the greater their ability to negotiate (manipulate?) lower prices for the cattle they buy, leaving ranchers like Bill increasingly at the mercy of a few large corporations.

Much of the beef industry accepted the consolidation of the beef-packing industry with ambivalence, lamenting the fewer buyers of their products but believing it better to learn to compete in this new industry structure than to fight it. The largest association of ranchers (the National Cattlemen's Association) even merged with a meatpacker organization in 1996 so that the beef industry as a whole could better compete with other industries.[42] Bill sees this as an infiltration of beef packers into an organization that once represented only ranchers. Just a year earlier, the World Trade Organization was created.[43] All of these events seemed to work against independent US ranchers, with the government playing a significant role.

Bill argues that the US government (1) fails to enforce regulations to protect farmers from corporate power, (2) allows meatpackers to import cattle from any country, process it, and then export the beef with a "Made in the USA" label to other countries, and (3) forces all ranchers to pay money into the beef checkoff program, which is intended to promote beef consumption, but a large part of it goes to the National Cattlemen's Beef Association, which is partly run by beef packers. Given that no one seemed to be advocating for independent ranchers anymore, they decided that an organization needed to be created. It would be called R-CALF USA (Ranchers-Cattlemen Action Legal Fund, United Stockgrowers of America), and in 2001 Bill Bullard would be its CEO.

Bill was an advocate for the independent rancher long before the advent of R-CALF USA. During the 1980s farm crisis he helped South Dakota farmers and ranchers facing foreclosure and bankruptcy. Earlier in his life Bill noticed the government organizations that loaned farmers money were foreclosing on those loans before giving farmers their right to contest a decision. Most ranchers were unaware of these rights, and as Bill insisted upon them for himself, he attracted media attention. Other ranchers began contacting Bill, asking for help—and help he did. "I would travel upwards of 250, 300 miles to sit at the table of a farmer-rancher who was experiencing problems and go through their financial statements and their work plans for getting out of their financial predicament. Then later, I'd travel back to represent those farmers and ranchers at hearings before their lenders. I'd leave a farm or ranch with a dozen eggs or zucchini, or bread in the truck. These people had no money. They were in dire straits, so I did not charge. I was doing it out of my own pocket." In these consultations he saw the government dealing harshly with farmers. The government could claim rights to the revenues from cattle sales to pay back loans, but not even allow ranchers to access some of this money to buy basic groceries or cover healthcare costs.

When R-CALF USA was being formed to represent independent ranchers, they needed someone who understood ranching, who understood politics, who understood business, and who had demonstrated a passion for helping farmers. Bill was the obvious choice. "It allowed me to make the full circle from being a cow-calf producer to representing cow-calf producers across the nation. It was my opportunity to give back." He didn't even need to apply for the job. They recruited him.

R-CALF USA's slogan is Fighting for the U.S. Independent Cattle Producer, and the reader may wonder why "independent" is included. The reason is that livestock producers are increasingly dependent on the corporations who process the food. Most chicken and hog farmers today are not really "farmers," at least in the conventional use of the word. They don't own the animals or the animal feed, only the land and facilities. Nor do they have much autonomy in how the animals are raised. The corporations bring them young livestock and the feed the farmers must use, and dictate to the farmer exactly how the animals should be raised. The farmer is compensated based on the growth rate of the animals. This compensation is largely nonnegotiable, and the contracts the farmers must sign are usually confidential and written to leave the farmer at the mercy of the corporation. If farmers complain about this situation, they can expect punishment from the meatpacker.

People like Bill regret the loss of independent poultry and hog farmers, and they see beef corporations trying to do the same thing to the cattle industry. Today, if you want to produce hogs, poultry meat, or eggs, you must either work for a meatpacker or try to sell your products locally. R-CALF USA wants to make sure this doesn't happen to ranchers, which is why they focus on *independent* cattle producers. "The first objective was to explain to the decision-makers that there's a demarcation point between those who raise and sell cattle in the cattle industry, and those who purchase those cattle and manufacture beef. Up until that time, the beef packers were in Washington saying they represented the entire supply chain from the cow-calf producer to the beef packer, when in fact their interest was—and oftentimes is—diametrically opposed to the economic interest of the producers who were trying to maximize the value of their animals."

R-CALF USA wants a clear line between the ranchers and the meatpackers, and thus wants to prohibit meatpackers from owning cattle. It also wants to prevent the meatpackers from manipulating prices, and in speeches Bill frequently remarks that since 1980 almost half of our beef farms and ranches have been lost through low prices. The independent hog farmers did not fight the good fight against meatpackers, and as a result the number of hog farms has fallen by 90 percent. Bill notes that US ranches are the last livestock sector that is not owned and dominated by meatpacking corporations. It is the "last frontier" for the meatpackers, and Bill doesn't want them to conquer it.

It is also fair to say that R-CALF USA's members are fiercely independent people, "so independent that we represent a group that is least likely to join any organization. Generating sufficient membership to maintain a viable organization has been a challenge for us for seventeen years. I do meetings across the country. More often than not, someone will come up and say, 'I have never joined an organization before, but I'm going to join you.' I think in our industry they believe they've been deceived by the conventional organization, who they see representing the interest of the meatpackers, who have an interest contrary to their own."

Though independent ranchers would rather stick to their cattle and not have to battle the World Trade Organization and multinational corporations, they feel surrounded, and like a herd of cattle forming a circle to protect calves from wolves, they formed organizations like R-CALF USA and the Organization for Competitive Markets (OCM). They believe that the American consumer supports independent ranchers, but almost no one else is on their side.

Bill notes the USDA has long operated to the benefit of meatpackers, not ranchers, and the lobbying power of meatpackers allows them to unduly influence legislation. Once some ranchers took a meatpacker to court and the jury awarded a large settlement, only to have the judge reverse the decision and force the ranchers to pay the meatpacker's court costs. Even the judicial system seemed to be on the side of the food corporations. (It isn't that the judges were bribed, but that the wave of neoliberalism that began in the 1980s has created the pervasive idea that what is good for corporations is good for the nation.)

Agricultural colleges have received fierce criticism from people associated with R-CALF USA and OCM. Most states have a university with an agricultural economics department, whose faculty are trained to study market power issues. Neoliberalism is embraced in these departments also, resulting in rare objections to the consolidation in the meatpacking sector. The economists have their reasons, of course, but some in the farming and ranching community see this orientation as betrayal of the land grant mission of agricultural colleges. If agricultural colleges are supposed to help farmers, how can they not object to a system that prompted a 90 percent fall in hog farms? Sometimes, when farmers take a meatpacker to court, no agricultural economist volunteers to serve as an expert witness for the farmers. Yet meatpackers have no trouble hiring one to represent them. One of the authors (Bailey) receives one email about every three days from a specific producer, arguing that his agricultural college is failing in its job to serve the interests of independent farmers. Given that R-CALF USA and similar groups feel opposed on all sides, it is understandable why the groups exhibit such a strong personality. Bill is clear that R-CALF USA decided it needed to be more aggressive than other groups. "Too many organizations were in the business of insuring self-perpetuation. They wanted to engage in the issues, and they wanted to manage those issues, but when it came to a choice of winning the issue or perpetuating the organization, they would always decide to back off from the issue and live to fight another day. Our members viewed that to be a series of compromises that the conventional organizations were making that were eroding the strength of the producer sector in the livestock industry. This organization needs to be more aggressive. It needs to stop compromising on important issues. It needs to fight to win on behalf of its members. We were willing to put it all on the line to win."

Bill is a kind and polite person, but in speeches he is stern, and his picture on the R-CALF USA website is intentionally serious. They don't compromise, they won't change the subject, and they won't stop fighting. For this reason R-CALF USA is considered radical within the beef industry, and to stop the trend in the livestock industry and reverse it would be a radical action. "It's a shift in who benefits from having policies that are intended to ensure that we have food security—safe food—and a healthy economy. I see myself as committed, straightforward, unwilling to compromise on the issues that are vitally important to our members. We are seeking changes and we know what happens if you do nothing. We have lost industries like the steel industry and the textile industry because no one had the will or courage to stand up and protect the integrity of those industries. We're here to protect the integrity of the US cattle industry. We're not going to quit until we get the job done."

Individuals like Bill do not seem very radical to the ordinary American, especially compared with others interviewed for this book. We include people like Bill to point out that they are fighting a similar fight as some of our other radicals. They are fighting dominance of the food sector by the World Trade Organization and multinational corporations. The blend of corporate dominance of the food industry and globalization has transformed the US pig industry from hundreds of thousands of independent farms to one where one in four pigs raised in the United States is now owned by a Chinese company. Given the thin line between the private and public sector in China, we could even say that a quarter of all US pigs are now owned by a communist country.[44] In 1958, the year Bill Bullard was born, who could have even imagined that? Radical, indeed.

Welcome to Venezuela

Like Oakland, California and Chiapas, Mexico, Venezuela also has persons who feel abandoned by capitalism. Instead of being the minority, they are the majority. They too sought a different food system, but because they had a powerful ally in the person of Hugo Chávez, they sought to transform not just a neighborhood, but the whole country.

Venezuela shrugged off its dictatorship and established a democracy in 1958. By then it was exporting large amounts of oil, importing much of its food, and borrowing money from other countries. When oil prices plummeted in the 1980s, the nation earned less money from oil exports but still had debts to repay. To avoid bankruptcy, it sought a bailout from the International Monetary Fund (IMF). The bailout wouldn't be free, though. In return for the money, Venezuela would have to undergo a number of "structural adjustments." These included wage cuts to its employees, reduced spending on public programs, selling some of its natural resources, privatization of services formerly provided by government, and other actions that forced many Venezuelans into further poverty.

These "structural adjustments" are common concessions countries accept for bailouts. They are changes the IMF deems necessary for loan payback. The expansion of the private sector and retreat of social programs is referred to as "capitalism" by many, and "neoliberalism" by most of its critics. As the United States, United Kingdom, and other developed nations who controlled the IMF embraced neoliberalism during the 1980s, they thought nations like Venezuela should also adopt it if they wanted to pay back their loans. If Venezuela did not adopt neoliberalism voluntarily, the bailout would be denied until it did adopt it. Sure, Venezuela would resent the coercion, but Venezuelans would thank the developed nations, it was thought, once they experienced the bounty that neoliberalism had to offer.[45]

To Venezuelans, this forced neoliberalism seemed like a new form of colonization. Developed nations and their multinational corporations exerted more control over their government than their own politicians. Venezuelans saw their wages cut and their social programs end, so that money could flow to the richer countries. When the country's resources were privatized, the new owners were foreigners.

Though they still voted, and the country was still technically a democracy, it didn't feel like a democracy. There was no one in power to appeal to for help as the nation slid into greater poverty. If Venezuelans appealed to their elected officials to end the cuts in government funding, those officials would remark that it was the IMF that demanded the cuts. Venezuela imported most of its food, and if it wanted that flow of food to continue, it must oblige the demands of the richer countries.

Presidential candidate Carlos Andrés Pérez rode this resentment against the IMF to victory in 1989, referring to the IMF as a bomb that kills people. Yet, upon taking office, he complied with more neoliberal reforms in exchange for more IMF loans. Disappointed in Andrés Pérez and realizing they were unable to retake their government through votes, the people sought to do so with action. A rebellion began in the city of Caracas, which later turned into a riot resulting in the death of about four hundred protestors by police. To some, it seemed "the West" was not only responsible for controlling the government, but now had blood on its hands.

Since government was no longer under their democratic control, Venezuelans mobilized for a change—one that would respond to the needs of the poor majority of the population. At the same time they began constructing their own radical forms of self-government at the grassroots level. These two paths would converge a decade later, at the end of 1998, with the inception of the Bolivarian Revolution.[46]

Most Venezuelans felt abandoned by their traditional leaders in the 1980s and 1990s, so new leaders emerged to challenge the existing order. The most notable, of course, was the military officer Hugo Chávez. After leading a failed coup in 1992, he became a folk hero, and in 1998 he became president. Now rejection of Western policies did not just echo in the streets of Caracas, but was magnified in President Chávez. To fulfill campaign promises, Chávez rejected neoliberalism. Although he demonstrated solidarity with the US people, he displayed hostility to Western economic and political powers. He had to show his citizens that the days of neocolonialism were over. This is why he embraced Fidel Castro, communist leader of Cuba. This is why he sought to construct a new type of economy: not capitalism, not communism, but democratic in radical ways.[47]

Christina Schiavoni, from Little Italy to Venezuela

Venezuela makes frequent appearances in world news, but news stories barely scratch the surface of what is really going on. Because Venezuela refers to itself as "socialist" and allies itself with Cuba, reporters use a vocabulary similar to that used to describe Russia in the Cold War, giving Americans a distorted picture of how the Venezuelan government has operated since the rise of Chávez. Moreover, few good sources are available in the English language. Lucky for us, we have a terrific source in the person of Christina Schiavoni, a PhD candidate at the International Institute of Social Studies (ISS) of Erasmus University in the Netherlands.

Christina grew up in Boston's North End, known as Little Italy. Though a city kid, she would say "a farmer" when asked what she wanted to be when she grew up. Food was a culturally binding activity in her community, and she also had fond experiences on her relatives' farm in Maine. Even when she realized a farming career was not in her future, the idea of being connected with agriculture always appealed to her. Today she is a scholar-activist, displaying a passion for activism on social justice issues that began when she was in high school, especially issues regarding the global food system. "I got into activism around different environmental and social justice issues and really saw almost everything connecting back to food and the exploitative global food system that was impacting the environment, human rights, animal rights, and many of the issues I cared about. I decided that I would make that the focus of my time in universities." She attended Cornell University's agricultural school, studying international agriculture. Initially she wanted to focus on helping farmers in developing countries, but she soon learned that these farmers were already adept at their trade. If they struggle, it is usually because of external constraints, like government policies or an inability to receive a fair price.

This piqued Christina's interest in public policy, and at the same time she was becoming aware that developed nations like the United States also had food problems. Wanting to satisfy her lifelong interest in agriculture, as well as her newfound interest in the US food system, after graduation she spent a year working on a community-supported agriculture project in a low-income area in New York. Food would be grown locally, but instead of being sold to affluent areas, it was taken to areas where fresh, healthy food was hard to find and sold at more affordable prices.

From there she began work at WhyHunger, an organization seeking to end hunger by building a social movement for food justice, addressing the root causes of poverty, and working to make access to nutritious food a human right. "I started off on their hunger hotline, where people could call from anywhere in the country when they were in need of food and other forms of assistance. That was very eye-opening about the many cracks in our system that were allowing people to go hungry in the US" She knew there were holes in the system, but now understood that these holes in the social fabric needed more than just a patch.

By the time of the 2007 food crisis, when world food prices rose considerably and the number of undernourished people in the world rose by over 100 million,[48] Christina was working on WhyHunger's international programs. "It was really a time of tremendous growth for the movement, pushing us to think, how can we be stronger? How can we be more effective in our work?" As part of this program she attended a World Social Forum in Venezuela, where civil society organizations opposed to neoliberalism meet to converse and form strategies. This year one of the themes was food sovereignty, and she looked forward to attending a session on "land-grabbing." Some Venezuelan farmers had also planned on attending the session, and when they all arrived to learn it was canceled, they began conversing. Christina engaged in perhaps the most interesting dialogue of her life.

The farmers described the changes in their lives under the reforms of the Bolivarian Revolution, headed by Hugo Chávez. "I still remember my first conversation in very broken Spanish at the time. They were explaining to me that all their lives they, and their parents, and their grandparents had been very marginalized. They had never mattered to the government or to anyone in power. For the first time they actually felt like they did matter. They felt like they had the ability to shape their own lives and become community leaders. They were organizing their communities. They were coordinating with the government to make sure that they could get educational services, health services, and other types of services that they needed. The energy with which they were talking really was contagious." Now, with Chávez, their lives were valued by the government. Now oil revenues were used to help them. Now they had a chance to flourish.

A sense of cooperation began developing in their villages, a new form of democracy—not a democracy in the sense of "one person, one vote" but a form where each person has an equal ownership and control in the workplace and community. The farmers praised Chávez not just because the government allowed the local communities autonomy, but because Chávez was making sure that revenues from oil exports were going to fund social programs, like healthcare and education. They spoke with energy, and this energy seemed to be revolutionizing their economy and nation.

As they spoke, Christina pondered how difficult it was to make substantive changes back home. "I was coming from the US context, where every step along the way often involved a confrontation with our government's policies. So often in the United States I felt like we were putting out fires. We were trying to prevent cuts to food stamps. We were trying to prevent farm foreclosures. All these emergency things. It was so hard to have the conversations and do the really transformative work that we wanted to do." Like Venezuela, the United States had problems with its food system, problems Christina had personally seen, but the US government seemed largely uninterested in the problem. Movements in the United States, like those Christina was involved in, were busy putting out fires, while in Venezuela there seemed to be possibility for far deeper transformation.

This conversation started a deep interest for Christina in the Bolivarian Revolution, the political movement started by Chávez and named after Simón Bolívar, who helped South Americans achieve independence from Spain in the early nineteenth century. Though she would one day return to Venezuela, at this point she had to return to the United States. She took her interest in Venezuela with her and eagerly kept abreast of how the Venezuelan food system was evolving. "I started paying attention to how the process was being portrayed in the news in the US, which was often just the very opposite of what was happening there. That was just so frustrating. It seemed to be doing such a disservice to the people and the process, . . . withholding information that I think was actually very useful to a lot of communities and people trying to work toward change in the US. I started following the process, trying to work in solidarity with Venezuela, and also trying to start building more links between food sovereignty work in Venezuela and in the US." She developed lines of communication between US and Venezuelan food movements, sent delegations to Venezuela, and invited Venezuelan farmers and community leaders to the United States. "I found that working on Venezuela could be so polarizing. Some people just hear it and they think dictatorship and communism and all sorts of bad things." As the United States increasingly cast Chávez as a dictator, WhyHunger's board of directors discouraged any further collaboration. However, Christina could not help studying Venezuelan politics, so she continued to do so, just not during office hours.

The Erasmus University at Rotterdam, impressed with her writings on food sovereignty, had been recruiting her for some time. She had resisted joining the academy. "I had a lot of my own baggage around academia, and a lot of stereotypes seemed to be coming true. I felt like there was a lot of talk, and a lot of it felt so detached from things." Finally, she agreed to become a student so long as she could study Venezuela as part of her research. The university approved, and she enrolled. Her hobby now became her profession. Currently completing her doctoral research project, Christina has become one of the leading English-speaking scholars on the Venezuelan food sovereignty movement. It was a privilege to hear her describe Venezuela's radical food experiment.

Christina's time in Venezuela taught her that the farmers she talked to at the World Social Forum years ago were not an anomaly. The people once referred to as "marginals" now had new opportunities to improve their lives, and were no longer treated as second-class citizens. "Just before the Bolivarian Revolution, 60 percent of the population was living in poverty. In the United States we would talk about a high standard of living and all this development in Venezuela in past decades—but it was really quite exclusive, marked by huge inequalities. As I made friends with regular Venezuelans—the ones who had been part of that 60 percent— they would often point out [that] the subway used to only be for those who could afford it. This plaza that we're hanging out in, even though it had been a public space, it had only been for those who could afford to take the transportation here, and then once you got here, you had to be able to afford the shops and cafes. This had only been for certain people. Just having my friends point out all these different spaces and areas that had been exclusive and now were for the broader population was really striking—this idea of putting people in boxes."

The revolution gave people identified as marginal their first real shot at education, and they embraced it with enthusiasm. Christina recalls visiting a bio-control laboratory at a cooperative that was transitioning from industrialized agriculture to agroecology. The lab was researching the use of beneficial pests in place of insecticides to control crop-destroying insects. Christina's group was waiting for a lab technician, looking for someone who looked like a technician. "There was a grand-motherly looking woman outside watering and cleaning. Finally she asked us—what are you waiting for? We said, 'Oh, we're waiting for the lab technician to come.' She said, 'Oh, that's me.' We felt really embarrassed because . . . it didn't occur to us for a second that it could have been her. We got into the lab, and she put on her lab coat. She started talking to us about things in such a technical way that I was not able to translate very well. This woman was speaking so technically." Looks could be deceiving in this new Venezuela.

After the lab tour Christina started asking the woman about her life. The lab technician had grown up very poor and wasn't even given the opportunity to finish elementary school. At an early age she became a mother, and then a grandmother, all the time struggling to feed her family, never expecting to be given an opportunity to better her life. With the Bolivarian Revolution came educational missions, where she was allowed to attend elementary school and high school after that, followed by college. Later she attended a bio-control program in Cuba, becoming the lab technician she is today. This is just one example of the many opportunities made available by the revolution to people once derided as marginal.

If all Chávez had done was divert more money to the poor, that would not be radical. What is radical is the new economic system the revolution sought to develop. We previously met Karissa Lewis of Oakland, California, a woman of color fighting for minorities' access to healthy food. Karissa and her affiliated organizations believe that the marginalized in America will rise only through social movements created and led by themselves. Likewise, the revolution propagated a similar philosophy of economic development referred to as endogenous development (endogenous, meaning "proceeding from within"), where the people, working in democratic community structures and in partnership with the government, create and lead the formation of a new economic system. It is similar to the Indigenous planning discussed previously.

Consider the transformation of Venezuela's food system. First, different forms of property rights are envisioned. Much of the agricultural land had previously been owned by a relatively few people, and some large farms (referred to as *latifundios*) would leave land idle even though nearby residents had no food. Beginning in 2001, the Law of Land and Rural Development introduced reforms whereby unused land would be handed over to "the people," which usually meant cooperatives run by local residents.

The land would now be managed by cooperatives, meaning the cooperative members were both owners and managers, but also in partnership with the government. The cooperatives would receive subsidies to purchase farm inputs like fertilizer, acquire machinery, and help marketing their products, along with better access to education and healthcare. Educational programs include not only basics like literacy, but also instruction in how to run cooperatives. Most of the cooperatives wanted to produce food using agroecology principles, and to help them, the government sent them experts from Cuba, a country that has mastered the art of organic farming because of the difficulty of acquiring industrial inputs like chemical fertilizers and pesticides.

The new cooperative farms are not like the state-run farms of the Soviet Union, where all property was owned by the state and decisions were made through a hierarchical chain of command. It is the cooperative members themselves who make the vast majority of the farm decisions, and the members are quick to assert their independence if the government attempts to dominate them. At the same time, the government supports the cooperatives only if they are actively contributing to the economy. The participants refer to it as comanagement between the state and the people.

While socialism is often depicted as a centralized form of economic activity, Venezuela has been trying to make economic power and decisions more decentralized, more democratic. Christina remarks on the effects her experiences had on her, "someone like me, going to Venezuela and saying wow, it's actually possible for the people to work together with their government to address hunger. To me that's a beneficial thing because it makes me come back to the US and want to try to do things differently and want to try to effect change, and it makes me inspired. Maybe to some of the powers that be, that's threatening—people can go and see this other way of doing things." Much of the new food economy in Venezuela reminds Christina of what she saw in New York with community-supported agriculture, where locally grown food was brought to poor communities in

New York. In Venezuela there are people-to-people programs that work to connect small farms with urban communities lacking affordable, healthy food. Some of these communities have their own trucks and distribution systems and will travel to small farms to acquire food and then transport it back to their communities for distribution. Because they know the communities well, they understand the communities' food needs and thus know what to look for at the farms.

Rather than selling based on market forces, they sell at "solidarity" prices. These are prices deemed fair in that they compensate farmers for their costs, are low enough to be paid by the poor, and do not fluctuate as much as regular market prices. For example, if there is a shortage of potatoes, market prices would rise, but solidarity prices would not, ensuring poor communities can still afford the potatoes that are available. When there is a surplus, market prices fall, but solidarity prices do not, so that farmers can still receive sufficiently high prices to cover their costs. By negotiating stable prices with one another and not taking advantage of each other according to market conditions, consumers and producers protect each other from market shocks. "The idea is to try to blur the lines between producers and consumers. They're also very clear that this is not just a marketing project. This is really about trying to construct a new food system and bridge the urban-rural divide that has been quite deep in Venezuela for a while. It's a very transformative project. It's coming from the bottom. At the same time, these are people who had been working in state institutions and are still tapping into the state in different strategic ways. They're doing it on their own terms so that it's very much controlled by the communities involved. I find that another example of a pretty radically different way of doing things," says Christina. In fact, the relationship between buyers and sellers is so different that in some communities buyers are not referred to as "consumers" but "prosumers," in that those purchasing food are not passive consumers but active agents, doing their part to bridge the rural-urban divide and create a sustainable food system.

Cooperative farming, in comanagement with the government, has extended to seafood as well. We already met Dominique Barns, CEO of New Wave Foods, who is creating synthetic shrimp to reduce the need for shrimping in the seas, where trawling plows the sea floor, disturbing the marine ecosystem. Fishing villages in Venezuela share Dominique's concern about trawling and have long resented the damage caused by large fishing boats. They used the Bolivarian Revolution to ban large trawling ships and support artisanal fishing methods. The government provided equipment, such as boats and nets, and fishing cooperatives were formed. According to Christina, these communities now have a thriving fishing industry and higher fish stocks.

Although this book focuses on food, it should be noted that this new economic system used in the food sector was extended into other parts of the Venezuelan economy, including manufacturing sectors like textiles. The Chávez government passed "communal power laws" (note: Americans' conception of a "commune" differs from its Venezuelan use) that encouraged communities to organize themselves politically. The communities established a plan for how they would use public funding to contribute to the economy, and if the government approved, they were given funding. The communities were given considerable discretion in how they were organized, but there was one ironclad requirement before any funding would be given: the decisions had to be made democratically. The councils representing communities, for instance, had to be elected. So while Chávez did acquire great political power during the revolution, from the perspective of some Venezuelans it was offset by a flood of local democracy unseen in Venezuelan history.

The alternative food system that Venezuelans have been attempting to build may sound strange to Americans, but there are a number of similarities to the local food movement in the United States. Abandoned lots in cities are being converted into gardens, especially in areas that have experienced hard economic times, like Detroit. Often gardens are started without consulting the owner of the lot, earning it the name "guerrilla gardening." Part of the motivation is aesthetic, but partly because—like Venezuela—people are hungry and the land is just sitting there.[49] Like Venezuela, the local food movement prefers agricultural systems described by terms like organic, sustainable, regenerative, permacultural, resilient, and agroecological. The US local food movement is attracted to the word "cooperative" and repelled by the utterance of "corporation." In Oklahoma we can purchase locally produced food from the Oklahoma Food Cooperative, and in Colorado Taber Ward (the goat dairy farmer we met previously) is attempting to establish a cooperative of small goat dairy producers to produce and sell pasteurized goat milk. Just as Venezuela is subsidizing local food production, the United States does as well. Examples include the millions of federal dollars spent connecting local farms with school cafeterias,[50] and the government grant given to Taber Ward to investigate the feasibility of a goat cooperative.

Though they are not ubiquitous in the United States, you can find communities pursuing a worker-cooperative business model similar to those in Venezuela, where the workers are also the owners and decisions are made in a democratic fashion. Cooperative businesses also tend to focus on providing opportunities to low-income areas and prefer environmentally friendly production practices. Examples include the Evergreen Cooperative Initiative in Cleveland, Ohio, and the Isthmus cooperative featured in Michael Moore's documentary *Capitalism: A Love Story*.

Despite these similarities, Venezuela differs from the United States in the degree to which it promotes the cooperative system. In the United States the worker-cooperative is an unusual form of business, and few young people would even know what a worker-cooperative is. It is tolerated, and sometimes encouraged in the United States. In Venezuela, for those supporting the Bolivarian Revolution, it is an end-goal for most all economic production.

Another difference concerns the importance the revolution places on food sovereignty, which describes Venezuelans' ability to both feed themselves and make their own decisions on how food is produced. So important is agriculture and food that when Venezuelans rewrote their constitution in 1999 through a participatory process, it included a special section on food. From the Constitution of the Bolivarian Republic of Venezuela, Article 305:

> The State shall promote sustainable agriculture as the strategic basis for overall rural development, and consequently shall guarantee the population a secure food supply, defined as the sufficient and stable availability of food within the national sphere and timely and uninterrupted access to the same for consumers. A secure food supply must be achieved by developing and prioritizing internal agricultural and livestock production, understood as production deriving from the activities of agriculture, livestock, fishing and aquiculture. Food production is in the national interest and is fundamental to the economic and social development of the Nation. To this end, the State shall promulgate such financial, commercial, technological transfer, land tenancy, infrastructure, manpower training and other measures as may be necessary to achieve strategic levels of self-sufficiency. In addition, it shall promote actions in the national and international economic context to compensate for the disadvantages inherent to agricultural activity.

It is in the realm of food sovereignty that Christina has been able to wear the activist hat in her scholar-activist persona. Though she has no official role in the Venezuelan government or communal system, issues occasionally arise where she can use her unique skills to contribute to the revolution. "Venezuela actually passed what I think is the world's most progressive seed law. It's a law that bans genetically modified organisms from being produced in Venezuela. It also gives special protection to seeds developed by indigenous and Afro-descendant communities throughout Venezuela and promotes agroecology in very concrete ways." In an effort to promote agroecology and food sovereignty, the government passed a seed law in 2015 that bans genetically modified organisms (GMOs) from the country. The idea is that most GMOs are designed to be used in conjunction with industrial inputs like pesticides, whereas in Venezuela there is a push to try to farm without such inputs, much like Cuba. Also, they are trying to avoid what happened in Mexico, when GMO corn bred with local corn varieties, resulting in genetic contamination.[51]

The law faced opposition in the Venezuelan National Assembly, which since 2016 has been dominated by conservative parties who challenged the law by charging that it was unscientific. Christina and others decided to solicit support from scientists around the world to help preserve the law. This was a case where a scholar-activist understood the needs of Venezuelan communities because she was living alongside them and was able to help them through her contacts as a scholar.

If readers are attuned to world events, they might be wondering why Venezuela is currently being featured in major news headlines as having a difficult time feeding its people, even when its constitution expresses food as a human right. Indeed, Venezuela has experienced some difficulties in the last five years. Christina does not see the current food problems through rose-colored glasses. Chávez died in 2013, and a little over a year later, oil, which was funding much of Venezuela's economy, plummeted in value.[52] Nicolás Maduro succeeded Chávez, but with less money from oil sales, and perhaps less political talent, he is facing much greater opposition.

Venezuela's problems might not be as bad as presented through Western media lenses. Here Christina can help offer some perspective. Consider the stories that tend to reach Western audiences. Food is now scarce. People wait in line for hours for food, and about 10 percent of the population only eat two meals a day. Food scarcity is manifested in Venezuelan waistlines, as the average Venezuelan has lost around eighteen pounds. The humans of Venezuela might not be dying due to starvation, but animals in their zoos are. People who own homes are searching for food in garbage cans, and some find they can only acquire their basic necessities by smuggling goods in from Colombia or Trinidad. The Maduro government was depicted as comical when it suggested that Venezuelans solve the food crisis through urban gardens and raising chickens at home, appointing a minister of urban farming who raised sixty laying hens himself. The problem goes well beyond food. Medicine is equally scarce, and people are increasingly resorting to spiritual healers when the modern medicine they need is unavailable.[53]

If those were the only news stories you saw, then yes, Venezuela would seem to be suffering a humanitarian crisis. However, this is the same country that was given an award by the United Nations in 2015 for nearly eradicating hunger. In 2013 and 2012, the nation was also recognized by the United Nations for its great leaps in reducing hunger and poverty. By the end of 2015 it was estimated that the average Venezuelan was consuming 3,092 calories per day, helping to put the eighteen pounds of weight loss recently experienced by Venezuelans into perspective. Perhaps Venezuelans are importing food from Trinidad and Columbia, but maybe this is because some food is being illegally smuggled out of the country in the first place. While Maduro has encouraged urban agriculture, it was not actually suggested that this would solve the problem, and the establishment of the Ministry of Urban Agriculture was welcomed by many social movements.

Shortages of some goods do indeed exist. Christina has written that we overlook exactly which goods are scarce. They tend to be specific processed food staples as well as things like diapers, soap, and toilet paper. She argues there is no overall shortage of food or other basic goods. Milk is hard to get, but yogurt and cheese are not. Coffee is missing from the grocery store shelves, but not tea. Besides, walk into the streets of Caracas and you can easily purchase prepared coffee on street corners and in cafes. The specific nature of these shortages point to distribution bottlenecks which tend to occur for specific foods provided by large companies, not foods provided by the grassroots food system established under the revolution.

Moreover, it might not be a coincidence that some of the large companies whose food products have gone missing from supermarket shelves are owned by opponents of Maduro. For example, precooked corn flour is especially scarce. The company Polar is the dominant provider of this flour, and the family that owns Polar is not only the country's wealthiest family but a staunch opponent of Maduro. Consider that researchers have documented a positive correlation between the size of shortages and politically important events, like elections, suggesting the shortages are improvised by opponents of Maduro to hurt him politically.

If you have heard rumors of people eating dogs in Venezuela, well, Christina has heard them too. She lives in Venezuela, and when she went into the rural and urban communities to ask if the rumors were true, the only dogs being eaten were hotdogs. When a UN expert, Alfred De Zayza, traveled to Venezuela to assess the situation, he reported that although there were shortages and distribution delays, there was no humanitarian crisis. He also described the recent coverage of Venezuela by the mainstream media as "theatrical."[54]

Capitalists now use Venezuela as their textbook case of how socialism fails, usually pointing to the problems inherent with price controls. In addition to solidarity prices established between urban communities and farmers, the government has set price controls on food, and they might be set so low that it is impossible to produce food profitably. For example, some farmers are required to reserve 30–100 percent of their production of certain foods for state-owned stores, where the products are sold at low prices. However, this requirement is just for certain crops receiving state credit, like corn. State credit helped provide the farmers with resources to produce the corn in the first place.

It is common for capitalists to invoke Hayek's *Road to Serfdom* and argue that socialism always becomes dictatorship. Those arguments seemed eerily accurate when the government in 2016 called for forcing some workers away from their current jobs to work in the farm fields. Yes, this sounds like forced labor, and would have been horrible if it were true. The program was actually voluntary, and Christina considers this perhaps the most egregious example of misinformation by the mainstream media thus far.

The mainstream media has remarked that you are sent to jail if you protest against the government, but Christina counters that much of the violence by the opposition has been ignored, and that many people within poor communities actually believe there have been too few arrests.[55] To its critics, Venezuela is simply repeating the mistakes of communist Russia and China in the twentieth century. To those propelling the Bolivarian movement forward, that criticism is just spin devised by media that either do not care to learn the truth or are unwilling.

Those of us watching Venezuela through the filter of Western media assume that support for the Bolivarian Revolution has waned. Christina lives with the Venezuelan people and assures us it has not. Why? For one reason, Venezuelans are better off now than before the revolution. Rather than seeing the revolution as a failure, many believe it did not go far enough in transforming the food system, noting that the new grassroots production and distribution system is working fine. It is the food provided by large companies, often owned by the opposition, that is failing to deliver.

Cracks in the food system are indeed showing and may be exposing the system's faults—or it could be the result of sabotage from those in opposition. Earlier, when Chávez was in power and oil prices were higher, the revolution delivered dignity to people who were once called "the marginal." As the revolution began to take place, they watched the middle and upper classes repeatedly attempt to destroy it from within. Entrenched interests within the government were always intent on profiting off the changes and preventing the new farm cooperatives from achieving success. This is why Chávez, Maduro, and supporters of the revolution frequently refer to big business as the enemy. Sometimes when the government would expropriate land intended to be used by the local community, the land would instead be managed by state-run corporations. Often replete with corruption, the corporations might bar the people from entering the land, sell what they found on the land to enrich themselves, and hire community members at a low wage, rather than give them the land to manage as cooperatives. When this happened, the communities had to assert themselves and insist the land be given to them, sometimes even occupying the lands, refusing to leave, and farming as they saw fit.

The revolution can be thought of as a two-sided political battle. On one side there was Chávez, his entourage, and the marginals. On the other side were the elite, who resisted the reforms and favored the old system, attempting to sabotage reform. The elite were often an entrenched part of government administration. While some parts of government were moving mountains to help the poor, other parts were trying to destroy the system from within. The marginals and Chávez needed each other. Without Chávez the radical new food system would have been sabotaged from the beginning. Without the marginals, Chávez might not have survived an attempted coup in 2002.

From this perspective, those supporting Maduro today may see Venezuela's current woes as having little to do with the revolution itself, and everything to do with its enemies.

Alas, this book can provide the reader no closure on the Venezuelan food situation. The fate of the revolution is a chapter yet to be written. Christina emphasizes that grassroots movements are actively mobilizing in the face of current challenges, in some cases seizing opportunities to radicalize efforts toward food sovereignty, as with the recent passage of the new seed law, as well as the current people-to-people efforts across the urban-rural divide.

> I find it incredibly inspiring and instructive that in the face of so many challenges right now, from shortages of key items to new economic sanctions imposed by the US government, movements are not only implementing emergency responses, together with their government, but pushing forward in their efforts toward broader societal transformation. If they can do this right here, right now, in these circumstances, then I think that's a message that we can do it too, in our respective locations. I think one key lesson is the importance of community organizing. One of the reasons why communities have been able to respond so rapidly with grassroots solutions is that they had already been organizing themselves over the course of the revolution. Another key takeaway is the importance of broad and bold visions and mechanisms toward achieving them. I think it's radical to have articles of the Venezuelan constitution guaranteeing everybody the right to food through a largely domestic, sustainable food supply. It's radical to say that food should be a basic human right and that countries should be able to supply at least a portion of their own food—and that it be sustainable. The challenges we're seeing today show exactly why this goal is so important. I feel honored to be here bearing witness to the tireless efforts toward these ends, and to support them in what ways I can. I encourage fellow food radicals to question the headlines and lend their solidarity.

Yet there is one lesson from Venezuela that outsiders are failing to recognize. It's that if you foster a society with extreme inequalities, things are bound to erupt, as they did in Venezuela, paving the way for the Bolivarian Revolution. While many analyses have focused on the figure of Chávez and more recently Maduro, what they miss is that the revolution came about through decades of popular struggle. Some of the most interesting developments related to food sovereignty in Venezuela—those Christina has been documenting and working to support—are similarly coming from the bottom up, from those who had been most exploited under the prior system. It is their stories and struggles, together with the broader lessons of the Bolivarian Revolution, both positive and negative, that Christina plans to bring back to the United States, she says, to inform much-needed movement building efforts at home.

Those who wish to avoid the recent path Venezuela has taken should remember that the revolution was given its force by a class of Venezuelans who felt oppressed by the upper classes and felt neglected by the political system. To avoid such a revolution happening elsewhere, then, means to ensure that everyone feels included in a nation's economic and political system. But of course, if you build an inclusive democracy, much of the revolution is already achieved.

Hannah Dankbar and Rivka Fidel, Scholars and GMO Activists

Would you eat a genetically modified banana? What if you were offered $900 to do so? In 2014, Iowa State University made this offer via email to female students and staff between the ages of eighteen and twenty-four.[56] Some students did volunteer,[57] but the experiment never took place because the university was challenged by a small group of concerned students. One can debate whether these students are radicals, but in addition to being scholars, they are definitely activists, and their story illustrates the difficulty of trying to be both in a university setting.

The banana itself may not seem particularly radical to some. The Bill and Melinda Gates Foundation recognized that people in areas like Uganda have serious vitamin A deficiencies. Some bananas have a gene that produces generous amounts of beta-carotene, a compound that the human body converts to vitamin A. Although Uganda grows over a hundred different banana varieties,[58] most do not have this beta-carotene-producing gene. To the Gates Foundation this suggested a simple solution: take the gene that produces vitamin A from one banana species that grows in Papua New Guinea and insert it into bananas grown in Uganda. This new genetically modified (GM) banana could then be propagated throughout

Uganda, allowing its people to continue consuming a beloved staple food without the blindness associated with vitamin A deficiency.

But is the new GM banana safe? To many scientists this was a foregone conclusion. Since the gene already exists in another banana and that gene is beneficial to humans, inserting it into a different banana would only provide benefits. When Iowa State University (ISU) offered females $900 (a very high dollar incentive in such a setting) to eat the bananas, it was not trying to determine if the banana was safe, but the extent to which the beta-carotene produced by the banana would be converted to vitamin A in the human body.

A small group of Iowa State students saw the issues differently. They recognized that it would be the first ever institutional feeding trial of a genetically modified food (except for the feeding trial we are all participants of, since much of what we eat is produced with genetically modified crops).[59] One of the females receiving the invitation to eat the banana was Angie Carter, a graduate student studying sociology and sustainable agriculture. Angie knew that human feeding trials had really never been conducted, so she did not see this as an ordinary research project, and she was not going to just assume it was safe.

Angie had reason to believe that Ugandans did not necessarily want the GM banana. Bridget Mugambe is Ugandan and a policy advocate for the Alliance for Food Sovereignty in Africa (AFSA). In an open letter to both the Gates Foundation and ISU, Bridget opposed the feeding trial. The letter contained the usual verbiage about GM crops not being proven safe, and an argument about the complex role vitamin A plays in human nutrition. Given the differences between the genetics, diet, and lifestyles of Ugandans to those of Americans, she also argued that the experiment might provide little insight into how the banana would impact the health of Ugandans. Written by Bridget and the AFSA, the letter was supported by 127 different organizations, many of them African, and twenty notable individuals.

In a YouTube video Bridget explains that Ugandan bananas are not sweet like the Cavendish varieties Americans consume. Commonly referred to as matoke, they are steamed, mashed, and eaten as a starch at many meals, much like cassava and potatoes. Ugandan children do not even like the bananas until they are seven or older. If the goal is to improve the nutrition of children by introducing a genetically modified banana, how will that work when young children do not want to eat it? The letter ends with a plea for Ugandan food sovereignty and for the Gates Foundation to not take actions that might interfere with the genetics of staple crops. Instead, Bridget argues, if better nutrition is the goal, the Foundation should encourage greater food variety, not genetic tampering with staple foods.[60]

All of this suggested to Angie that she should share the email invitation and Bridget's letter with her ISU friends to discuss what, if anything, should be done. A half dozen or so people were invited to Angie's house, all of whom were studying sustainable agriculture and shared Angie's concerns. Two of these students were Hannah Dankbar, studying community and regional planning at the time, and Rivka Fidel, studying agronomy—two food radicals interviewed for this book. Although we will reflect on the university administrator's position and the overall lesson from this story, what happened next is told largely from Hannah's and Rivka's point of view.

As Angie, Hannah, Rivka, and others discussed the issue, they all shared concerns about the safety of the feeding trials; the banana's implication for agricultural sustainability, food security, and food sovereignty in Uganda; and who would possess ownership of the GM banana. Rivka notes,

At the time, it was all women, all friends and colleagues from within the Sustainable Agriculture Program. We did not form a specific group or give ourselves a title, but we were all interested in this study and concerned about it. We each had various nuances to our concerns. We had some concerns in common: we could not find any evidence of this banana ever being tested on any organisms before, no record of any safety testing. As sustainable agriculture students, we were also concerned about the implications of this banana for sustainable agriculture in Uganda and with sovereignty. What would introducing this banana do to local ecosystems? What would it do to society? What would it do the economics of the region? Would this banana be more expensive to grow than the traditional bananas? Why did the researchers feel the need to introduce a gene to a banana that is grown in Uganda as opposed to encouraging Ugandans to diversify their diet? Were they being myopic in their approach, and just looking for a quick technological fix to what appears to be a complex problem?

It is important to note that at this point, neither Hanna nor Rivka was against the experiment. Additionally, neither was unilaterally opposed to GMOs. They simply felt there needed to be more awareness and discussion of the study, and they had both the skills and the enthusiasm to make such a conversation happen.

A number of questions needed addressing, they decided. What safety precautions were being taken to protect the health of those who eat the GM banana? What procedures were being used to make the study relevant to Ugandans, as opposed to college faculty and staff? All university research must be approved by the university, so what factors did it consider when it granted approval for the study? The students wanted these questions addressed publicly so that others could become aware of the study also, and to encourage a conversation on the issue. A public dialogue was envisioned, where invited speakers would present their thoughts, answer questions, and facilitate an exchange among all concerned parties. The students didn't necessarily expect the administration to have all the answers, but they did want to ensure that these questions were at least considered when the research was approved.

The students were not planning a rally or a one-sided conversation. The dialogue was not to be a platform for them to amplify their opinions, but to gather multiple perspectives in a calm, rational exchange. The title of the event was ultimately Transgenic Bananas? A Dialogue on the Ethics, Impacts, and Alternatives—very academic, hardly provocative.

Nor was the dialogue to be a debate on GMOs in general. The Monsanto Corporation was not to be put on trial or even mentioned. The questions simply concerned the safety of the feeding trial and its relevance to the health of Ugandans. Issues like food sovereignty would arise, certainly, but this was not because the students wanted to debate whether GMOs threaten the food sovereignty of all nations. If the feeding trial showed the GM banana to successfully provide vitamin A, the implication is that the GM banana is a simple, technical solution to Ugandan vitamin deficiency. Yet the actual raising of the banana in Uganda might alter the diversity of crops grown, and reliance on foreign produced crops might leave the nation with less control over the plants providing its food. The students felt this should be an item of discussion, too.

Convinced that such a critical dialogue was needed and such questions needed answering, the student group delegated different tasks to the members to make it happen. Some searched the scientific journals, checking to see if this GM banana had ever undergone an animal feeding trial before, or if any human feeding trial had ever been conducted (the answer was negative to both). Other students approached the dean of the agricultural college, the lead researcher (a professor of food science and human nutrition), and the food science department chair. Concerns mounted when these faculty and administrators, though not rude, were generally unresponsive.

The lead researcher did not return the students' emails and was frequently unavailable for comment, so it was some time before the students could talk with her. When they did, the researcher was polite but provided no answers. Rivka recalled, "she seemed to want to help me, but she said that she was not approved to discuss the details of the study with the public or the media. She is an expert in her field of nutrition and specifically vitamin A nutrition. She was asked to participate in this study as a researcher because of her expertise. Knowing what I knew from the media and as she talked to me, she was just doing her job. Talking with the media, or curious students, seemed to be beyond what she could do." Although free speech by faculty is protected by tenure, the students knew that controversial issues like GMOs can make university administrators nervous, and those administrators prefer caution. Sometimes administrators would prefer not to answer a question, even if it makes them seem nontransparent, rather than give an answer that comes under public criticism.

Efforts to reach the agricultural dean through email were also frustrating—one email after another was ignored. Only later, after the celebrity activist Vandana Shiva visited the campus to speak on sustainable agriculture to an audience of over seven hundred students did the dean respond.[61] The email exchanges concerned the critical dialogue to be held on the banana trials. Instead of picking one or two of the panelists, the dean wanted to select five, in addition to helping the students compose the questions. From the students' view the dean was attempting to control the dialogue, which of course, would mean it was not a dialogue at all.

Why would the dean suddenly take so much interest in the students' activities after the Vandana Shiva speech and seek so much control over the dialogue? Perhaps the dean had attended Shiva's speech and grew concerned over what she heard. Shiva is a renowned critic of conventional agriculture, especially GM crops (the student introducing Shiva was Angie Carter). Probably the best-known anti-GMO activist in the world, Shiva spoke on the benefits of sustainable agriculture compared to conventional, stressing the benefits of biodiversity over monocultures. The vitamin A issue was addressed specifically when she argued that the easiest way to increase its intake is to stop killing "weeds" like amaranth with pesticides, and value it for what it really is: food. Instead of genetically modifying the same monocultures to possess more of the vitamin, and by diversifying our diets instead, we can simultaneously improve our nutrition while using less pesticides and less tillage. That is essentially the message of sustainable agriculture and the students' vision for an effective food system.

Other parts of Shiva's speech addressed the GM banana specifically and might have frightened the administrators. The ostensible purpose of the banana may be to alleviate vitamin A deficiency, Shiva remarked, but the real reason is to assert control over the cultivation of bananas by the West. Going further, Shiva contended that the lead researcher "has no expertise in biosafety of any kind" (and this is true, but the researchers probably believe there is no biosafety threat to begin with) and mentioned the researchers' affiliation with a biotechnology corporation, thereby suggesting the researcher was being influenced by money. At one point, Shiva asserted, "I don't think this university should facilitate a biopiracy project. Just on that one ground these trials should stop."

At the conclusion of Shiva's speech, before the question-and-answer session began, the audience was then told by Angie that if they want to learn more about transgenic bananas, they could attend the upcoming critical dialogue and were told when and where. It was called just that—a "critical dialogue"—and presented only as an information session. It was not depicted as a protest against the transgenic banana. Angie did say she hoped to see the audience there to "continue this conversation."[62] Did that mean a simple conversation about the transgenic banana, from people of all different viewpoints? According to Hannah and Rivka, yes. Could the ISU administration have interpreted it to mean a conversation criticizing GMOs in general and the transgenic banana in particular? Perhaps. To Hannah, "it was clear [the dean] perceived our panel as an attack, not as a simple way to raise awareness. Through our correspondence, when we showed her the questions that we were going to ask, she expressed concerns that we would be putting whoever showed up who was pro-GMO on trial and criticizing them. That was absolutely not our intention. We put a lot of work into those questions to avoid such a situation."

All the administrators and lead researchers contacted by the students declined to participate in the critical dialogue, nor would they suggest someone to represent their views. The dialogue took place with only three panelists selected by the students. There was no one representing the supporters of the GMO banana or the feeding trial to be conducted, as the dean insisted on choosing these persons, but then ultimately provided no one. Rivka noted that "the critical dialogue had gotten good attendance and we got good media coverage. We felt that a lot of our questions, parts of our questions, I should say, had gone unanswered because the panelists had done their best to answer the questions during the critical dialogue, but they ultimately were not the ones that the questions were directed towards."

Up until this point the students were never allowed an in-person meeting with the dean, and shortly before the dialogue the students approached another one of the administrators to ensure her that it was indeed a friendly conversation, and that those involved in the GM banana research were not going to be "put on trial." This administrator expressed some concern that some of the questions did not just pertain to vitamin A absorbability of the banana, but other issues not relevant to the ISU research. According to Rivka, "she used the word 'science' a lot. She'd say the questions you're asking do not pertain to the science. It seemed to me she was implying my questions were unscientific. I found this frustrating because social science is science. They were trying to play both sides. The response to us planning our panel was to write up a letter to the editor claiming that this technology would help save lives in Africa. When we asked them about the details—sustainability and food sovereignty—which very much play into saving lives, just make sure you're continuing to save lives and do it in your best way with a long-term perspective. They backed away from the question and would say that doesn't pertain to the science anymore."

Here we have something of a contradiction with ISU's interactions with the students. When communicating with the students, the administration was clear that the only purpose of the research was to determine the bioavailability of vitamin A from the GM banana. Any implications for Ugandans was outside the scope of research. Yet when the administration publicly expressed support for the project, it proudly touted the banana's ability to help Ugandans, once stating in an *Ames Tribute* editorial that the banana was developed by people "who wish to address vitamin A deficiency in millions of women and children worldwide."

A few days after the dialogue, the dean authored an editorial expressing ISU's support for the research and the lead researcher.[63] Was the critical dialogue so opposed to the GM banana feeding trial that ISU needed to publicly express support for the researcher? Fortunately, a video of the dialogue was recorded and posted on the internet for the public, and readers who watch it will agree that it was anything but an anti-GMO rally. It was respectful, thoughtful, and was not even completely against the feeding trial. Of the four scheduled speakers, one was unable to attend, one was difficult to understand because of poor-quality audio, one expressed concern about Uganda's food sovereignty, and the fourth believed the feeding trial should be held. The room was packed, with about eighty people in attendance, all of whom were attentive and curious, never disruptive. It was interesting, informative, calm, and polite—certainly nothing that a university should fear. If anything, it should make a university proud.

To understand why university administrators were so reluctant to participate in the dialogue, try to consider the issue from their point of view. These are mostly scientists who researched and taught in narrow fields before being promoted to administrative positions. Very few are activists or even outspoken in their field. The person doing the GM banana feeding trial was one of the foremost nutrition experts but was probably uncomfortable discussing broader topics like food sovereignty and the politics of GMOs. Such scientists have devoted their adult lives to mastering highly technical topics, leaving little time for studying the broad and complex arguments made by anti-GMO activists. The university wanted to focus solely on the conversion of beta-carotene in the GM banana without having to confront all the other baggage that comes with GMOs, but the students were insisting that ignoring such considerations was irresponsible. "In our Sustainable Agriculture Program there is a heavy emphasis on systems thinking, of looking at the big picture of food," Hannah states.

It isn't the case that scientists only want to focus on their own specific research questions while disregarding the implications of their research. This just happens to be an instance when the university did not believe that a wider discussion was necessary, whereas students like Rivka and Hannah did. Neither Rivka nor Hannah is against all genetic modification, but they believe it is being adopted too quickly and without adequate evaluation. In interviews they mentioned the precautionary principle, which states that activities with uncertain or disputed effects should be avoided. Rivka notes, "I'm inherently a cautious person and have a strong belief in the precautionary principle. If there is a perceived risk, even if the percent that something could happen is low, you should do everything in your power to further minimize and avoid that risk. The developed technology has only been used in agriculture for about twelve years. That seems like a long time, but we're dealing with very complex systems that have chemical, biological, geological, human components to them. I feel that we need to understand genetics in general, and genetic coapplications far better than we do right now." European activists have been particularly avid about government adherence to the principle,[64] and the principle has even found a home in Article 191 of the Lisbon Treaty, which is the international agreement forming the constitution of the European Union. The reticence of the European Union to adopt GMOs compared to the eagerness of the United States is partially due to the precautionary principle.[65] Rather than saying the students behaved like radicals, we could say they were aligned with European ideology and practice—but at an American university.

Perhaps the university believed that nothing would make the students happy, and that the GM banana feeding trial would continue to be opposed regardless of how well the students' questions were answered. Sometimes activists are thought of as fanatics, people who "can't change their mind and won't change the subject." Rivka states, "there's a lot involved in being an activist. I think everyone should pay attention to the political sphere and what's going on at their institution. What they choose to do about it is a much more personal choice. For a lot of us who are involved in activism, it is because our drive to do something good and to make a difference is just that strong, and activism is the best way in the foreseeable future for us to do that. I've spoken to people who would say that if you feel your institution isn't doing enough, or your local government isn't doing enough, you're obligated to be an activist no matter what."

If the university had investigated some of the students, it might have discovered that they are indeed activists, having participated in a range of activities. At least one of the students had protested the Keystone Pipeline by blocking a major university intersection.[66] When the Monsanto chief technology officer visited the university to speak, some of the students attended with bags containing gas masks and signs. During the speech they donned the masks and lifted their signs into the air, one of them reading *conventional ag = chemical ag*. Some of them were members of ActivUs, a university group "committed to achieving environmental and social justice on the Iowa State campus . . . through means of public education, grassroots organizing, and non-violent direct action." One of our interviewees had been the president of the organization. If the students did hold their public dialogue regarding the GM banana research, was the university fearful the students would be disruptive there?

It is easy to see how a university administrator might have these fears, but it is also clear from the video of the dialogue that took place that these fears were unfounded. Hannah, Rivka, and their friends are indeed capable of activism, but they are equally capable of participating in a thoughtful and polite exchange of ideas. Hannah asserts, "there should be an emphasis on research, and outreach and education. People shouldn't be ashamed of doing research on GMOs, and we shouldn't be splitting ourselves in these camps. Having these critical dialogues is important."

The critical dialogue came and passed, but it did not achieve the students' objective. They still wanted assurance that their questions were considered in the research design. The researchers and administrators once again were contacted to see if they would answer these questions, whether in a recorded interview or an article. No public communication would be allowed by the dean. Only a small, unofficial private meeting would be permitted, and at this point the students were finally able to record the dean's responses to certain questions. Still, it was not a public statement made by ISU, but just answers recorded by the students. Because the meeting was private, it was impossible for other concerned people to ask questions and voice their concerns.

Rivka, Hannah, and the others were frustrated, and they had difficulty understanding why ISU would not choose transparency in researching such a controversial issue. The group discussions then began to center on the need for transparency in science, and how knowledge does not thrive unless people are free to express skepticism and ask pressing questions. As sustainability activists, they felt their questions warranted consideration by ISU. As scholars seeking knowledge, they decided they must insist on answers. As they remarked in an *Ames Tribune* editorial, "Open and honest discussion is integral to scientific research. Without it, the scientific process itself is in jeopardy." After the summer of 2015 passed and the students reconvened for the fall semester, they decided more action was needed.

So they started a petition. Its goals were modest; they only asked that ISU publicly answer seven questions about the research. They wanted to know some details about how the bananas would be prepared, how differences in physiology between Americans and Ugandans would be accounted for, how the study compliments other approaches to solving vitamin A deficiencies, and the like. They were not opposing the research, but the petition did state that *if* "these questions could not be answered in a transparent manner that justifies the sociological and biological claims made about the study's impacts, we believe the banana study to be an inappropriate use of state funds and lab space."[67]

The petition received about one thousand signatures but no response from the ISU administration. There was reticence to implement a second, larger petition, or to escalate their struggle with the university, so the students stopped pressing the issue. It was important to them that they voice their concerns, but they did not want to appear to be obstacles to the scientific process. They backed off. Another group more willing to make a ruckus took over. The Community Alliance for Global Justice (CAGJ) administered a larger version of the petition in November 2015, using the activist social media platform *Credo*. Their goal was not to ask for transparency and answers to the students' questions, but to discard the research project as a whole. The petition was aimed not just at ISU, but at the Gates Foundation as well. Some of the students signed it, and some helped collect signatures, but this was done on an individual basis. It was not the deliberate result of coalition-building on the part of the students, but because one of the students happened to know a CAGJ member who was actively protesting some of the projects conducted by the Gates Foundation, and CAGJ had corresponded with some of the students through email as the students conducted their research. It was the CAGJ that approached the students about conducting a second petition. On February 15, 2016, after gathering 57,835 virtual signatures, the CAGJ hand-delivered the names to the Gates Foundation. On the same day, the students delivered a banana-shaped memory stick to the dean's secretary containing copies of those same petitions (figure 3.1). There was no response from ISU.

By now the reader might be asking what happened to the women who volunteered to eat the GM bananas? The feeding trial was approved by ISU and participants were already recruited by August 2014.[68] The trial was delayed for some time. When our student "radicals" started asking questions about the research and planning the critical dialogue, it was as if ISU no longer wanted to discuss the research.[69] During the students' April 21, 2015, meeting with the dean, they were told the experiment would still be held, and between March and June 2016 it was.[70]

Although this group posed quite an obstacle to ISU research, one could argue that ISU should have been proud of their efforts. They were employing the very same critical thinking skills taught in classrooms across campus. In classes, some of the students had participated in role-playing exercises where they would pretend to be panelists representing different private and public organizations and would answer questions

FIGURE 3.1 Students delivering the second petition to cancel the GMO experiment (Hannah Dankbar: top row, third from left; Rivka Fidel: bottom row, right)
Image courtesy of Rivka Fidel

regarding whether certain GM crops should be introduced into a region. They were taught to understand the GM technology and its role in society, discuss the issue intelligently, and to be an active participant in society. Hannah declares, "we find this work rewarding, and we appreciate the opportunity to take what we're learning in the classroom and have conversations and apply it to the real world, so we're not just sitting at our desk reading about theory all day. While we're at grad school, we're actually able to step outside of the classroom and engage with the world. We're lucky enough in the Sustainable Agriculture Program to have a lot of professors who are accustomed to having students involved in activism, and often even reward that and appreciate that work." Their engagement with this issue seems such a direct application of what they had learned in college. In hindsight, perhaps ISU administrators feel the students were taught too well!

The students' research and investigations required they be in constant contact with one another, and every few weeks they would meet as a group or conduct a phone conference. It required studying the issue and employing critical thinking skills. The dialogue required corresponding with administrators, making reservations, advertising the event, writing introductory statements, and developing strategies for keeping the peace should disruptive pro- and anti-GMO activists attend. Even if the university disagreed with the students' conclusions, it should have applauded their thoughtful work and their efforts to be good citizens. Hanna recalls, "some people viewed us as radical, but we saw ourselves trying to create a dialogue among scholars. We were graduate students, many of us working to becoming researchers, so wanting to create a dialogue about food and agriculture doesn't seem that radical to us."

If a small group of students questions university research, to what extent are researchers and administrators obliged to assuage them? In regards to the GM banana, the university believed it could ignore the students. It was wrong. Because questions were not adequately answered, the students felt morally compelled to start their petition, and that petition would prove to be sufficiently powerful to stymie the university's research plans.

Some readers may conclude that if the students wished to be taken seriously by the university, they should have worked within the system and avoided all forms of activism, to appear less of a threat to the university. However, this puts the students in the uncomfortable position of having to choose between being an activist and being a scholar, which is unfortunate, because an activist without knowledge is dangerous, and a scholar without conviction can be used for nefarious means.

Students need space where they can express their moral views in nonviolent though pesky ways, in addition to the many places they are provided

to express themselves as scholars. Looking back on Thoreau's civil disobedience to protest slavery, few of us conclude he was in the wrong, and
most of us admire both his activism and his writings. After refusing to pay
taxes that would be used to support a government that allowed slavery, he
was placed in jail. Thoreau the activist then became Thoreau the scholar
when he penned *Civil Disobedience* about his protest,[71] an essay that would
inspire both Mahatma Gandhi and Martin Luther King Jr. If we want our
students to become great people, we must give them the space to do so.

In one sense ISU did provide the students a platform to be both
scholars and activists. Understanding the impact of GM technology
requires a multidisciplinary approach. Scientists are needed, yes, but
other fields also need to be represented, like community planning,
anthropology, and sociology. The graduate program in sustainable agriculture at ISU is multidisciplinary in nature, and so this group of
concerned students (to our chagrin, the group never gave themselves a
name) was an ideal crew. Hannah notes, "we were used to all coming
together, coming from different disciplines, and talking to each other
despite our differences and backgrounds." Though diverse in their
specialties within the Sustainable Agriculture Program, the students
shared two commonalities. One is a high value placed on sustainability, of course, and the other is an enthusiastic involvement in social
issues. As Hannah explained, they are not all activists, but they all embrace activism as a worthy endeavor. They do not criticize activism in
general or use the word "activist" as a pejorative. Unlike in most agricultural programs at universities, the professors at ISU are accustomed
to students being activists and sometimes reward active engagement
with important food issues.

In some ways the Sustainable Agriculture Program was radical, at least
compared to most agricultural colleges. There are two different agricultural cultures at play in universities: the cultures of conventional agriculture and sustainable agriculture. The agricultural colleges at land grant
universities generally adhere to the conventional agriculture culture—
they are happy with the technologies developed in the last fifty years and
eagerly adopt new ones—and some even teach classes on how to defend
conventional agriculture against activists who would speak out against it.
The reader might remember the hostility toward Amory Starr's critique
of conventional agriculture at Colorado State University, and that it is
smaller non-ag schools like the one Katie Michels attended that tend to
have organic gardens, not the big agricultural schools.

Those adhering to the goal of a sustainable culture believe that agriculture must develop a different philosophy if it is to continue feeding the world. Although both cultures are optimistic about the ability of technology to improve food, they disagree on the merits of individual technologies. Whether big corporations are helpful or harmful is also in dispute. Students like Rivka and Hannah believe that not all problems can be fixed by working within the system. Sometimes you must lift a sign into the air and halt traffic. But they also want to take some of the same courses as other students in agricultural colleges, and to participate in scholarly exchanges. Iowa State University has a nurturing environment for such students in its Sustainable Agriculture Program, but that environment does not extend to the entire university. Given that a few students were able to pose such an obstacle to a university research project, perhaps it should.

Fergal Anderson Says Power to the Peasants

Some readers might find it surprising that Rivka and Hannah would protest the use of advanced technologies by an enormously rich philanthropist to solve a developing country's nutrition problem. However, there is an undernoticed movement to reject solutions from nongovernmental organizations, experts, and institutional science, and to instead seek solutions from peasants (note that "peasant" is not considered derogatory by those receiving the label). Fergal Anderson is an Irish farmer we briefly met earlier, but before he was a farmer he was a curious student eager to better understand what it takes to help developing countries and solve world problems. His studies and travels exposed him to different genres of solutions. One was an external approach where experts from the outside come in to help, and the other was an internal approach where the people needing help organize themselves and seek their own solutions. We have seen this dichotomy previously. Karissa Lewis argued minorities in the United States must organize themselves, where "organize" means to lead their own political movements and identify their own solutions. Venezuela sought endogenous as opposed to exogenous development strategies.

In his younger years Fergal was unsure which strategy was best, so he sought to learn more about both of them. With his partner, Emanuela, he volunteered with a locally based association in Guatemala that worked to empower indigenous and marginalized communities there in organizing their food production systems, infrastructure and representation at the local government level. This also took them to Mexico, where they learned that outside philanthropic groups were not always welcome in indigenous communities. Their travels also exposed them to the concept of agroecology, where small peasant farmers shunned industrial inputs and farmed in harmony with nature. The desire of these communities to produce their own food and chart their own destiny for their agriculture—instead of allowing global markets to make the decisions—exposed Fergal and his partner to the concept of food sovereignty. "We went out and spent a lot of time in villages, working with the people who were going out into the indigenous villages and working with the farmers on the ground. That was where we came across these ideas of agroecology, food sovereignty. The ideas that we were talking about with the local people made a lot of sense . . . when we thought about it in our own context—for me particularly—in Ireland."

Years later would find Fergal taking these ideas back to Ireland, becoming something of a peasant farmer himself and developing a movement aiming to champion food sovereignty in Ireland (Food Sovereignty Ireland). What is important here is to recognize that these ideas were not just borrowed from a few scattered farmers across the Americas. They have been cultivated by groups of peasant farmers all across the world, representing one of the most powerful farmer groups that people in the developed world have never heard of: La Via Campesina.

In Mexico Fergal encountered the Zapatista movement, which began in an armed uprising of indigenous peoples in 1994 in the Chiapas region. For five centuries these groups had experienced oppression and exploitation by outside forces. This includes the political elite of the country as well as transnational corporations that systematically stole resources. Tired of both direct and indirect colonization, the 1994 uprising adopted the battle cry "Enough!" and foreshadowed Hugo Chávez by rejecting neoliberalism and encouraging cooperative farms. The Zapatistas believed the North American Free Trade Agreement (NAFTA) would bring ruin and rejected the trade rules of the World Trade Organization. They called for debt forgiveness, arguing that debt is largely a tool of the powerful to further dominate the vulnerable. The Zapatistas aim was to give indigenous communities control and self-determination through direct democracy, empowering them to develop their own schools, agriculture systems, and other elements of everyday life that reflected their cultural and historical realities.

The date of the uprising is important: January 1, 1994—the same day NAFTA officially took effect. This is no coincidence. The neoliberalism that began in the early 1980s was associated with a rise in corporate power and decline in rural agricultural areas. Just as Bill Bullard saw his fellow ranchers and farmers lose money year after year, farmers in developing countries witnessed the same phenomenon, and both noticed that at the same time a few corporations were acquiring greater and greater power. Farmers across the global South (a term replacing "developing" or "Third World" countries) began organizing against neoliberalism. These organizations began working together, and in 1993, a year before the Zapatista uprising, they founded La Via Campesina (Spanish for "the peasants' way").

In 2007 La Via Campesina brought farmers from around the world to protest the G8 meetings in Germany. By this point, anytime the largest countries convened, it was viewed by many peasants as another dose of neoliberalism, so global civil society movements including activists, NGOs, and the "peasants" organized huge summit protests to denounce the nondemocratic nature of such organizations, as well as the policies they were proposing.

Fergal Anderson was there also, fulfilling a requirement of his MS degree in public advocacy and activism to intern at an activist organization. "It was the first time I'd ever encountered this international movement of farmers. We met people who were there from India, and Turkey, and Latin America. They were sleeping in tents in the field with the rest of the activists. It was a massively inspirational kind of experience to meet those people. They were grounded in the struggles. . . . I didn't see any of that sense of detachment. They were completely on the same wavelength . . . and not working on some kind of institutional agenda. It felt much more real. They were coming from the other side of the world—and sharing tents. Very different from the big NGO lifestyle happening in other places. They were talking about food sovereignty and with great dignity, wisdom, and strength about these big international issues." He found the event inspiring. These farmers were both the victims of neoliberalism and activists at the same time. It was as pure a grassroots movement as an international organization could ever be.

The concept of "food sovereignty" has been mentioned several times, but not its origin. La Via Campesina introduced it at the World Food Summit in 1996 as "the right of people to healthy and culturally appropriate food produced through sustainable methods and their right to define their own food and agriculture systems," explicitly rejecting the previously dominant concept of "food security" while proposing an alternative framework. We have seen these notions previously, with Karissa Lewis in Oakland, California; Rivka Fidel and Hannah Dankbar at Iowa State University; Venezuela under the Bolivarian Revolution; and to a lesser extent, Bill Bullard in the United States.

As the farmers explained food sovereignty to Fergal, he saw much wisdom in it.

> All I saw around were problems. I saw very few solutions being offered. But they were talking about food sovereignty. . . . I thought they were actually talking about a solution. They're talking about a solution and they're the people who are least likely to get listened to. People say this is the last place they expect a solution to come is from: the peasants. The solutions are about the leaders and politicians and experts and NGOs. In fact, what they gave with food sovereignty was a very powerful opening: this idea of solidarity and not competition, the idea that you have a right to define your own food and agricultural systems—radical ideas actually, but quite simple ideas. You have an obligation not to interfere with other people's rights to define their own food and agriculture systems. These are simple things, but actually very fundamental things. It opened up a whole new way for me to think about how we could organize ourselves, more democratic organization, an evolutionary framework.

Fergal volunteered to help Via Campesina however he could. Soon he found himself organizing delegations and providing logistical support and was offered a full-time job at Via Campesina's European office in Paris. Here Fergal was working on many of the same problems as the Gates Foundation, but proposing solutions using an opposite strategy. The Gates Foundation seeks technical solutions to problems, while La Via Campesina relies on peasants for answers. The Gates Foundation works as an army: experts design a battle plan, execute it with precision, evaluate the outcome, and then adjust accordingly. La Via Campesina is more democratic, more flexible, more informal, and more focused on empowerment and autonomy.

It is here we can now develop a better appreciation for what Hannah Dankbar and Rivka Fidel were trying to accomplish. They opposed the use of a genetically modified banana in combating vitamin A deficiencies in

Uganda. It may be hard for some readers to understand why intelligent people would take such a stance (and Hannah and Rivka are incredibly bright), but Fergal would stand with our two Iowa students for a simple reason: there is no evidence that the peasants of Uganda want this banana. Indeed, our section on Hannah and Rivka suggests Ugandan peasants do not want it. So how do peasants in Uganda wish to combat vitamin A problems? This book can't tell you because we haven't asked them, and Fergal would not want us volunteering solutions until we have first done so.

Fergal found working at La Via Campesina inspiring and meaningful, because it treats peasants with dignity, gives them sovereignty over their own lives, and frankly seems to work. When he moved on to Brussels next, his partner Emanuela moved with him and began working on an "open" farm that would organize community gardens and occupy land intended to be used for a supermarket. So while he was supporting peasant agriculture, Emanuela was actively engaging in it. As time went by and Fergal worked at his dream job, he grew frustrated at being stuck in the office, behind a computer, conversing through Skype rather than in person. The person who previously held Fergal's position had quit to become a farmer, and eventually Fergal would follow her lead.

After quitting his job, Fergal traveled Europe, visiting different types of farms employing agroecology. He and Emanuela "were looking to visit people who were trying to do similar things, in similar stages. We ended up visiting lots of different places, big communal farms, farms with people who live on hills all on their own growing gardens, or people who were trying to set up CSAs. We saw different types of organizing and saw the diversity of approaches. In practical terms we were always kind of thinking in the back of our heads—we're going to have to get land somewhere. The more we went through and realized that getting a bit of land was going to cost a lot of money, we began to think, well, there's land sitting here in Ireland." Their European tour convinced them that they too wished to be peasant farmers. Fergal's family owned thirty acres of land, most in trees but some in fields, so they moved to Ireland to farm using agroecological principles, selling to local communities, and fighting for food sovereignty in Ireland.

One might argue that food sovereignty has been lacking for some time in Ireland. Like India, like Sri Lanka, like Africa, like regions throughout the Americas, Ireland was colonized by the English for centuries. Many of us learn in school that millions died during the Irish Potato Famine, caused by a potato disease. This disease did occur. It wiped out most of the potato harvest for years, but the island actually produced enough other foods during the period to feed everyone. The problem was that these other foods were produced on land controlled by the English, and the food was exported to increase the wealth of the British elite. The real reason so many Irish died and emigrated is that the English gave them so little land on which to grow their own food, and the only crop that provided for caloric needs on the limited land was potatoes. So when the potatoes rotted, so did the primary food supply. What is important to note is that the Irish did not want a potato-based food system—they adopted it by necessity because the island did not possess food sovereignty.[72]

With the advent of globalization, Irish land is now being converted to grazing land for beef and dairy production, the vast majority of which will be exported to Europe, and the proceeds used to import other foods. "There's been no discussion at all about how we use the land in terms of environmental impact, or social impact, or impact on the local economy. We've hollowed out the entire local food system. The farmers in this area would very rarely even eat their own animals, or have any access to their own produce. They just sell into the global market. And at the same time, they're not making a living off their production. Their income is almost entirely dependent on their association with the European Union." Fergal sees much danger in basing agriculture on just two products (beef and dairy) and on making the whole agricultural economy dependent on external inputs while exporting into volatile global markets. After all, one cattle disease could eliminate their food production system, just as one potato disease did less than two centuries prior.

In agroecology, the key to a resilient food system is diversity in plants and livestock products, something Ireland sorely lacks. Yet Fergal is doing what he can to encourage diversity and is starting on his own land. Today he and Emanuela (figure 3.2) run Leaf and Root farm.[73] "We grow I think about sixty different types of vegetables on the farm . . . annual crops, which is probably more than would be economically sensible. We are interested in growing lots of different things. Part of the fascination for us is to see what different crops can do. We often let things go to seed because we're interested in seeing the whole life cycle of a plant."

He and Emanuela are encouraging independence from the global food market, and Fergal is starting in his own community by selling locally, both directly to consumers and to a local restaurant called Loam (loam being a type of soil). Following agroecological principles, he has no need

FIGURE 3.2 Fergal and Emanuela on Leaf and Root farm
Image courtesy of Fergal Anderson

for chemical fertilizers or pesticides. "I suppose I regard it as normal now, but I think it probably is radical. The food sovereignty movement certainly is radical because what we're trying to talk about is completely outside the narrative of what the government wants to talk about. If I really get down to the discussion about how I see the use of the land in Ireland, my neighbors, they'd think it was completely radical. One of the things I've been thinking a lot about recently is the conception of the landscape. You have an idea about the landscape in Ireland in particular as being the cow in the meadow and the green grass. We've kind of taken that image and made that parcel of images part of our identity. That is an image which I feel is a history of colonial expropriation and exploitation of the landscape. There's a whole struggle there in changing people's perception of the landscape and what it looks like now, and what it might look like if it was covered in oak forest, or if it was farmed in a different way (figure 3.3). So those are radical ideas because they are asking people to completely transform the perception of the place around them. You're

FIGURE 3.3 Leaf and Root farm
Image courtesy of Fergal Anderson

challenging very conservative mindsets in the farming community. That's not straightforward."

Can Fergal and Emanuela really make a difference? Can peasant farmers stand up to the wave of globalization and the corporations riding that wave to world dominance? "What we're trying to do with food sovereignty is to start a conversation about changing farming from a very much profit-driven industry to something that is more embedded in the social, cultural fabric of society and which reflects the needs of the environment and its people that live in the space. It's more about the people, and the place, and less about profit and production."

Let us return to the Zapatista movement discussed earlier. The reader probably assumed the Mexican army swiftly suppressed this uprising. Well, the army tried but did not succeed. Today Chiapas is something of an autonomous region. The official laws of Mexico do not officially apply, and the indigenous peoples have developed their own informal laws. At the same time the Zapatistas are not seeking independence from Mexico. So, yes, a movement based on wisdom of the peasants and indigenous people can achieve great success—it is the dominant force in an area of 74,715 square kilometers! That's nearly the size of Ireland itself, though Fergal's strategy is not armed insurrection, but peaceful persuasion.

Dan Brown Serves the Maine Course

Not all food sovereignty advocates are seeking a revolution in the food system. Some just want the ability to be self-sufficient and sell food to a neighbor.

For Dan Brown of the state of Maine, food sovereignty initially meant providing food for himself. "When I hear the term, I think of it on a very personal nature. Food sovereignty for me is growing as much food as possible for myself to feed myself. Knowing your farmer and knowing where your food is coming from is part of that. You don't have to grow everything yourself, but working together and bartering and trading or buying or selling is part of that self-sufficiency." Growing up just outside of New York City, he would often visit his uncle's small dairy farm. He would have loved to have taken over the dairy after his uncle died, but his aunt insisted it was not a career he should enter, noting, "There is no life here," and she sold the farm instead. So Dan worked a variety of jobs, including positions at grocery stores, milk-processing centers, and driving trucks.

Trucking took its toll on him personally, taking him away from home and his daughter. He quit but had to accept lower-paying jobs, which presented their own challenges. Dan struggled and, except when with his daughter, felt lost.

Then he met his current wife, Judy, who resurrected his love for the farm. Judy was a homesteader, meaning she strove to be as self-sufficient as possible. (If anyone thinks this is an odd lifestyle, just go to YouTube and type "homestead" and be astounded at the number of postings). Judy gardened, raised a variety of livestock, and was especially adept at making dairy products from the cow she milked. For all of his adult life Dan had purchased most of his food from conventional grocery stores, but when he tasted Judy's food, raised on her land and prepared with her own hands, he caught the homesteading bug.

They joined in marriage and he joined her on the farm. For the first time in his life he found work that he loved, work that gave him meaning. "She was the driving force that figured most of it out before I came along. The minute I was exposed to it, I couldn't imagine anything else." They were quite good at it, producing most of the food they ate. Dan eventually decided they needed to figure out how they could farm full time. By this point it was the only life he could imagine.

Their first customers for raw cow milk came easily. People just started showing up at the farm. "The two first clients were just local neighbors.

They heard through the grapevine that we had a cow, and they literally just pulled up the driveway and said, 'Do you have any extra? Could we buy a half-gallon of milk?' I had no clue how to go about it, what to put it in. They brought a gallon pickle jug and we just poured some milk in their gallon, glass pickle jar. That was the very beginning of it all. We didn't seek them out. They drove up the driveway and said, 'We hear you have a cow. Do you have any extra?' "

Dan and Judy also started raising hundreds of laying hens, and decided they produced enough to sell off the farm, so they became a vendor at the local farmers' market, where they quickly sold out of eggs and all the raw milk their cows could produce. Everything was going well. It looked like they might be able to soon make a profit, which for any farm is a triumph. The only problem (if you can call it that) was the number of his customers who wanted a farm tour, something Dan could not do because he was too busy working. (However, as we previously saw in the case of Taber Ward, a dairy goat farmer, this interest in farm tours can be used to a farm's advantage).

After a month or two of selling at the farmers' market, problems began when a shopper asked Dan (shown in figure 3.4) how long he had had his license. "I went, what license? I really didn't know anything about it. I was kind of naive." He was just a guy with a few cows selling milk directly to customers. "It's very important to a lot of people around this area of knowing where your food comes from. That's one of the things that I tried to bring to this is knowing your farmer. Knowing where your food's coming from. They said, 'Do you have your milk tested?' I said, 'No, I don't need to have my milk tested.' I milk my cow every day. I know if my cow is sick. It's a one-on-one relationship. . . . I think a lot of people around here like that aspect of knowing where their food came from. And that's why we were so successful." The idea of needing a license never crossed his mind.

Not a week later, Maine's Department of Agriculture, Conservation, and Forestry (hereafter, the Department) called the farmers' market and said Dan could not sell raw milk there. Dan called the Department to understand what he could do. The answer was very clear: if he sold from his farm and did not advertise, he was welcome to sell whatever farm products he wanted—including raw milk—and wouldn't be breaking any laws. So that's what he did. Dan and Judy milked their cows and relied on people to find them—and find them they did. The farm was doing well and once again an actual profit seemed possible.

FIGURE 3.4 Dan Brown with two of his cows
Image courtesy of Dan Brown

Then in 2009 a new administrator for the Department of Public Safety, John Morris, decided to interpret the laws differently. Of course, this new administrator didn't know about Dan until he read an online review from someone who purchased steaks from Dan's farm. "A couple of gentlemen from Rhode Island pulled up in the driveway and wanted some steaks. We didn't have a lot of beef down at the farm stand and we sold them a few big, giant, two-inch T-bones. And they bought some cheese. They wrote a write up in an online review. The inspector went out of his way to track me down and find where my farm stand was. That one incident was what started this whole train."

The new administrator visited the farm and informed Dan that he was now considered a milk distributor and would thus need both a license and the expensive equipment that large milk distributors use. "He said, 'Don't worry about it, all you have to do is get your license.' But that constituted stainless steel tanks and all these different upkeeps that don't sound like much, but for one to four cows, it just isn't feasible. You're not going to put in a $20,000 milking parlor to milk one cow. It just doesn't make any sense from a business standpoint. That was never really an option for us. We literally closed the doors on the farm stand."

This was bewildering. How could Dan suddenly be a milk distributor if he was only doing what the Department told him to do and no law had changed? Later he would learn from a FOIA (Freedom of Information Act) request that the state government was apparently attempting to harmonize enforcement of state laws with federal health laws because the feds threatened to remove funding for meat inspection programs if the state did not cooperate. It would also be revealed that the federal government was pressuring the state government to shut down sales of raw milk in the state. They couldn't really do so, because many people in Maine sold raw milk under the radar.

After John Morris informed this farmer of three cows that he was in fact a milk distributor, Dan called some other local food producers to seek their advice. They urged him to fight back and promised to have his back. Some of them were affiliated with an organization called Food for Maine's Future, which itself is affiliated with the La Via Campesina organization that inspired Fergal Anderson. They helped Dan recognize that according to the law, he *should* be able to sell milk from his farm, and that what the Maine government was doing was unlawful, unfair, and arbitrary. Start selling again, they said. If the government raided his farm and tried to confiscate his food as was done in other states (Maine isn't the only state to confront these issues),[74] they said, "We will get one hundred people to set up tents in your yard, and we won't let them take your food." Dan believed them. "They were so passionate about it that I believed they'd stand behind me, and they did. They literally gave me the strength to put my foot down and say no, we weren't going to take this anymore."

With such eager support, Dan agreed to fight. He reopened his farm stand—again, on his own land, with no advertising—and resumed selling. When John Morris returned to the farm, perturbed that Dan wasn't obeying his orders, Dan understandably became frustrated, telling him that because he was not enforcing the laws as written, Dan no longer recognized his authority. Dan sternly ordered John Morris to leave the farm. Up until then Dan wasn't really a radical, but he was one now.

The local farmers and Dan formed an organization called Local Food Rules, meant to support Dan but also to push back against the new interpretation of the laws. The new reading was affecting other farms as well, preventing farms from processing and selling poultry meat directly to consumers.

Local Food Rules decided to fight state laws with local laws. In Dan's town of Blue Hill they proposed, and voters eagerly passed, a local ordinance in 2011 that stated:

> Producers or processors of local foods in the Town of Blue Hill are exempt from licensure and inspection provided that the transaction is only between the producer or processor and a patron when the food is sold for home consumption.[75]

Other towns in Maine passed similar ordinances. Normally a town cannot exempt itself from state or federal law, but Maine has a home rule clause in its constitution that occasionally allows such actions. "After the ordinance passed, I went back to the farmers' markets. The minute I went back to the farmers' markets—and we know this because of the Freedom of Information Act—the next day there's a memo from the Department of Agriculture saying it looks like we've got our test case. That's when they really ratcheted it up and decided to use me as an example to put a stop to this." So began the lawsuit.

Before we get lost in all the details, let us summarize these events. A small farmer with one to three cows wants to sell raw milk directly to consumers, a practice employed with some frequency throughout the district in which the farmer resides. The federal government decides this is not acceptable, so it puts pressure on the state government to suppress the artisan milk industry. The State of Maine then has to choose whether to comply with the federal government's demands, or fight them on behalf of its small farmers—and it chose the former. However, Dan, other local farmers, and a number of towns decided that they would fight back, so they passed an ordinance that did allow a farmer to sell raw milk directly to consumers. The state responded by suing Dan—and the administrator who signed the lawsuit had even sold raw milk himself! Dan knows this because he purchased cows from the administrator, and has personally seen people scoop milk out of the bulk tank (where raw milk is stored) for purchase. Moreover, farms all over the state were selling raw milk to people. Dan was singled out to serve as a warning to others. The case went all the way to the Maine Supreme Court, which ultimately ruled against Dan. So today he does not sell raw milk—but plenty of other people do. All around him are local farmers selling raw milk directly to consumers.

Maine's government cannot do a thing about the sales because there is no way for them to know about the transactions. Dan had the misfortune of having someone write a favorable review of his farm online, and then had the audacity to stand up to the government. It made him a target then, and makes him a target now.

This is an issue bigger than Dan, and about more than raw milk. It is regular people wanting more freedom in how they acquire food. It is about a basic human right, in the same spirit that La Via Campesina seeks to give developing countries the same sovereignty over their food supply. It is also an opposition to intrusive government and corporations. When Maine's Local Food Rules group learned that the federal government was the main impetus behind the crackdown on raw milk sales, combined with a perception that large food corporations have a profound influence over regulatory agencies, it seemed evident that the case against Dan involved more than the safety of raw milk. It was about big corporations trying to stop local food producers from gaining market share in the food system. The "little guy" was being suppressed by a Leviathan formed by a partnership between the government and corporations. Though Dan is no political radical like Amory Starr, in a sense he was fighting a similar battle, and he isn't the only soldier.

The tension between federal laws, state and local laws, and common sense is growing. Wyoming passed a Food Freedom Act that allows people to sell poultry directly to consumers for home consumption, yet the USDA's Food Safety Inspection Service believed that federal law compelled them to visit a Wyoming farmers' market and make a vendor dump out all his jars of chicken chili.[76] North Dakota recently passed a similar law, and it remains to be seen if some of its vendors will also be harassed by the federal government. These bills are peculiar in that they allow the sale of poultry meat but not pork, beef, or lamb because federal law requires they be processed in a USDA-inspected facility. However, at the time of this writing, a bill was being considered in Congress that would allow states to set their own rules for slaughtering all livestock, so long as the meat is sold only within the state.[77] The State of Maine is continuing to lead the local food sovereignty movement, and though its effort to add Food Sovereignty to its constitution failed, it recently passed a bill giving towns, not the state, authority to regulate sales of local foods.[78]

Advocates of food freedom can thank Dan for taking the fight all the way to the Maine Supreme Court. Though the court ruled against him, so many rose in his defense that it is clear food sovereignty is desired even by residents of wealthy countries. "If wanting to sell or give milk to my neighbors is radical—that's what other people's viewpoint is—then yes, I guess I am a radical. Am I radical? I don't think so. Am I different from the mainstream? Sure. I understand that I'm not the norm in today's society. Am I a radical, or is it just radically different than the status quo? What's happening to our food system is not good for our population, for our health, for our economy. I guess that's where I go on that radical side of it. We need to be more radical."

Dan is no longer in the business of being radical. His fight was long, exhausting, and he now just wants to be left alone on his farm. "I know a little bit more about the machine and the system, and it was a brutal couple of years." It took a personal toll on him because his struggle against the state became so personal. Not only was he personally invested, but his interactions with the regulators became testy. They would pester him in situations where they had power. For instance, there was a lobster shack (they are called lobster pounds in Maine) that didn't have the permits necessary to operate. They purchased ice cream sandwiches from Dan. The state regulators told the pound that if they didn't stop buying from Dan, they would be shut down. So the pound was allowed to skirt the law, but not Dan, in what seems to be arbitrary enforcement. Tit-for-tat, Dan pestered regulators when it was in his power to do so, like having a video camera follow regulators when they visited the farmers' market or asking them to complete a public service questionnaire before they asked any questions (something within the rights of Maine citizens before they have to answer any of the regulator's questions).

These years were exhausting not just because of the uncertainty regarding the lawsuit and the frustration of dealing with the regulators, but also because of the amount of time he had to spend researching. This includes learning how to pass a local ordinance, understanding the local laws, and using the FOIA to acquire information the government did not freely share. He fought, lost in court, and so now hands the banner over for someone else to carry. People all around him are still selling raw milk. Because he knows the state watches him, he cannot. He still farms. "I am not in the dairy business anymore. I still farm full time, but we just change the aspects of it. We have one cow and do the milk for ourselves. We still make the cheese and the dairy and all that. I have twelve chickens as opposed to four hundred. And we just do other things on the farm." Dan found a farm product that the State of Maine approves of and involves far less hassle from government regulators: medical marijuana.

4

The Fork

Dan Durica, Who Dances with Rabbits

People today are adjusting their lifestyles in search of a more ethical diet. They are paying higher food prices to ensure better treatment of livestock, are patrons of local food suppliers, and are planting more vegetable gardens. Most of these lifestyle alterations are minor, requiring little sacrifice. Food radicals won't stop with marginal changes, but will adopt a way of living vastly different from the norm. Otherwise, they wouldn't be radical.

Dan Durica, for example, is a resident of the Dancing Rabbit Ecovillage in Missouri. From the age of seven (except for a few years in college) he has always gardened and shown a keen interest in nature. Of course, many of us garden: about one in three households raise food in gardens.[1] And who doesn't like nature? How Dan differs from the average person can be illustrated in his response to Styrofoam. Most of us use it frequently, without really thinking about it. To Dan, Styrofoam is a lamentable symbol for what is wrong with the modern world. "I just assumed that people would never create something that didn't ever go away. I didn't know that was even possible. Why would you make something like this . . . that never breaks down?" Styrofoam isn't biodegradable—perhaps after millions of years, but for practical purposes, once it is made and used, it becomes permanent trash. When Dan first learned of Styrofoam's permanence as a kid, it blew his mind. He could not fathom why anyone would want to create or use anything that becomes trash for an eternity.

This realization is one of the things that set Dan on a different path, a path that today finds him living in a community committed to, in their words, "radical environmental sustainability." Thanks to the community's austere lifestyle, Dan's carbon footprint is about half the average American's,[2] and part of this reduction involves his approach to food.

Developing a concern for environmental issues in high school, Dan studied environmental science at Bowling Green State University and became an activist, protesting toxic waste incinerators and involving himself with several activist organizations, including Earth First! "I studied environmental science and thought I might get a job doing something related to solving environmental problems. It wasn't really that cut and dried. I learned that they were grooming you for working for a corporation or company to help them meet the environmental regulations and stay within the bounds of the law. I learned a lot about environmental issues, and that was great. But I found that it was hard to find a job where you're actually doing something good."

Though his major and involvement in activism helped him meet like-minded people, he eventually concluded that he could have a greater impact simply by changing the way he was doing things in his personal life. "I kind of felt not as effective when I was doing political activism. I think that protests have their place, and at the right times and with the right numbers of people, they can be really effective. I became focused on trying to change the way people live and the way I live to reduce my impact on the planet. Getting involved in community gardens and trying to promote and teach people about growing their own food . . . that became more of a way that I felt like I could be more effective in changing the world." Instead of using activism to challenge the behavior of others, he began challenging himself.

Some of these changes involved food, including what and how he ate. Like our radical Liz Specht, he concluded that meat was wasteful, so he became a vegetarian. Like Styrofoam, plastic doesn't biodegrade, so he ceased using plastic utensils. Heading out on a road trip, Dan would bring his own food so that he wouldn't have to eat fast food. Gardening once again became a part of his life, and at community gardens he would teach others how to grow their own food.

Food also became his job. After college he worked in a cooperative bakery, which taught him not only about baking bread but about running a business and working with others to make decisions by consensus. (Notice that consensus-based decision-making is practiced by many of our radicals who show an interest in local food and social justice.) He not only worked in a cooperative, but lived in cooperative housing, testifying to his desire to belong to a socially harmonious culture. Dan believes that people can live in peaceful concord with each other and the environment, so long as power is equally distributed among the people, which is why he is so eager to live in a community that operates by consensus. "We have a village counsel, which is elected by the membership. The village counsel itself operates by consensus. By the time proposals get to us, they've already hashed it out by getting community input. There's been some preprocessing to get to some proposal that we think is likely to pass and that is likely to be a good compromise to what the sentiment in the community is."

It isn't surprising that Dan would eventually find himself a member of an ecovillage dedicated to sustainable living and consensus-based decision-making. When he first heard about Dancing Rabbit Ecovillage, he liked what he heard. "I was looking into a place to live, but I wanted to live in a place that was already established. I'd been through the effort to try to start one with friends, and it was difficult. The starting is difficult. Moving to something that's already what you want it to be is a lot easier. Dancing Rabbit was just getting started." If he joined an ecovillage, he wanted to join one that was firmly established. About ten years after his first interest, he met someone who had lived there and still liked what he heard. Given that it had flourished since his first contact with the village, he decided to give it a chance.

The reader might be asking: what, exactly, is an ecovillage? We already met one. Chapter 2 of this book described Katie Michels's ecovillage at Middlebury College. Dancing Rabbit is quite different, though. For one, it is a permanent community, not a temporary residence for college students, out in the country in Missouri. This isn't a hippie commune, it isn't a religious order, and they don't consider themselves a sovereign nation. People have regular families and work regular jobs. What makes them different is that they go to greater lengths to minimize their impact on the environment, and they do it in a spirit of solidarity.

Much as a typical neighborhood allows each household to live however it likes, but within the community covenants, people at Dancing Rabbit have their own houses and separate jobs. The covenants they agree to are more stringent. You can build your own house, but you must use reclaimed lumber so that no new forests will be destroyed. Even better, some build their own houses out of straw and mud. Their houses are heated with wood, but only wood discarded by others. You can use a motor vehicle, but instead of owning one you must use one of the village's shared vehicles. To minimize use of fossil fuels, you cannot connect your residence to the electricity grid but must instead rely on solar panels.

This consumer asceticism may sound demanding (and to most people it probably is). The ecovillage is zealous only in achieving its objectives, not in how those objectives are met. For instance, it relaxed its requirement on using only reclaimed lumber once a market for certified, sustainable lumber became available. People can now connect to the electricity grid, but they use it only when their solar panels do not generate enough energy. This was necessary to allow people to work jobs like computer programming remotely, as there are few jobs available in the surrounding community. Dancing Rabbit's ecovillagers are not trying to separate themselves from the world, but to become better stewards of the planet.

To the greatest extent possible the village wishes to be self-sufficient. Members are also realistic, knowing that complete self-sufficiency may be impossible. To promote trade between village members, they have their own currency, referred to as Exchange Local Money, or ELM. This is a digital currency, with almost $100,000 in circulation, which members use to trade with one another. Dan sells some of the food he grows to members using the ELM, and he can take that currency to buy things from other members, or use it to rent one of the ecovillage's vehicles.

This currency does not lock in its residents to trade only with each other. It has a one-to-one exchange rate with the US dollar, so if you want one ELM you simply pay one dollar. This fixed, one-to-one exchange rate means there is technically little difference between using the ELM or the US dollar to trade within the community, so this is not like a community trying to create its own, sovereign currency. However, it is a symbol of the ecovillage's ethos and a constant reminder that they are trying to live differently than the typical American. The vast majority of trades within the community are made with the ELM.

Dancing Rabbit's food strategy is to grow as much of its own food as possible, eliminate most all food waste, and adopt diets known to produce less carbon emissions. "I would like to set up a system here where we were growing our food more collectively and sharing in the effort to grow food like some other intentional communities do. Part of the benefit of living in a place like Dancing Rabbit is being able to share resources. If I were to live on a farm out in the country on my own, I would have to buy my own tractor. I'd have to buy my own pickup truck, own my own equipment. Here we could buy those things collectively and share them in growing all our food for ourselves. That's my dream and vision for what I would like to eventually see at Dancing Rabbit. We're pretty far away from that right now—experimenting with a grower's co-op and growing food on a larger scale collectively."

The residents are not naive and do not blindly believe that local food is always more climate friendly. Ecovillage residents have found local food production methods and distributors that they do believe lower their carbon footprint, though. Go to their website and you will see they have done their homework on the sources of their carbon emissions. Mindful of their diets, they tend to eat less meat in their meals than the ordinary American, but they do consume meat when they believe it ecologically friendly.

The village actually has some of its own livestock. The animals are integrated into their food production system in an environmentally friendly manner. Much of the arable land in the village is in the federal government's Conservation Reserve Program (CRP). "Our land is highly sloping and it's been eroded over decades of conventional farming. We've inherited this poor land. It's a big challenge in growing food here." The CRP is designed to pay landowners not to farm compromised land, giving it the rest from tillage it needs to restore its carbon content. So when village members want to take land out of the CRP for raising food they have to pay the government a fee.

Some, like Dan (figure 4.1), have done this, but are using farming methods that will improve the soil—methods we learned about from Ray Archuletta and Jeff Moyer. Dan is establishing a vineyard on some of this land. "In my vineyard I'm doing sort of a mixture of growing grapes and growing vegetables, and having stock running through, and building soil in a way that I feel is sustainable and fast to restore the land into productivity." Chicken manure is also used as fertilizer by moving around portable chicken cages, and cover crops are planted and then plowed into the soil to improve soil structure and nutrients. Other community members have hogs, goats, Muscovy ducks, and a donkey to guard the livestock (yes, donkeys really do make great bodyguards for livestock, protecting them from critters as small as raccoons and as large as coyotes). For this community, livestock is not a climate-intense indulgence, but a key component of an ecological agriculture that reduces the village's carbon footprint.

In other parts of the village, permaculture agriculture is being established, like an edible forest. "You're emulating the different layers or the levels of the canopy of a forest. Everything that you plant is useful

FIGURE 4.1 Dan inspecting his vineyard
Image courtesy of Dan Durica

in some way. Instead of just letting a forest grow on its own, you're planting taller trees that produce nuts. Then you might have below them a shorter tree that produces some kind of fruit. And then below that a shrub that's producing something else that's edible. Then on the ground you'll have something else that you can use. That's the kind of agriculture that a lot of people here are interested in. You're going be able to restore the land, and it becomes a self-perpetuating system. It doesn't require tilling all the time or weeding. At some point it just thrives on its own and you can just go in there and harvest the nuts, or the fruit, with minimal effort."

This polyculture (figure 4.2) reflects the way nature works, where different types of organisms grow together in harmony—the type of biomimicry Ray Archuletta spoke of. In many ways the edible forest is similar to the forest envisioned in the feminist utopian novel *Herland*.

Go to YouTube, type in "Dancing Rabbit Ecovillage," and you can spend hours watching its residents give tours of the village and illustrations of how they live (Dan himself has a fascinating YouTube channel called *Hardcore Sustainable*, where the authors learned how to self-pollinate

FIGURE 4.2 Polyculture system at Dancing Rabbit Ecovillage
Image courtesy of Dan Durica

small stands of corn). You will see strongly built houses, but they won't look like your typical suburban residence, because many are made with straw and mud using straw bales and natural plaster. Clothes will be hung out on lines to dry, for that uses less fossil fuels than electronic dryers. Solar panels embrace the roofs, and you won't see a manicured lawn, but lovely gardens and trails seemingly made by wildlife.

Though food is grown all over the village it currently produces less than 10 percent of the food villagers eat, according to Dan's best guess. Being 100 percent self-sufficient in food is hard, and Dan points out this is because most people are growing vegetables, which are mostly water, as opposed to staples like beans and grains. Being strictly organic farmers, they would ideally be able to sell large amounts of produce to people outside the village, but being in such a remote location makes this difficult. They simply have few people living around them.

The village is located near Rutledge, Missouri, which has slightly more than a hundred citizens. This is the challenge of living so radically differently. Dancing Rabbit's location was chosen partly because it does not have building codes, allowing its members flexibility in housing construction

FIGURE 4.3 Environmentally friendly housing at Dancing Rabbit Ecovillage
Image courtesy of Dan Durica

and design, like those in figure 4.3. "It allows us to do the experimental, natural, and more sustainable kind of building that we do." It also doesn't have many people around to trade with. "There are more farmers than there are buyers here. We're so far away from any sympathetic market. The idea of transporting food like vegetables and selling them at a farmers' market—I'd have to go to a large city to find a good market. It's just not worth it to go that far." Their ultimate goal is not to export large amounts of food, though, but to attract enough residents such that Dancing Rabbit can have a self-sufficient food economy.

In a previous chapter we met Fergal Anderson, who works with a group called La Via Campesina, meaning "the peasant's way." Some readers may have been surprised that people would enthusiastically identify themselves as "peasants." In many ways Dancing Rabbit has given nobility to the term "peasant" because of the way they have chosen to live: growing much of their own food, living in self-built natural houses, using few fossil fuels—and they are doing it by choice.

It would be a mistake to believe these are individuals with an overly-romantic view of the past, or holding anti-technology perspectives. They are scientifically sophisticated and eager adopters of any new technology that helps them live in harmony with the environment. Even though a significant portion of the American public disagree with scientists about climate change,[3] every single resident of Dancing Rabbit sees climate change as anthropogenic (or related to human activities). Though most all energy production in the United States comes from old-fashioned fossil fuels, Dancing Rabbit gets most of their energy through solar technology. Their houses and lives may seem primitive to some, but their community infrastructure is arguably quite progressive.

Perhaps the reader is wondering where the name "Dancing Rabbit" came from? It turns out their most frustrating pest is rabbits. Every garden must have a rabbit fence surrounding it for anything to have a chance at growing. But they don't kill the rabbits or even resent them, for they are trying to live in harmony with nature. Dancing Rabbit Ecovillage is doing more than that: they are *dancing* in harmony with nature, for community members do it with great joy.

Dan and his neighbors have chosen to radically revamp their lifestyle to live more ethically, to pursue a more meaningful life. "I think we are viewed in the ecovillage and sustainable community movement as one of the most radical communities functioning and successful. We have the covenants. When you're surrounded by and have a community of people who are radical, living that radical lifestyle and moved here because they wanted to live it, they are keeping on top of each other and wanting to implement even more things to cover different areas of sustainability and make ourselves even more sustainable than we were in the past." What separates Dancing Rabbit ecovillage members from the average person is their greater awareness of the impacts of modern life—including the modern food system—on the environment. They pay greater attention to the choices they make. You might say their personal values have greater clarity, and they are intent on ensuring their lifestyle is consistent with these values. It is for these reasons that ecovillages are often referred to as "intentional living" communities.

We can learn something from Dan without having to adopt his lifestyle in full. In addition to changing the way we farm, in addition to being politically aware, we can transform our world through our personal actions and our interactions with other individuals on a one-on-one basis. We can better shape our environment to match our values—ensuring what is on our fork is consistent with what is in our soul.

The Where and What of Eating
Bob Moje's Architecture of Eating

We previously met Dan Durica at the Dancing Rabbit Ecovillage. To prepare for the interview the authors viewed many of the village's YouTube videos, where residents would describe the joys of ecological living. As the videos transitioned from one member to another, one could not help but remark on how everyone had a healthy weight—with envy we might even call each of them lean! This isn't because Dancing Rabbit is an ascetic community dedicated to denying themselves food. They may limit fossil fuel intake, but they don't believe that a hungry belly is necessary for harmony with nature. Their relationship with food mimics their relationship with the environment: balanced, rich, and healthy.

There is something about the ecovillage's culture that promotes a healthy relationship with food. What that "something" is, though, is hard to say. Our interaction with food is so complex—so sensitive to the context in which we live and eat—that identifying even a few key habits to maintaining a healthy weight is difficult to do.

One of the greatest human feats is the near eradication of polio, a disease that causes paralysis. The disease resigned America's thirty-second president to a wheelchair, and gave Sir Walter Scott a lame leg.[4] The cause of the disease, once discovered, was simple: a virus. The cause led to an inexpensive solution: immunization. Today, across the world, polio is 99 percent eradicated.[5]

If only obesity were so simple. From one perspective, it is: burn more calories than you consume, and you will lose weight.[6] How to do that, however, is not so simple. Convincing yourself to take a polio vaccination does not take much willpower or money: gaining access to and eating a healthy and nutritious diet does. The more we research obesity, the more complex it becomes. For decades it was believed that exercise would help burn more calories. In some contexts it will, but new evidence suggests that the body often burns roughly the same number of calories regardless of our physical activity. (Exercise still promotes good health, however, even if it does little to shed pounds.)[7]

The key to a healthy weight might reside in factors seemingly unrelated to calories. For example, researchers have uncovered an undeniable correlation between stress and obesity. Suffering childhood trauma increases likelihood of obesity,[8] and so does not getting enough sleep.[9] Children who feel safe and loved are less likely to be obese. Spending more time around the dinner table with family members and participating in the cooking process also leads to healthier weights, especially if kids see their parents eating healthfully and exerting gastronomic discipline.[10]

Correlation, of course, is not causation. Different outcomes may ultimately be due to genetics. Genetics for intelligence might lead to more career opportunities, a less stressful life, and more resources to ensure a stable, happy family. Still, if you want to have a healthy weight, it pays to mimic the behavior of healthy, lean people. Parents may not be able to control the genetics they bestow upon their children, but they can reduce stress with love, they can make sure their kids get plenty of sleep, and they can make family meals a nightly tradition.

Even the best of parents run into a problem though: their kids aren't always with them. Only around 40 percent of a child's body-mass index is determined by genes and family environment.[11] A complex combination of factors determines the remaining 60 percent. Part of that equation includes what takes place in a space where kids spend most of their time when not at home—school. Schools are something every community builds and runs. In an era where 17 percent of children and adolescents are obese,[12] designing schools in ways that can combat and prevent obesity is an opportunity for a socially responsible solution.

Bob Moje of VMDO Architects doesn't just believe in the idea of designing schools for health: he lives it. An architect by profession, his passion is improving schools. For forty years he has led a revolution in school design, giving teachers an ideal environment to use their skills. His work involves far more than sketching clever building plans. It requires understanding how students learn, how schools are run, and how to foster innovative teaching methods. Designing schools involves both blueprints for the buildings and plans for school operation.

Architects have a knack for seeing the big picture, and recognizing a human's unconscious response to the environment. We will need such people to curb childhood obesity, because excessive weight is linked to behavior. School cafeterias can pile more broccoli on plates, but much of that healthy food will be thrown away because many children don't want to eat it. Food portions can be reduced, but this harms children who are not obese, and will lead to more snacking immediately after school. Children can be educated about healthy eating . . . well, we've been doing that for some time (with both kids and adults). More exercise might help, but the majority of school time must be devoted to education. That is why there is a growing body of research on integrating physical activity with education, with the recognition that movement can enhance learning.

School decision-makers must look beyond what is served and think more deeply about the minds and bodies of students. "Everybody's focused on academic performance," Bob Moje points out. "One of the things that has suffered is lunch, as we have tried to cram in more learning, so that students can do well on the test. Lunch is considered a necessary evil that we have to get through as fast as possible so we can get back to the learning." It is a stressful time for both children and teachers. "A student is rushing around from class to get there, and she barely has time to eat, and she's so anxious she doesn't want to eat even when she has lunch. And that's a sign that there's a problem. The signs are flashing all over the place."

Children are marched in like Prussian soldiers and given only about twenty minutes to eat. This results in only about seven minutes of eating time after organizing students and waiting in line for food. The food selection is often sparse, and teachers have to shout to keep the kids from shouting. The resemblance to a prison cafeteria is troubling.

This is the opposite of the pleasant family meals we are told are so good for children. Children are taught to eat food quickly, getting it out of the way to make time for recess, suggesting to children that meals should not be an enjoyable activity. "All of the digestive science says that you cannot possibly know that your body has eaten, and whether it's had enough food, in seven minutes. Quickly swallowing and overeating is a habit that we're building into students. I think that's one of the major factors in obesity. It's not just the quality of food, although that's certainly an issue, but it's the norm of the eating process. In public schools in America, we are unconsciously training our children to be perfect fast-food consumers. Pull up at the drive-in window, have an ordered box of food presented to you, put on your lap. You start eating before you pull away from the drive-in window and have mostly consumed everything before you get to your second red light." Many kids have trouble eating all their lunch in such a short time and find themselves craving snacks immediately after school. The kids don't like these lunches, and neither does Bob.

How do you design an environment that promotes better eating? How do you provide school lunches akin to the proverbial family meal? For Bob the solution was discovered partly by accident. He recalls renovating a school with limited space for the cafeteria, forcing his firm to adopt an unusual approach to serving lunch. In one area was the regular cafeteria familiar to us all, but it was too small to serve everyone efficiently. In another location they built a café, with a smaller selection but still plenty of healthy options. Without enough seating room in the cafeteria for everyone, students were allowed to eat in other places—to choose their lunch sites.

As Bob attended lunches to observe students' behavior, he noticed something profound: there was less fighting, less bad behavior, and more smiles. He had attended schools that used a red-light system to inform students when they were too loud, and others that used a bullhorn to silence students. In the new structure there was no noise problem—partly because students were dispersed, but partly because each individual was quieter. What struck Bob was that the scene looked like a *normal* lunch, and it inspired radical new ways of designing schools. "VMDO Architects specialize in educational institutions, because we believe the environment children are educated in has a profound effect on them. . . . I try and look at things with a critical eye, and one of the things that seems broken is the way we feed children in school and the unintended consequences."

The designs (see figures 4.4 and 4.5) are especially compelling because they involve so much more than structures. The buildings are indeed beautiful, to be envied by any poorly funded school system. The genius resides in how the facilities are integrated into teaching strategies, and how they are informed by modern research. In schools like the Buckingham Country Primary and Secondary Schools in Virginia, food is not something to be gulped down in record time to make way for the next influx of students, but is instead an enjoyable experience.

> The notion was to change the whole eating dynamic to a happier place. So the cafeteria, if you will, was conceived as a dining room similar to what a nice restaurant would be; all glass on two sides. It has a dining terrace outside; it's connected to a garden where the children can grow food. You enter it through a beautiful lobby. The acoustics are very carefully worked out where there's a tremendous number of acoustic partitions and decorative things hanging from the ceiling so that the sound level is humane so everybody can have a conversation without it being overly loud. There's different types of chairs, and tables, and seating arrangements that the children have a choice to sit at. The kitchen is exposed so that the children can see the food being prepared. There's not a line—it's more like a food court. There's a window at the entrance. There's a window into

FIGURE 4.4 Blending a cafeteria with a classroom at Buckingham Primary & Elementary Schools in Dillwyn, Virginia

Photo by Alan Karchmer/OTTO

the bakery. The school bakes its own biscuits so that the odor will also permeate the experience.

Bob notes that because most cafeteria food is precooked, it does not generate the pleasant smells that arouse the appetite. "The odors that you get [in school cafeterias] are mostly from the processing of the food, not the cooking end of it. You get the antiseptic smells of the cleaning, not of the food itself." If you want children to eat whole-grain bread, it is much better for them to smell the bread being cooked. A bakery where the smell of freshly cooked bread entices the children to choose fresh over processed food was installed. Bob stresses that the smell is just as important as the actual food.

The food in the cafeteria line is carefully placed to nudge kids to choose healthier foods. "There's how you display the food. The children are showing up, get their food, and they're hungry. If the first thing that they see is a selection where they can pick up some apples, and those apples are freshly sliced so they're all crisp and clean, and they don't have to worry about peeling them, or biting into them, or what the core's going to

FIGURE 4.5 School garden at Discovery Elementary School in Arlington, Virginia

Photo by Alan Karchmer/OTTO

be—they just pick them up and eat them, they will select those. Make the healthy options more prominent and easy to select. You give them some choices on selection, maybe they like apples, but maybe one little plate has five slices on it, maybe another one has seven, maybe another one has three. Those are all engaging thought in the eating." When ice cream is provided, it is always the last item on the line. Calling it a "line" is incorrect though, for the cafeteria is designed more as a food court.

Some of his schools have a garden (figure 4.5) where kids can learn where fresh fruits and vegetables come from, and his firm designs strategies for how the garden can be integrated into the educational curriculum. The use of gardens is said to be especially helpful for summer school programs, so much so that graduate students are conducting research on their impact on student performance.

The main point of the school design is to promote "intentional eating," where students not only learn about food but are taught to take responsibility for their choices. This requires Bob to work in tandem with principals. "Every single morning one principal mentions some of the things that are going to be available in the cafeteria that day, and then has a subtle line at the end of it: 'I hope you make a healthy choice.' That subliminal message that's planted at the very beginning of the day is powerful. If you go to that school and you're interacting with the students, I witnessed this myself: kids in second grade will run up to her and say, 'I made a healthy choice at lunch today,' with a big smile on their face."

The design strategies rely on behavioral economics, or what has become known as the "nudge" approach, a term made famous by the book *Nudge*. This is a philosophy that encourages healthy behaviors while preserving personal autonomy. Students choose what they eat, where they eat, and how much to eat—*but* the cafeteria is designed to nudge them to choose healthier choices. This type of nudge is not like when your mother says, "You don't have to eat your vegetables, but it would make me very happy." It is a nudge that makes you choose the better option because, in that environment, you actually *want* the better option. Hopefully, by choosing healthy options when young, children will continue to do so as adults.

This is a rather radical change in viewing our responsibility toward children. Instead of saying to ourselves that it is our duty to put healthy food on children's plates, we say it is our duty to design the proper environment for them to choose to practice healthy eating habits. This respect for children's autonomy emerged from a research collaboration with public health researchers. Bob says he has learned a few key aspects of eating behaviors in children:

- The body is naturally wired to know what it needs. Yes, the body does crave sugar in greater portions than it needs, but when it is lacking certain nutrients, the body will naturally crave foods containing them. Placed in the proper environment—many healthy choices, not an abundance of unhealthy foods—kids will select the foods their body needs without having to be educated to do it.

- People, even children, understand portion control. In the proper environment, children will eat enough to restore their body but will not always eat in excess when given the opportunity.

If these two assumptions seem misguided, Bob would have you note that obesity is a relatively recent phenomenon. The key to returning to the healthier weights of our grandparents, Bob thinks, might be to return to something closer to their food environment, where our voluntary food choices were in harmony with physical needs.

In one school Bob went even further in recreating the pleasant family meal. One particular school was struggling with test scores and needed more time for teachers to spend with children. "A very progressive assistant superintendent in charge of instruction and I proposed the idea. What if we just turn the whole thing on its head, and say your lesson plan will be developed by what you're doing? What's the most important lesson you're trying to teach that day, and you do that at lunch with your class, and you eat with your class? And lunch is a common experience eating with that whole group, thinking around what the lesson of the day is that you're trying to learn." The lunch break was extended and additional planning periods provided for teachers. The teacher would gather the students around to discuss class topics. The idea wasn't to replicate in the cafeteria what is normally done in the classroom, but to teach differently. In some instances, the students would actually bring food in large trays for everyone to the table, as if it were a real family meal. Though you might suspect that students would resent the classroom being extended into the cafeteria, according to Bob, the younger children actually are excited by it.

This healthier environment goes beyond the cafeteria, and Bob cares about more than just food issues. His goal is better education in addition to better health, and this too is stamped on his architectural sketches. When describing the justification for his plans, he reels off factoids about educational psychology, demonstrating his awareness of how students learn. Other times he shows his awareness of human physiology. One school was designed so that students had to travel two flights of stairs between each class. The brain starts shutting down if the body doesn't move after fifty minutes, he explained, and two flights of stairs is exactly the amount of physical activity to rejuvenate the mind. What might seem to a visitor to be an inconvenient design of classes is actually a deliberate strategy to keep students alert.

Bob expresses a frustration with the slowness of change in education, and he is apt to politely observe its faults. "The schools are broken. They are broken in so many ways, and simply copying what has been done before is a sure path to failure." School lunches are a factory process, kids are bored at school, and schools keep copying what has been shown to fail. Is what Bob is doing radical? "I think it's common sense. It's astounding what we are not doing. This is simple stuff." He sees what he and his firm are doing as common sense, backed by science—and he is right. Studies have shown that schools with longer lunch periods have lower obesity rates in their students,[13] that the physical environment of a cafeteria does impact eating behaviors,[14] and that children do seem to eat healthier when they learn about cooking and gardening.[15] Kids from homes with regular family meals are less likely to be obese and more likely to eat healthy,[16] so it is likely that mimicking these pleasant meals at school will have positive effects. Bob's designs are backed by science because science is incorporated into the designs from the beginning. When he redesigned the primary and secondary schools in Buckingham, his firm partnered with public health researchers to bring health-promotion knowledge into design strategies. What makes Bob's architectural firm unique isn't just its ideas, but the importance placed on ensuring the ideas are inspired by the science of health.

Bob may not think himself a radical, but to us he is. He is pioneering a system of food in schools that may be ordinary in the home, but far from ordinary in schools. "The culture of eating is fundamental to humankind. It has to with developing civics, developing cultural habits that make the human race better, more sophisticated, more loving, more caring. The culture of how we share food, and the process of eating together, needs to be considered. We're screwing it up, and we need to reform this before we make an unrecoverable mess out of it." There are now established guidelines for school architecture that promote healthy eating.[17] These ideas are catching on.

Katie Plohocky Brings the Food to You

Let us suppose that with the vision of people like Bob Moje, and a greater willingness of the public to fund education, we can fix the problem of food in school. There would still be much to worry about for many children, as food problems often abound at home. The government estimates that 16 percent of children are in households classified as food insecure, meaning the household has difficulty acquiring enough healthy foods to meet basic needs.

Part of the problem is money. Almost half of US citizens do not make enough money to achieve economic security, meaning they cannot afford basic needs while also maintaining enough savings to protect themselves from poverty. Many cannot afford to save at all.[18] Even if they have the money, access to healthy foods is often lacking. We previously discussed food deserts when we met Karissa Lewis, who lives in a food desert in Oakland, California. Such deserts can be found all across the country. The map in figure 4.6 shows the locations in the contiguous US states where access to supermarkets is limited by both low incomes and long distances to grocery stores, while also taking into account whether individuals have vehicles to travel to distant stores.

Katie Plohocky knows what it is like to face food insecurity. She was once a single mother raising three kids on a small income. "I have . . . walked some of those roads that customers or clients that we work with have. I understand being food insecure. I understand the embarrassment of having to ask for a handout or ask for food. I have been homeless before and have not had transportation. I've had to rely on the bus or a broken-down car. I've been a statistic. I've lived a lot of statistics." Unlike many in similar positions, she was able to break from the poverty trap and become a commercial real estate agent in Tulsa, Oklahoma, where she found herself becoming involved with city boards regulating local economic development. As part of a Tulsa development initiative, she helped develop a shopping center for new, local businesses and personally witnessed the same food security challenges that she faced years earlier. She began fostering relationships with various organizations seeking to hydrate Tulsa's food deserts, which gave her a greater appreciation for income disparities across regions. For example, some schools would have smart boards in classrooms, while others had plywood covered with chalkboard paint. When she saw this inequity, Katie naturally felt a longing to help the disadvantaged areas.

To rectify these problems, she joined more community boards, began initiatives and foundations, and promoted entrepreneurship as a way out of the poverty trap. "We're hoping that we can spin projects off into jobs and businesses for people to start. I think that's the only way we can solve food insecurity—by creating living-wage jobs so people can actually buy and afford their own food." Doing this requires community involvement.

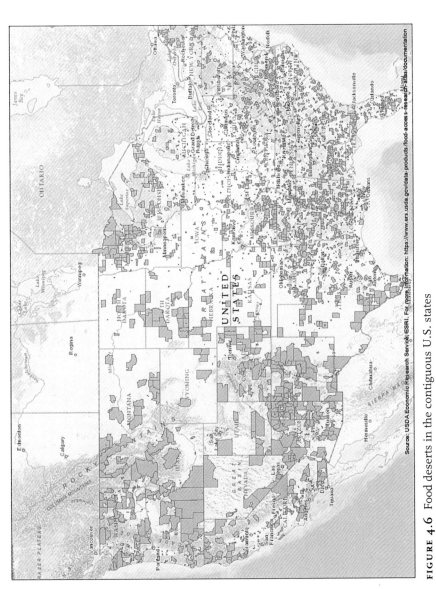

FIGURE 4.6 Food deserts in the contiguous U.S. states

Map made available by the United States Department of Agriculture (2017).

Another problem she identified was that most people just don't understand the challenges low-income households face when trying to acquire food.

To help the food secure put themselves in the shoes of the food inse-cure, she led "Getting to Grocery" tours in Tulsa. "We'd have people meet up at a bus stop, and we'd take the nearest bus to a grocery store and give them the daily allowance of food stamps for a family of four. We also assigned them some diseases, so they would have to figure out—if I'm lactose intolerant and I have high blood pressure—how do we shop for our family with specific food needs and meet everybody's wants as well? It was eye-opening. They were shocked. In order to get back on the next bus and transfer without having to buy another bus ticket, you'd have maybe thirty minutes shopping. It was racing through the store." The real educa-tion for these participants came at the checkout line, when they realized they didn't have enough money for what they believed they needed, and found themselves having to take healthy foods like bananas and potatoes out of their cart. Considering that many of the participants were commu-nity leaders, this exercise went a long way in helping Tulsa' policymakers understand not only what a food desert is, but how being food insecure feels to its residents.

You can go to any city and find people who are on multiple boards and philanthropic organizations. That isn't what makes Katie a radical. What distinguishes her is that she goes much further, devoting her life to knowing the economic disadvantages personally and helping to meet food needs through her own sweat. She has conducted surveys of people living in food deserts and sought help from neighboring colleges to ana-lyze the outcomes to better understand community needs and challenges. She also personally attended impromptu block parties held in these areas. People would decide to have a party and simply block off the streets with their cars, without a city permit. The grills would come out, the sprinklers would be turned on to keep kids cool, and the neighbors would feast to-gether. Katie would scout for such parties and would offer people a free tomato plant if they completed a survey. In addition to the survey, she would engage them in conversation, asking what they would like to see in a grocery store, what type of fruits and vegetables they like, what diet-related diseases they have, and the like. These conversations testified to how food and social problems were intertwined. "A lady once told us that she had an easier time finding a gun than an apple in her neighborhood." These conversations also impressed upon Katie the lack of food education, as some kids would be unaware that a cantaloupe comes from a plant.

In addition to block parties, Katie would interview people in libraries, churches, and other community areas.

Like Karissa Lewis, Katie's long-term goal is to give residents of food deserts the ability to feed themselves. It is a travesty, an injustice, she contends, that hard-working families have difficulty buying healthy food. Until economic opportunities are created, such families will experience food insecurity—an unacceptable situation. Katie took it upon herself to bring food to the food insecure.

The research she conducted told her that over eighty thousand people in Tulsa County live in food deserts, and that many who have incomes of only $15,000 to $20,000 per year are forced to pay high prices for unhealthy foods from convenience stores. Most people see this problem and casually remark, "Yeah, but what can you do?" Katie saw the problem and converted a horse trailer into a mobile grocery store. "We just need to take the food to the people and expedite food access. There's a lot of money being spent on food, and where they're buying food is convenience stores. They're paying high prices. They're buying bad food. And they're still spending that money. Our thought was, we'll just give them an option of healthier food where they can spend their money, their SNAP [Supplemental Nutrition Assistance Program] dollars. So the SNAP community was our target market, to give a place to buy healthier food options with their dollars and be able to stretch those food dollars. Our prices would be much lower than the convenience store."

Katie transports the mobile grocery (figure 4.7) almost daily to different neighborhoods. Some of the food she sells is grown at her farm, and some she purchases at retail grocery stores. Acquiring this food takes up much of her time. In addition to the farming, most days she spends six hours shopping in retail grocery stores, taking advantages of sales, varying prices, and variety. Jokingly, she refers to herself as a penniless philanthropist, as virtually all of her life is devoted to her food projects, leaving little time or money for anything else.

The mobile market visits some seventeen locations each week and incorporates incentives that allow customers on SNAP, formerly known as food stamps, to purchase more local fresh produce than they could at a convenience store or even a grocery store. "We incentivize for those healthy options using the Double-Up Food Bucks program. Anyone using our store, we matched their purchase—dollar for dollar—up to twenty dollars every visit with free fruits and vegetables. A lot of them will get eggs, milk, cheese, bread—whatever they need—and then all their

FIGURE 4.7 Inside Katie's mobile grocery store
Image courtesy of Katie Plohocky

vegetables and fruits are free." As a result, 38 percent of the market's sales
are in fresh produce.[19]

The mobile market is effective, and Katie was recently recognized as
a Significant Woman in Oklahoma Agriculture, but she sees it only as a
stepping stone to a more effective food system. Buying retail and then selling retail is a poor business model, she concedes, but right now it is the
best she can do. Ideally she would purchase on the wholesale market, but
that requires buying at least $15,000 worth of food each week, a volume
she cannot yet meet. The long-term goal is to create community-owned
grocery stores that will put her mobile market out of business, and to use

these stores to establish a local food distribution network that will serve people the current for-profit food system does not.

Katie's mobile market is innovative, but it is also a throwback to the first half of the twentieth century. The country was more rural then, with over 20 percent of the American workforce on the farm, and traveling to the store was even more difficult. Entrepreneurs discovered they could make money by taking food to the farms. "Rolling stores" (figure 4.8) were built on bus frames and stocked a variety of basic goods. Some households had little cash to pay for food and would barter instead. People bartered with chickens so frequently that some rolling stores would have chicken cages mounted on the top.[20]

Much has changed since the days of the rolling stores. Adjusted for inflation, food prices are considerably lower. During the days of rolling stores, the average household would spend 20–40 percent of its total income on food, compared to around 10 percent today.[21] Today's farms are bigger, more efficient, more specialized. Our food distribution system is brutally efficient, able to process, store, and transport food using far less resources than a century ago. Our radical friends have criticized the industrial food system frequently, but this same food system has given the average household better access to food than at any time in history.

FIGURE 4.8 Rolling grocery store in 1937 Alabama
Figure under public domain at the National Archives and Records Administration (NAID = 280052)

Yet Katie does not serve the "average" household. The conventional food system is a marvel in many ways, but it has neglected the economically disadvantaged—and what the system neglects, Katie nurtures. In interviewing Katie, we saw that correcting these faults in the food system will require more than just improving food production efficiency.

Establishing a healthier, more just food system will require communities, philanthropists, and governments to partner together, something that is currently difficult to achieve. "People are doing a lot of things, but if we don't work together and we don't connect all of our projects or all of our dots, we can't really find a sustainable solution to food security and food access. We really all need to work together and we all need to take a holistic picture or view of it. It's all connected. Food is connected with health, is connected with moving and parks. It's connected with public transportation, living-wage jobs, quality of life. It's all connected, and we need to treat it that way and not just isolate each problem and try to deal with it in an isolated vacuum. We need to see how what we do here affects downstream or even upstream."

As we have seen in the case of our radical Dan Brown, federal regulations that treat small mobile markets the same as big corporations limit the ability of local food systems to flourish. State and local governments must do more also. City governments should be willing to do more than just pass resolutions. "We're missing infrastructure. Oklahoma really is more of a darling for commodity crops—wheat, canola, and cattle, big cattle. Our produce is kind of the red-headed child. Nobody pays much attention. Even when we are doing the Double-Up Food Bucks program and we're writing a big grant to help spread it across the whole state of Oklahoma, we couldn't get the Department of Ag to support it officially. They were afraid the cattle and the commodity crops would be mad if they did." Powerful producer groups see the local food movement as a competitor for both consumers and government resources. Even nonprofit groups need to collaborate better, Katie said, and focus more on improving lives than claiming the glory of being the sole group to fix a problem.

Perhaps society will begin to take these problems more seriously and work together for solutions. At the time of this writing, however, it is considered a victory if government doesn't cut spending on social programs. Until the political landscape changes, we should be grateful that political gridlock doesn't stymie the efforts of radicals like Katie. "It takes time for solutions to become viable. You're kind of testing some things out. I think that's the ability to move on a dime if something's not working. You can quickly not do it and make a change. Or sometimes things pop up that we weren't expecting, that really is a solution that we can implement immediately without red tape. We're kind of playing, or we're experimenting. I do think in some ways what we're doing is radical, saving the food, integrating it all into the solution chain. We had problems securing food for the store? We're like, 'Well, let's just start a farm; we'll grow our own. That'll solve that problem. In order to keep prices low, we'll glean from farms who have too much, and we'll take volunteers down and create a teaching mechanism for people to get out in the field and learn some agriculture and be able to take food home with them.' When you're food insecure and you are just taking food, it's different—when I've worked for the food, I care more about it. I'm more apt to eat what I've just picked out of the ground. That goes for kids too. If they've planted it or they've picked it, they're going to eat that carrot because they've participated in that." Until we can get our act together and enact long-term remedies, Katie is there with short-term patches—and a short-term patch is better than no patch at all.

Into the Wild with Wildcrafter Jackie Dill

What should you do if you have little money, you don't have Katie Plohocky in your area to operate a mobile market, and the food made available from food pantries and government programs isn't enough? One answer is to follow the path of our distant ancestors: venture into the wild, and forage for food. Most of us wouldn't dare: how do you know what is edible and what is poisonous? Again, take the lead of our ancestors and learn from our wise elders—people like Jackie Dill.

Jackie's father was Native American, Cherokee specifically, and though she was raised in Oregon, she spent most every summer with her Cherokee grandmother in Arkansas. "My grandmother's name was Elizabeth Childers. My family is Childers and Ross." Elizabeth possessed an encyclopedia of Native American botany, a wealth of information that allowed her family to find ample nutrients from wild plants almost anywhere in North America. When Elizabeth gained a daughter-in-law (Jackie's mother) who had almost starved to death during the Great Depression, she passed this information down, and they both passed it along to Jackie. "It's a part of my heritage. I love doing this. I was taught this by my grandmother who was Cherokee, and also my mother who was not. It was just a way of life. It was something that we practiced. It was normal to us. It's like you're born into it." Now Jackie passes the torch to others.

Throughout her life Jackie has used her family's teachings to gather much of her own food, not just because it saves money and is often delicious, but also because it is a part of her identity. It is in her stomach, and in her soul. As she retired from working, her income dwindled, and today she says she acquires more than 80 percent of her food from wildcrafting. It was later in her adult life that a Cherokee woman approached her and remarked that wildcrafting—collecting plant materials from the natural environment for use in food, medicine, arts, or crafts—was a dying art, and that Jackie should teach it to others before it became extinct.

After being granted permission from the Cherokee Nation to give lessons, she soon attracted a following from a remarkably diverse set of students: rich and poor, liberal and conservative, young and old. They come from such strikingly different backgrounds that Jackie prohibits any talk of politics or religion during their walks, in order to preserve harmony and keep them focused on nature. Some are city people who want to learn more about the natural world. Some are survivalists, some are country folk who want wild foods to accompany what they grow in their gardens, and others are botany enthusiasts. Sadly, a number study under her because they cannot afford food. "They come because they're hungry. They come because they're frightened." Jackie remarks that, even with government programs and food pantries, with cuts in government services and a healthcare system that favors the rich, many of her students need every dime to pay medical bills, so they save money by learning how to eat wild plants.

A few conspiracy theorists come to her, wanting to be prepared for an apocalyptic future, but these are the few that she turns away. Jackie wants to help people with real problems, and there are so many of these individuals that there is no time to humor the eccentric.

We joined Jackie for a class at St. Francis of the Woods, a rural Catholic retreat in Coyle, Oklahoma. What surprised us is that we didn't even need to enter the wild, for she spent half an hour identifying edible plants on the retreat premises. Little green plants that are normally considered weeds in the yard were actually edible. A tree nut we had never seen before can be used to make a tea or flavoring for ice cream. There were even edible flowers, and that night St. Francis of the Woods hosted a wildcrafting dinner that consisted almost exclusively of foraged foods. It was delicious!

Foraging, as it is sometimes called (though Jackie insists on the term "wildcrafting" for what she does), has become a surprisingly popular hobby for many. Crowd-sourced websites exist where users indicate on maps where wild, edible foods can be found. In New York City it is illegal to forage for food, so instead a "food forest" was created on a barge, where visitors can take a variety of edible plants, medicinal herbs, and fruits—for free. Featured in a *New York Times* video,[22] it is described as a call to action to address issues like food insecurity and food justice.[23] Foraging has become so popular in contemporary culture that it was made the source of humor in the comedy *The League*, where the character Andre brags about being an urban forager, and while scouting the ground for edible plants he remarks, "Mushroom caps and . . . oh, no, that's a condom."[24]

Other foragers are just in it for the money, and there is money to be made. A good forager can make a living collecting wild mushrooms and selling to restaurants. Wild mushrooms can elicit such a high price that the business can be cutthroat. As foraging entrepreneurs venture into the wild looking for mushrooms, they sometimes run into marijuana growers—with unpleasant outcomes.[25] Foragers for the valuable fiddle-head plant in Maine have started trespassing on private property, even foraging at night to evade detection, becoming such a problem that the Maine legislature has considered passing laws to protect landowners.[26] People are even starting to scavenge from roadkill, and some states like Oregon are passing laws to make eating roadkill legal.

Jackie is different. She is not collecting plants for resale to restaurants, and she charges a much lower fee than others do for lessons. Her motives are not financial: she wishes to preserve her Cherokee heritage, to give the food insecure the means to acquire adequate, nutritious calories, and to help people develop a healthier relationship with the earth. Students are frequently reminded not to take more than 10 percent of a plant, as living in harmony with the earth requires that *both* humans and the plants continue to live. "We do not want you to wildcraft more than 10 percent of any plant—that's the line. You've got to leave most of it alone because if you don't, you will come back next year and it will be gone."

After the Great Depression, once canned food, flushing toilets, and other amenities became widely available, people lost interest in nature, Jackie laments. Once those individuals take her class, though, they develop a better understanding of the bounty nature provides, and how vulnerable nature can be to irresponsible humans. "They don't realize the relationship with their food, or their relationship with the medicine they take, or just the earth around them. They find out all of these things you can eat out there and how nutritionally valuable it is. They find out the medicines that we make work very well. They open their eyes to where all this comes from. At one point in time, this is how everybody was. This is no longer." Her students begin to take sustainable agriculture more seriously, and when they flush their toilets at home, they want to know how that water is treated before it is released into rivers.

Wildcrafting goes beyond food to include medicines as well as natural dyes. A number of local residents have found that her herbal salves help their skin heal in ways even their dermatologists find amazing. Jackie herself has lupus, and says she does well self-medicating, using only remedies her grandmother taught her.

Great care is taken to warn her students of the dangers of incorrect plant identification, and learning to wildcraft properly takes many years of study. "I took it farther than my grandmother's teaching. I want to know more. You never know enough. Never. It's a never-ending education. The day you die, that's when it ends. But up until then it's always changing. It's always new plants. There's always new things. There's so much to learn." While Jackie gave us a tour, a few of her new students accompanied us. One of them, a young woman, remarked that she learned what she could and could not eat simply through trial and error. Eat it and regurgitate, stay away from the plant; eat it and feel fine, it's okay. Jackie sternly pointed out what a foolish strategy this is. "So you eat this for five years, and then six years down the road you find out your liver's not working properly or your kidneys aren't functioning properly. It's not instantaneous that things cause damage to you." Just because a plant does not make you sick immediately does not mean it is safe. The toxins can build over years, eventually causing organ failure. Watching Jackie interact with aspiring wildcrafters, it is clear that she cares dearly for their safety and well-being. If she thinks a student is particularly low on money and at risk of practicing wildcrafting without the necessary knowledge, she will offer lessons for free.

"Having the knowledge requires 100 percent identification, nothing less than 100 percent. If you can't do that, then you don't eat it. If you can't do it, then you don't put it in your mouth. That's how serious that is. And that's what we teach." There are some plant families that she teaches only to those who have been studying under her for many years. The carrot family is an example. Some are fine, but the family also includes hemlock, the poison used to kill Socrates, and offers too great a risk for misidentification.

Jackie's teachings began with only five students twenty-five years ago, but now she has a "tribe" (as she calls them) of five thousand in Oklahoma alone. The internet has given her an even larger virtual tribe. She jokes that she is an author of wildcrafting books even though she is a poor writer, because you can now easily hire editors and self-publish online. Both of her books, *Oklahoma Wildcrafting: The Beginner's Guide* and *Eat Your Weeds: A Cookbook,* have helped preserve her grandmother's teachings. Her Facebook group Oklahoma Wildcrafting has over 2,480 members from around the world. People daily post pictures of plants, allowing Jackie and other members to chime in on identification. "Books are wonderful. But pictures in books many times are taken in people's gardens. They're not taken out in the wild, where we have droughts, or we have excess rain, or there's too much shade or too much sun. Plants react differently in how they grow and what they look like sometimes." Books and the internet cannot replace the teachings of a practiced wildcrafter.

Fortunately there are other Native American wildcrafters helping to preserve their ancestor's wisdom. Like Jackie, they are not only acquiring much of their calories from the wild, but are teaching others to do the same. "People say this tastes amazing! It's because naturally grown foods, and wild foods, are so intense. The flavor . . . everything is usually so intense. And it's the quality. Many times I say they are beyond organic. And they are." For some wildcrafters, it is about "decolonizing" their diet, in much the same way that our radicals Amory Starr and Fergal Anderson seek to help groups take back their food heritage after having Western food cultures imposed upon them. For Jackie, this sentiment does not stem from a resentment of Western culture, but love of her grandmother's culture, as well as a desire for people to have ample, healthy foods. "I think people are finding wildcrafting so appealing because we care. All of us care."

We are honored to have interviewed Jackie, for between our interview and this book's publication, she passed away. Her heart too full, it broke. "You take care of your people. I hope I just go out in the field somewhere picking something. Hopefully a new discovery. I'll go with a big smile on my face." During the interview Jackie seemed particularly pleased that we were recording her Cherokee grandmother's name, Elizabeth Childers, for posterity. Never could Elizabeth have imagined that, after centuries of disdain by white Americans for Native American ways, in the twenty-first century, her wisdom of the plant world would be admired by those very same people, marking a radical return to and appreciation for heritage and respect for the earth.

You've Never Heard of Amory Starr's Restaurant

Although the modern restaurant is said to have been invented in mid-eighteenth-century Paris, there were other places where people could order cooked food, like street vendors, taverns, and inns. What made these new "restaurants" different is that they catered to the wealthy, with extravagant decorations, scrumptious dishes, seating parties at individual tables, and menus with a larger array of items one could order. These new eating locations were more than just a place to acquire food: they were an experience, where meals were served in courses, unveiled during the meal like acts of a play.

Food radicals are today providing a new eating experience by creating new types of restaurants, ones that provide both unusual foods and an even more unusual experience. Recall Amory Starr, a food radical in many ways. She challenged the conventional food production system at Colorado State University, has actively opposed the globalization of food, and, more recently, has been part of the underground restaurant movement. For her this was not an innovative way of making money. It was a strategy of building political culture, locally.

It was 2003 and Amory had moved from Colorado to Los Angeles, hoping to develop into a more effective activist. By then she identified herself as an anarchist and still felt political to her bones, but the 2004 presidential election was demoralizing because the people who had worked to build third parties and nonelectoral politics were now unifying behind Democratic presidential candidate John Kerry. Not only were her fellow radicals supporting a candidate who was not antiwar, but they were bullying others into voting for him. There seemed no alternative movement to fight for, and she began feeling an urge to work in her neighborhood.

Then she heard a lecture by one of her mentors (Leo Panitch, a political scientist at York University) describing the vibrancy of politics in Jewish neighborhoods in the eastern United States and Canada. While most Americans today avoid discussion of politics, these communities in the early twentieth century actively sought dialogue with those of different political parties, calling each other on the phone to discuss politics, publishing several different newspapers in every neighborhood. These communities seemed to have a healthy, mature political culture that was lacking in Amory's neighborhood—so she set about trying to create that culture.

To begin, she threw a dinner party, inviting everyone she knew and not requesting an RSVP. When people arrived for the party, she simply began taking things out of her refrigerator and cooking items, simple foods that were organic and purchased at the local farmers' market. When people praised her cooking and asked questions about it, Amory realized that her guests did not understand the value in buying direct from farmers.

The party was a success, and Amory felt that it also served a higher purpose, a sense of political engagement that she was craving. She wanted to repeat the success, and others wanted to help, so they, in Amory's words, formed a "five-person democratic collective which used anarchist decision-making principles to decide what to cook." They decided they needed to request RSVPs, charge a small fee, and commit to using only seasonal ingredients from the local farmers' market. Postcard invitations were distributed personally to people at the farmers' market, yoga class, the Burning Man community, and friends. Those invitees would then share the invitation with others. Once a month thirty guests were allowed, with fifteen of those slots reserved for new guests, and the meals sold out every month. Keep in mind this was not a restaurant with a sign out front. This was Amory's house, and to know about the monthly dinner one had to be given an invitation or know someone who had been invited previously.

The guests were eager to learn more about the food, encouraging the chefs to tell the story behind every dish. The cooks made an annotated menu describing the ingredients, where the food was raised, information about the farmer, the history of the recipe, and the inspiration for the meal. As the months passed, the collective conjured new educational activities. One of Amory's favorite examples is the two maps they hung on the wall. One was a map of Los Angeles with the location of all the farmers' markets (seventy in 2007), on which guests were encouraged to add their own favorite food sources. The other was a map of California, where the chefs would post the names, the locations, and photos of the farms and farmers who produced the ingredients for their meal that night.

The collective named this food endeavor *The Viand*. More than just an underground restaurant, *The Viand* is a democratic institution intent on building political culture by educating and inspiring others to eat with a concern for the farmers and ecosystem that feed them. *The Viand* developed a zine (self-published magazine) to accompany the meals, with information on how to turn that political culture into political capital.

In addition to information about the farmers, the zine included recipes, news about US farm policy, and concepts like "slow food" and "food sovereignty."

Remember, *The Viand* was not established as an entrepreneurial venture. Amory's passion is politics, not running a restaurant. The objective was not just to educate people about food but to expose them to an alternative form of economic activity, one that begins with food but can be extended to the entire economy. It all links back to a previous chapter, when Amory confronted a group of Colorado State University agriculture students to warn about the dangers of industrial agriculture, which to her is a system where corporations exploit the disconnect between consumers and the farm by producing food in a way that consumers, if they understood the modern food system better, would never condone. Rather than depending on a food system that engineers nature, she wants a food system that respects nature in solidarity with farmers. This requires a food economy where people eat in season, buying from farmers they know and whose production methods they understand and approve.

This restaurant is not a capitalistic institution. It is not a business-customer relationship. This is evident upon entering, as a stranger will insist on hand-feeding you the first bite of food, instructing you to hand-feed the next arrival, a way of saying the person is no longer just a consumer, but a community member. Some readers may have chuckled when Amory described the restaurant's decision-making process as "anarchist," but this is probably because anarchism is poorly understood—it doesn't mean chaos. Nor should its symbol be a punk rocker with a Mohawk and brass knuckles. It means that the five chefs must come to a consensus on what will be served and the job each person will perform. There is no boss, so no one can be exploited. Many readers may remark that this sounds like a cooperative or an employee-owned business. That doesn't sound so absurd, does it? What Amory is trying to show is that an economy built on anarchist/cooperative principles is better for everyone except corporations that want to sell low-quality food at a high price to dependent consumers. She is teaching these concepts not only through writing—she is a talented writer—but through active engagement with communities and food, developing the type of personal knowing so essential to other food radicals, like Ray Archuletta's educational programs on soil health.

A dinner party that was meant to facilitate a discussion of economics also expanded to farmers' markets, home cooking, and the politics of food. This debut of an underground restaurant beautifully brought together various aspects of Amory's world. She had already been teaching the political economy of food to college students for a decade, and now she was running an underground restaurant to build political culture. The guests were yearning for information about food. Though she had always heard the call for political activism, always been interested in food, and was always eager to educate, at *The Viand* she found a place to do all three at once.

Dominique Barns Sells Shrimp to Google

After five years Amory left California, but she continued to host underground dinners in Massachusetts, New Zealand, Australia, and Berlin. When she started, there was no term "underground restaurant" to describe what she was doing. She first heard the term when co-chef Sybille Palmer showed her an excerpt from the magazine *Bon Appetit* using the term. She remarked to Amory, "I think this is what we have been doing." For readers interested in learning more about *The Viand*, Amory has written a beautiful book about it titled *Underground Restaurant: Local Food, Artisan Economics, Creative Political Culture.*[27]

Most underground restaurants are about the food, not politics, and the concept has taken off. The limited structure allows chefs to experiment with dishes and to sell food without the expenses of a restaurant, as the meals are usually offered at a person's house. Sometimes they are referred to as "supper clubs." The term "pop-up restaurant" is also used, but that typically refers to a one-time event held at a licensed facility. With the advent of smartphones and the sharing economy, it has become relatively easy to find one of these restaurants, with different apps serving distinct locations. Amory was doing underground restaurants before they became popular, and with a higher purpose than just sensory delight—that's what makes her a food radical.

A similar experience is available through the Feastly app, where chefs offer one-time meals you can book online. The event might be held at a restaurant or perhaps the chef's home and usually includes a very limited set of items to choose from. That is the point: you are not going to a restaurant, but choosing an individual chef who is offering a very specific meal. As Dominique (cofounder of New Wave Foods, making synthetic shrimp) was looking to make connections with chefs, she booked seats at an event that included vegan shrimp (figure 4.9) as a food option. "We talked with the chef: 'Hey, we're actually trying to make even better vegan seafood

FIGURE 4.9 Synthetic shrimp by New
Wave Foods

Image courtesy of New Wave Foods

shrimp alternative. Would you be interested in just staying in touch and working with us?'" This piqued the chef's interest, and it turned out that he was the vegan chef at Google!

Google is not just interested in awesome search engines and driverless cars, but sustainable food as well. Eric Schmidt (CEO of Alphabet, Google's parent company) has stated that a major "game-changer" of the future is plant-based proteins to replace meat, remarking that they, like driverless cars and mobile medical data, will significantly enhance humanity.[28] Knowing Google's interest in sustainability and his own interest in vegan shrimp, the chef tried the New Wave Foods synthetic shrimp, liked it, and became Dominique's first customer.

Today's chefs are known not only for their culinary talents but for their advocacy and activism: they are not just chefs but celebrities. Chef Jamie Oliver played a major role in tuning the public into concerns with finely textured beef (which you might know by its moniker, "pink slime"). In documentaries advocating organic, local food, chefs are often interviewed alongside activists and farmers, all paying homage to pioneering chef Alice Waters. Activists like Amory Starr have learned to be chefs to help punctuate their message, and chefs have learned to be activists to encourage production of the types of foods they wish to cook.

Transforming the food system requires us all to be a little radical—including the consumer. Jeff Moyer, researcher of organic food systems, remarked that his biggest ally is consumers buying organic food. Similarly, healing the oceans is going to require consumers to be a bit radical and begin buying synthetic seafood, like New Wave Foods' shrimp made from plants and algae. People like Dominique Barnes are leading the way, and they are collecting supporters like private investors and Google chefs. They need us, as consumers, to take some risks and to follow. Lucky for us, Dominique is making following as easy as possible by creating a synthetic shrimp that tastes almost identical to the real thing.

The How of Eating
Aruni Nan Futuronsky Says You Are How You Eat

She didn't grow up with the name "Aruni." It was a name given to her by her Yogi guru during her initiation as something that Aruni jokingly refers to as a Hindu nun. We know more about Aruni than any other radical because she has written memoirs about her life journey. "I'm a writer and a mindfulness coach. I work with people one-on-one to simply be in the moment." What a journey it has been! Decades of personal struggle were overcome through an eclectic blend of spirituality. She stuttered throughout her youth, was a lesbian growing up in an age when sexual orientation was a topic people did not discuss, and struggled with drug and alcohol addiction. "As a child of the sixties, I slipped into addiction with drugs and alcohol. Then it was the seventies. Then it was the eighties. Through the grace of something beside myself, I was blessed enough to get sober in the mideighties."

Her saving grace was her open mind and willingness to explore alternative spirituality. Though born into a Jewish family, by the age of thirty Aruni was a member of a community she describes as "radical lesbian feminist spiritualists."[29] The group would engage in rituals modeled on Native American tradition, publicly protest nuclear arms, and "pray for the health of our planet, peace for all people, the cleansing of the heated evils of racism, sexism, and homophobia, and ageism from our earth."[30]

Though she had a meaningful job as an English teacher and a close group of friends in her young adult life, she became increasingly disconnected. One night, after a fight with a lover, she found herself alone by the crashing ocean waves. The suffering she experienced throughout her life erupted, resulting in an atomic anxiety panic. She called out to the empty ocean for help, and a voice answered that it was going to be okay. Though she tried to dismiss the voice, a month later, finding herself banging her head on the floor, a similar voice called out again, this time through her own mouth, telling her she needed to attend a program to end her alcohol addiction. She did, and the twelve steps it involved helped her climb into a new life.

The twelve-step process is spiritual in nature, though not affiliated with any one particular religion. Step 1 emphasizes powerlessness over alcohol, but step 2 notes there is a higher power that can help. Step 3 asks practitioners to turn their will and lives over to God, defining God as "whatever or whomever they believe their higher power to be." It is step 11 that set Aruni onto the path of yoga mindfulness; it states, "Sought through prayer and meditation to improve our conscious contact with God, as we understood Him, praying only for knowledge of His will for us and the power to carry that out."[31]

How exactly do you use prayer and meditation to connect with a higher power? Aruni felt that she needed a spiritual guide to help her. When a friend recommended the Kripalu Center for Yoga and Health, she decided to attend a weekend retreat. "I came up to Kripalu Center because I wanted to not just think about spirituality. I didn't want to just think about mindfulness. I wanted to live it, I wanted to feel it. I knew that the only thing missing from the program I was working of recovery—was the body component." It would not be her only visit; she would ultimately become a disciple and then an instructor.

Readers may not be aware of the deep spirituality behind some types of yoga. Americans mostly associate yoga with an exercise involving a mat, stretching, yoga pants, and Dannon yogurt with fruit on the bottom. That type of yoga is a rather recent invention, a hybrid of Eastern and Western practices created during the Hindu renaissance and Indian nationalist movements in the last two hundred years.[32] "Americans, Westerners, we've latched on to the hatha yoga, the yoga-on-the-mat practice, which is wonderful of course, has zillions of benefits. The whole mindful, spiritual dimension of living yoga, what I teach as yoga off the mat, isn't as practiced."

The type of yoga Aruni undertook is more closely tied to Hindu practices developed more than six thousand years ago. History suggests it is the mother of Buddhism. Acknowledging that much of life is suffering, this yoga form offers a path to relief that involves a number of practices, including meditation, where the body and mind work in tandem to find freedom from suffering. The term "yoga" literally means "yoke," signifying the disciples' binding of their lives to asceticism. As in the early days of Christian monasticism, a few of the first yogis are said to have engaged in extreme self-denial, like staring at the sun until blind or imprisoning themselves in cages.[33] As with most modern monks and nuns, yogic asceticism today has more to do with moderation.

When Aruni's friend recommended the Kripalu Center, she casually added that the food was delicious and healthy, which was welcome news, given the sugary and processed snacks so common at the programs she had been attending. At the Kripalu Center, Aruni was not just provided different foods, but a different way of eating. On her first weekend retreat, she experienced "silent dining," where you eat as a group but without talking. It was enjoyable, she thought, as it allowed her to eat without the anxiety that comes with small talk among strangers. The retreat also involved yoga. It did involve a mat and stretching, but an even greater concentration on cultivating love and compassion for oneself and others. Aruni found herself crying during her first sessions, which the instructor explained was yoga's way of detoxing the body of held feelings.

One retreat was not enough for a full detox, though, so one summer she went to live and volunteer at the Kripalu Center, where she would help run the center in return for more lessons. The summer involved many of those silent breakfasts, and she began to realize that she ate less during the silent meals.

That summer wasn't enough, so she took a leave of absence from teaching and stayed another year, where she engaged in the Kripalu ashram program that would give her the name "Aruni." During this program she began consuming less sugar and noticed that if you abstain from sugar for months you begin to lose your cravings for it.

Aruni blossomed in the Kripalu ashram, in ways no brief summary can do justice to, especially since she describes it so well in her books. Earlier she described this journey as becoming a "Hindu nun," a simple description of what is really a more expansive journey. Later Aruni would reconnect with her Jewish heritage by joining a synagogue and often joins her wife at Quaker meetings.

What does all this spirituality have to do with food? In yoga the mind and body are not as distinct as they are in Western religions. Even when it was a nascent practice, in the days before Socrates, Buddha, or Christ, the mind was considered by Indian thinkers to be a part of the body, not much different from other organs.[34] Aruni explains that yogis believe that the body itself holds wisdom, and much of our suffering is mitigated by encouraging harmony between the body and mind. "Food is so cellular, so deep, so emotional. It's so much about how we were raised. When we talk about spirituality, we're talking about the wisdom of the body, and the spirit of the heart, and to bring those things into alignment. What I want for myself and my actions. That's the most spiritual thing I can do. If I intend to eat food as health, medicine, and wellness, and I eat junk all day, I'm going to feel pretty toxified and it's more than just physical because I've broken that promise to myself. A lot of that unity in yoga is of intention and action." Compulsive eating is all about the mind wanting food, but if you are in tune with the needs of your stomach, it will tell you when it is full—and the stomach wants far less food than the mind!

Today Aruni helps teach a number of programs at the Kripalu Center, one of which is called The Kripalu Approach to Diet, a seven-week program, where the first week involves online classes, followed by a five-day in-person immersion, with the other five weeks using online instruction and live Skype/phone calls. It is taught by a team; Aruni focuses on the *how* of eating, while a nutritionist and a doctor provide instructions on *what* to eat for a healthy diet.

Involved in the *how* of eating is mindful eating, and though we have not attended one of her sessions, she has created a YouTube video in which she leads a mindful eating session, using lovely images, soothing music, and a calming dialogue to demonstrate what mindful eating is all about.[35]

Words cannot relate the video's true essence, but we will do our best. It begins with surreal music, like a hybrid of a pipe organ and synthesizer, something you might expect to hear when waking from one world to enter a lovelier world. A picture of succulent grapes ready to be picked from the vine appears, and Aruni remarks, "The practice of mindful eating focuses on how we eat, not what we eat." The grapes transition to a cutting board, where someone is cutting kale, and the cutting board is surrounded by broccoli, peppers, onions, and carrots. Aruni continues, "As we allow ourselves to focus on each bite of food, the taste and the texture of food becomes a loving anchor, softly tethering you into the moment." The scenery moves from the cutting board to a panoramic field of corn, blowing in a gentle breeze. "Each bite becomes a doorway into the present moment. Rather than using food as a way to check out of the moment, eating becomes a way to check in."

She then gives suggestions on how to sit in a way that attaches one to the earth below and the heavens above. Students are asked to breathe and relax. Images transition from one food to another, sometimes on a kitchen table, sometimes growing in the field, sometimes cooking in a pot, sometimes on a plate ready to be eaten, and then back to the growing plant from which it came. Prayer is encouraged, accompanied by controlled breathing, and viewers are asked to scan their own body as a "compassionate witness," seemingly as a way of marrying the mind and body simultaneously, welding it to the present moment. "Imagine you could breathe in compassion, compassion for this practice of mindful eating. Imagine you could exhale expectation and self-doubt. Let yourself fill up with compassion as we prepare to practice becoming present, one bite at a time."

Only then are viewers asked to begin eating—but slowly. Before biting, they are asked to really look at the article of food, from every angle, and to smell it and to marvel at it. Don't just start chewing, let it sit in the mouth a bit, and perhaps even play with it and to dwell on its essence. Then the chewing can begin, but again, slowly, more thoroughly than usual, and to think about the changes in texture and flavor as the food is being chewed. It is as if the food is also being brought into the present moment, as the eater's mind and body already are, and is becoming one with the person before it even enters the stomach. Okay, swallow, but before the next bite, breathe three times, expressing gratitude each time: one for the body, one for the food, one for the work that brings food to us . . .

Notice how *deliberate*, how *intentional*, this eating practice is. Our architect Bob Moje discussed intentional spaces, and Dan Durica lives in an intentional ecovillage, but this is intentional living amplified. Mindful eating works best when paired with healthy eating, and much of Kripalu's dieting program involves learning to eat healthfully. The center is particularly known for food that is every bit as healthy as it is delicious. Aruni repeatedly stresses that Kripalu serves only *whole* foods, meaning minimally processed, high in vegetables, mostly organic, and, to the greatest extent possible, local. The executive chef has developed relationships with local farmers, trying to source organically to the extent the budget allows.

Recall that Dan Durica's Dancing Rabbit Ecovillage has trouble selling the organic food it produces because the surrounding market for organic food is so small. Dan also remarked that if they lived closer to the Maharishi University of Management, a Transcendental Meditation center also teaching yoga principles, they would easily sell more food, because like the Kripalu Center, it purchases large amounts of organic food.

Just as Aruni lost her craving for sweets after abstaining for a period of time, her students lose the taste for junk food, and though their craving for healthier, plant-based food rises, those cravings are more for quality in food, not quantity. "It's a lot about choice. It's a lot about lifestyle and certainly food—the problem and the solution. When people come here for the integrative weight loss program, people come motivated by everything. A big push is 'I just can't lose the weight.' What we try to do in our seven-week course is help people find the nourishment, the capacity to nourish ourselves, to feed ourselves real food, whole food, nourishing food, to look for sweetness in our lives separate from high-fructose corn syrup. Where else can you get sweetness? Is it in relationship? Is it from your dog? We don't know. We don't know that part—that's the exploration." The dieting system seems to work, but Aruni cautions that it does not work for every person all the time. The beauty of the process is that it benefits even the few who do not lose weight. For those few, the mindfulness practices help them to feel unashamed about their weight and at peace with their body. It also provides them with more energy and a more meaningful life. Mindful eating can be practiced with small steps; observing a few mindful bits at each meal builds our awareness and allows our process to evolve.

Mindful eating provides benefits to all who are open to the process because it is not a system that can fail in totality. Meditating may sound difficult to the novice, as we all know how hard it can be to control the thoughts pervading the mind. Ellen DeGeneres once joked that her attempts to meditate were stymied by the inability to get a television jingle out of her mind. Aruni also notes that meditation and mindfulness have a bad reputation. "I think it needs a new marketing agent, because the way I understand meditation and mindfulness, you cannot possibly do it wrong. It's bearing yourself to sit there and watch without judgment. Anytime you notice yourself carrying on, making up a thought which is not even happening, just have an anchor—be it breath, be it movement, be it the sensations in the body on the yoga mat, be it the texture of the food in your mouth. Let that anchor, that loving return, that reunion, bring you back, and let the thoughts go on without you." Can you not get a television jingle out of your head? You haven't failed! Acknowledging the thoughts that flutter amid the mind is an important part of meditating. What mindfulness does next is to accept those random, fluttering thoughts without judgment, and instead of scolding yourself for doing meditation "wrong," you forgive yourself.

Aruni is taking a practice that seems daunting at first and making it available to anyone. It is important that people like her show students that mindfulness can improve life without requiring one to become an enlightened guru. When people hear spiritualist Deepak Chopra remark that he meditates for two hours each day, they are intimidated.[36] When they attend one of Aruni's classes, they realize mindfulness is also useful in smaller doses.

This may indeed be a radical method of eating, especially in its simplicity. "It's every day, it's essential, and it's certainly life-changing. I go visit my family—they don't eat like this, and they don't think like this, and I think there's a lot of people who don't look to a more integrative way of living. In that sense, it is radical." The idea is catching on. Some restaurants provide silent-eating experiences, both to moderate caloric intake and to help the person focus on the foods' flavors. You know it is becoming popular when they make fun of it on television, as *You're the Worst* recently did with mindful eating. The character played by Aya Cash is trying to mindfully eat a plate of nachos, but having a hard time, saying, "My therapist says I have to practice mindfulness, so I'm focusing on the flavor of the food, the mouth feel, the (as she awkwardly struggles with the nachos that are sticking together as a bunch), the, reflecting, um (the struggle continues), swallowing . . . Jesus Christ! It's like trying to eat an area rug!" Her friend, befuddled by the idea of mindful eating, replies, "Eating slow? But, less food in mouth."

There are two popular TED talks on mindful eating with tens of thousands of views, only one of which discusses the practice as meditative eating. The other just asks people to think about where their food comes from, which is not the *how* of eating we are stressing here. Great Courses has a course on practicing mindfulness and devotes an entire lecture to mindful eating, concentrating on using the five senses to evaluate the food more than on facilitating compassion.

Not many studies have evaluated the impact on mindful eating on weight loss, but those that have find some support for its effectiveness.[37] People who practice mindful eating do seem to eat healthier,[38] in addition to losing weight, and have greater mental well-being.[39] Meditation is not the only "how" of eating that can help you stay healthy. There are a number of other self-hacks to reduce your food consumption without feeling the pains of hunger. Serving food on a smaller plate causes people to eat less, even when they can refill that plate as much as they like. Making your food look ugly can help.[40] Economist and author Steven Levitt once joked one should carry a jar filled with vomit, and every time they get hungry they can smell its contents, allowing its revulsive scent to suppress the appetite.[41] Or one can view the photos at the tumblr site *Someone Ate This*, which contains pictures of unappetizing foods. Studies have shown that imagining eating a food first, and then actually eating it, can reduce the number of calories consumed.[42]

A theme abounds in making a change to one's eating style—the deliberate decision to eat differently. Whether it is meditating, not eating in front of a screen, or intentionally performing acts known to reduce one's appetite, there is a reasonable chance that one of these might help you keep a healthy weight and live with increased vitality. Perhaps more importantly, unlike diet pills or unbalanced diets, actions like mindful eating certainly cannot harm you.

Alex Evers, Helping Kids Kick Obesity

Suppose you are a parent with an overweight child, and you have tried everything you can think of to help your child achieve a healthier weight—well, everything but mindful eating. You discard that notion because . . . how can you convince *a kid* to give that idea a go? You would need your child to hear it from someone other than a parent, other than a teacher. Children need to hear it from someone who is a hero, someone who has "kid credibility." Someone who can chop concrete bricks in half, issue a reverse hook roundhouse kick to attackers, and also talk to them about self-control and ethical living. Enter martial arts instructor Alex Evers.

Alex has a dojo in our college town of Stillwater, Oklahoma. Alex is at every kid-related event held in town. One of the author's daughters took lessons at his business, Stillwater Martial Arts. During one of these lessons, Alex entered the dojo with a blindfold over his eyes, guided by one of his friends. It was obvious he didn't have eye surgery. The blindfold did not look like medical material. What, then, was he up to?

He was working on his fourth-degree black belt, which has as much to do with self-improvement and philanthropy as it does martial arts. This belt requires students to set their own goals. Alex articulated thirty-one ambitious targets and began a blog about his pursuit. One of these goals was to spend two consecutive days blind, explaining the blindfold. Other goals were organize and execute an environmental cleanup project, mend three relationships gone bad, perform one thousand documented acts of kindness, and construct a strength garden.

The self-imposed challenges, in addition to the usual requirements for his next belt, signify someone who lives life deliberately. As with Dan Durica of the Dancing Rabbit Ecovillage, Alex is a living testament to the idea of intentional living. While many of us choose our values to coincide with an easy life, people like Alex, Dan, and other radicals in this book select their values first and then live life accordingly, regardless of how easy or difficult that path may be.

Of the many other requirements Alex elected to satisfy for his advancement to the next degree, some concerned food, like eliminating soda and constructing and teaching ten eating-related self-defense tips. One other piqued our interest: *eat mindfully*. How can the average person do this on a consistent basis, and how might kids be encouraged to do so as well?

The answer can be found in another one of his goals, which was to read *Savor*, a book on mindful eating. Coauthored by a Vietnamese Zen Buddhist master and a faculty member in the Department of Nutrition at Harvard University, the book applies the technique of mindfulness to eating and articulates the science demonstrating its effectiveness. Our unhealthy relationship with eating causes us to suffer, and Buddhism is a philosophy formed to acknowledge the causes of suffering—and mitigate them. *Savor* is clever, describing the Four Noble Truths of Buddhism (life is suffering, we can identify the cause of suffering, it is possible for suffering to end, and there is a path to free us from this suffering) and applying it to weight loss: (1) being overweight is suffering, (2) you can identify the cause of your weight problem, (3) reaching a healthy weight is possible, and (4) you can follow a mindful path to a healthy weight.

This path is described as the practice of mindfulness, learning how to become more aware of your thoughts and developing tools to resist the misery of regret regarding the past and anxiety over the future by focusing on the present. Earlier, Bob Moje taught us about environmental cues that influence our eating. Mindful eating asks us to become more aware of these external effects. Rather than habitually reaching for the soda, mindfulness challenges us to ask ourselves whether we really benefit from drinking soda. When we take everything about our lives into account, do we *really* want that soda? When we eat dinner while watching television, are we eating until our appetite is satisfied, or are we mindlessly eating until the television program is over? (Studies show we eat about 15 percent more calories when watching television!)[43] Practitioners of Buddhism monitor their thoughts and discard those that cause suffering. Practitioners of mindful eating scan their thoughts as well, filtering out those that cause unhealthy eating practices.

Living in the moment helps us to break free from the anxiety associated with eating and the guilt associated with overeating, so that we can develop a sense of self-compassion. By developing a more sincere and unconditional love for ourselves (in addition to love for others) we can better motivate ourselves to eat healthier. Just as you are more likely to help someone you love than someone you do not, you are more likely to help yourself by eating better if you nurture your own self-compassion.

Though the book *Savor* is new, the practice of mindful eating is not. From its beginnings, Buddhists developed specific rituals for eating (figure 4.10). From its earliest years of practice, monks and nuns received

FIGURE 4.10 Oryoki being practiced by a Buddhist Monk at Dorje Denma Ling in Nova Scotia

Photo was taken on February 15, 2008, by Davee and made available on Flickr creative commons license Attribution 2.0 Generic (CC by 2.0). Accessed September 12, 2017, at https://flic.kr/p/4uWJre.

a bowl upon ordination, which they were to use when begging for food. Over millennia the type of eating utensils evolved and diversified across sects. Eating liturgies were even codified.

In the thirteenth century AD, one Japanese monk, Dōgen Zenji, traveled to China and brought back with him Chinese monastic eating practices. With modification the practices became a form of eating called *ōryōki*, which means "just enough." The practice includes a specific set of bowls, each of a different size, so that all bowls fit into the largest one. The liturgies used while eating are said to be from the time of Buddha himself, and include blessing the food, saying chants, and expressing gratitude for the food. (You can watch a number of such rituals on YouTube.) The specificity and formality of the ritual is rigorous. Bowls must be arranged, and napkins must be folded. The process includes prayer, bows, and synchronization. The bowls, of course, are small, and the monks themselves display a healthy weight. The liturgies differ across sects and regions, but one version says that "two-quarters of the stomach are for food, one quarter is for drink, and one quarter is left empty."[44] An American might hear that and say, "But what if your stomach is three-quarters full but the television show isn't over?"

Alex is a Christian, not a Buddhist, but he knows a good idea when he sees one. Moreover, Alex is not referring to such formal eating rules when he practices mindful eating. Mindful eating for him has more to do with avoiding mind*less* eating. "It's about being mindful in eating, but really being mindful in life. I was eating, and I remember thinking—I'm not hungry, why am I eating right now? This doesn't make any sense. That triggered something for me. It took me awhile to make it a habit where it wasn't a natural thing that I'm watching TV, I need to be eating, or I'm on the computer, I need to be eating. I'd have nothing to do at home for another half an hour or so, and why am I walking to the refrigerator right now?" It got him thinking about how we choose to eat more for pleasure and boredom than need, and while in moderation that is not harmful, in excess it is.

Noticing how easy it was for him—an intentional living enthusiast— to eat mindlessly, he thought about the example he might be setting for others. His business trains people of all ages, but Alex is particularly skilled with young kids. In addition to martial arts training, he runs an after-school program and a summer camp, hosts birthday parties, and regularly contributes to community events for children. He may very well be the most popular person among the kids in his town. To really get through to kids about the importance of something, it is helpful to have someone with "kid credibility," someone they know, like, and admire. Alex has kid credibility in spades. "I know that there are one hundred kids who see me two or three times a week. Not to toot my own horn or anything, but I'm their superhero. For the four- to thirteen-year-old crowd, I'm pretty popular. I can break concrete blocks, and I can do cool stuff like that. It's very important for me to set as good an example as I can possibly set. If I tell the kids, 'We need to make sure that we're eating healthy,' I need to make sure that I'm doing the exact same thing. They're helping me out because that helps me stay accountable."

Being a martial arts instructor, Alex's job is to help people defend themselves. This includes much more than physical defense. Attend one of his classes and you will see kids learning to defend themselves against physical attacks, but in every class he also sits down with the students and talks about other challenges in life (figure 4.11). "We use something called a mat chat where we sit down and talk about something important that day. Maybe it's honesty, or maybe it's balance. When we talk about balance, we're talking about physical balance. What about balancing in our

FIGURE 4.11 Alex Evers, taking about food self-defense
Photo taken by Zuhrah Alwahabi

life? What about exercising? What about what we eat? I feel like kids are somewhat in tune these days with healthy things." One day it might be emotional self-defense, in regards to bullies, but on other days it might be food self-defense.

Has food become such a threat that we need to "defend" ourselves from it? Obviously we need food to live, but if we do not pay attention to what, or how much we eat, we can develop bad eating habits. Alex is saying that we need to defend ourselves not from food itself, but those bad food habits. In order to promote this type of self-defense, Alex not only provides lessons to his martial arts students but has organized a community-wide program to both create better awareness of obesity and prevent it. This work paid off in 2015, when the city of Stillwater officially declared January 28, 2015, as Kids Kick Obesity Day.

As part of this program he wrote a short manual titled *Top 10 Food Self-Defense Tips*, and chapter 3 is on mindful eating. It reads, "The key to eating mindfully is to savor each bite. Instead of trying to wolf your food down, take your time. Take your first bite. Chew for a while, swallow, put your fork or spoon down and enjoy the flavor you just experienced. . . . Take time to enjoy each bite. Be mindful of what you are eating, and how you are eating it. Be more mindful in your life, with everything, not just your eating habits."

This form of mindful eating asks very little of people, only that they pay attention to what they are doing. It may not sound like a radical idea, but given the obesity rates in the Western world, it is obviously not common practice. "It's radical when it's compared to what our standard is." Alex serves an important social role. Most people are uncomfortable adopting ideas outside normally observed behavior. No one will question you if you drink a diet soda, but eat mindfully in a restaurant, and you risk looking a bit odd—like a person caught in slow motion. Explain to others that you are meditating while you eat, and they may chuckle or worry that you "lost your religion."

Alex has performed the task of taking a useful idea and stripping it down to a more culturally acceptable notion. By the time the radical idea of mindful eating has been filtered by Alex, it goes from being a spiritual practice to simply a good eating habit. He took something that seems radical and made it seem commonplace. It is persons like Aruni who give us the tools to employ mindful eating, and persons like Alex who give them appeal with the masses.

Indeed, introducing positive change in the food system requires both radicals and the people who make radical ideas seem routine. We need people with names odd to the American ear like "Aruni" and ordinary names like "Alex." Our food system needs some people throwing out ideas that most would never conjure, and some people to point out that the radical ideas are worth considering and implementing.

5

Conclusion

BETWEEN RADICAL AND ROUTINE

THE ANCIENT CELTS would often bury nobility with wagons to help them travel to the next world. The Vikings performed a similar act, but with ships. Both had the same goal of honoring the deceased and aiding their transition to the afterlife, yet they had different concepts of transportation. The Celts mainly traveled by land; the Vikings by ship. They conceived of travel differently because their "lifeworlds," meaning their common-sense reality of the world, were different.[1] When they sought to understand the "truth" about the next world, they were faced with a dearth of information. They constructed their own form of understanding based on what they knew.

Had the Celts and Vikings met to discuss the "best" burial practices to secure a comfortable afterlife, perhaps they would have agreed that neither culture really knows much about it. Perhaps they would have just killed each other. Yet when the historian waxes intellectual about these ancient cultures, she does not hold one ritual to be more correct than the other. To modern-day historians, at least, both of their rituals are completely understandable, again, given their lifeworlds.

You could make similar remarks about the radicals interviewed for this book. In many respects they are ordinary people trying to achieve a common goal: a better food system. However, their background, life experiences, personality, and other dimensions of their lifeworld make them very different from the ordinary person, and often very different from each other. Some of our radical friends disagree on important issues. A number of our interviewees opposed GMOs, but we also interviewed a genetic engineer, along with his graduate student who was raised farming transgenic crops. We interviewed an animal rights activist, but also a rancher who contends that animals are not entitled to rights.

Like the Celts and the Vikings, these individuals see the world differently from each other. Once you get to know them, even if you disagree with them, you can begin to understand why they see the world as they do. Most books that take on agricultural controversies tend to espouse a specific viewpoint. Biotechnology is either a savior or a threat. Government is either the problem or the solution. For readers accustomed to such books, *Meet the Food Radicals* must seem schizophrenic. In one chapter we seem optimistic about the role of genetic engineering, while in other chapters we warn of the dangers posed by biotechnology corporations. In one place we praise the ability of capitalism to overcome food problems, while in others we seem to carry a socialist banner.

There is a good reason for this inconsistency: this book isn't about the authors or their views. It is about the radicals we interviewed. If the reader has made it this far in the book and can't tell what opinions, we, the authors, hold about the food system, then we have done our job.

This book was a pleasure to write because it allowed us to form relationships with people we had never met before, and to expose ourselves to new ideas rarely found at our university and in our academic circles. We now have a better understanding of what it means to be ahead of the curve, thanks to Amory Starr, and to consider the intersections associated with food inequality and the contemporary dynamics of the Black Lives Matter movement, thanks to Karissa Lewis. Our university is an agricultural school but focuses almost exclusively on conventional/industrial agriculture, so meeting Jeff Moyer allowed us to understand organic agriculture better. The state of Oklahoma is a major beef producer, so you won't hear much talk of meat alternatives in our agricultural classes. Meeting Liz Specht allowed us to understand the dynamics of what may occur between alternative food and livestock producers.

People often say you should "write what you know," a quote sometimes attributed to Mark Twain. We have done that before. For this book we were eager to learn alongside the reader, and so decided to let our radical friends become the teachers. Instead of communicating what we, the authors, think, we elected to devote our efforts to helping the interviewees for this book convey their message. We were excited with each interview at the opportunity to learn from so many different people. We hope we have done due diligence to their ideas and voices. The master historian can make ancient cultures like Celts and Vikings seem more human, more familiar. We hoped to do the same for people with radical notions about food.

But . . . why? *Why* should we study radicals? There are solutions to our food problems, we believe, and if they were obvious solutions, they would have already been implemented. Why not listen to some nonobvious solutions from people thought to have radical notions, then? What does it hurt to just listen?

Every feature of modern civilization was considered radical at one place and time. The French Revolution made democracy seem dangerous. Sadly, the idea of racial equality is a relatively recent notion. At the entrance of the Oracle of Delphi was the saying "Know thyself," which was meant to remind the Greeks that they were men, not gods. Yet today we extract nitrogen from the air to feed plants, are creating robots to work for us, and perform the very act of Providence by tweaking DNA.

Each of our radical friends has something to teach us, something useful to consider. Before those lessons can be turned into something useful, they must go through a filter before becoming accepted by society at large. It takes a nonradical, someone engaging in the "routine" to lend a radical notion credibility. Most Americans are not going to adopt Aruni's method of meditative eating unless it is first adopted and tweaked by someone like Alex Evers. Most Americans are not going to take anarchist political philosophy seriously, but they are more sympathetic when it is filtered into more pragmatic, reasonable forms, like those expressed by Dan Brown and Bill Bullard.

Why then can't we skip the radical? First, what is radical today can become commonplace tomorrow. We need the radical ideas in place as a potential goal. Second, what is unremarkable is often defined relative to the radical. The gene editing performed by Dan Voytas seems like only a small change compared to GMOs, where genes from one organism are inserted into another. Katie Plohocky's dream of community-owned grocery stores operating with some government support seems a reasonable method for addressing food insecurity, compared to the Bolivarian Revolution in Venezuela.

The radical and commonplace work in tandem. To understand the changes taking place in our food system and the changes to come, we need to understand both. The next time you meet a food radical, if the ideas seem extreme, don't reject them immediately. Listen. Ponder instead the parts of the extreme ideas that might be worthwhile and distill those ideas into a form that preserves their spirit while also being routine enough for society to accept.

Notes

INTRODUCTION

1. Online Etymology Dictionary, accessed September 6, 2016, at http://www.etymonline.com/index.php?term=radical.

CHAPTER 2

1. Ainit Snir, Dani Nadel, Iris Groman-Yaroslavski, Yoel Melamed, Marcelo Sternberg, Ofer Bar-Yosef, and Ehud Weiss, "The Origin of Cultivation and Proto-Weeds, Long before Neolithic Farming," *PLOS ONE* 10(7) (2015): e0131422, doi:10.1371/journal.pone.0131422.
2. Derek Hitchins, "Prof's Ancient Egypt," 2015, accessed June 13, 2016, at http://egypt.hitchins.net/the-three-kingdoms/the-tomb-of-sennedjem.html.
3. Chris Kennedy, "Display Your FFA Price, Pre-commit to an FFA Tag Today," August 2012, Alabama Farmers Co-op: Cooperative Farming News, accessed June 14, 2016, at http://www.alafarmnews.com/index.php/archiveshomepage/46-the-business-of-farming/3962-display-your-ffa-pride-pre-commit-to-an-ffa-tag-today.
4. The Voice of Agriculture, "American Farm Bureau Federation Golden Plow Award," 2015, accessed June 14, 2016, at http://www.fb.org/legislative/gp/.
5. World Ploughing Organization website, accessed June 16, 2016, at http://worldploughing.org/.
6. Genesis 2:15, New International Version.
7. Amy-Jill Levine, "Lecture 2: Adam and Eve," *Old Testament*, The Great Courses, The Teaching Company.
8. David Montgomery, *Dirt: The Erosion of Civilizations* (Berkeley: University of California Press, 2012).
9. Montgomery, *Dirt*.

10. Roger Claassen, Andrea Cattaneo, Vince Breneman, Robert Johansson, Shawn Bucholtz, and Mitch Morehart, *Environmental Compliance in U.S. Agricultural Policy*, June 2004, Economic Research Service, Agricultural Economic Report No. 832.

11. David Pimental, "Soil Erosion: A Food and Environmental Threat," *Environment, Development and Sustainability* 8 (2006): 119–37, doi:10.1007/s10668-005-1262-8.

12. Plant and Soil Sciences eLibrary. "Soils—Part 3: Soil Organic Matter," accessed August 22, 2016, at http://passel.unl.edu/pages/informationmodule.php?idinfo rmationmodule=1130447040&topicorder=6&maxto=8.

13. Shiping Deng, "Fertilizer Interaction with Soil Organisms," SunUpTV, October 23, 2009, accessed November 11, 2014, at https://www.youtube.com/watch?v=vasomO4JnTE. Deng is a soil biochemist at Oklahoma State University.

14. Richard Allen White, Eric M. Bottos, Taniya Roy Chowdhury, Jeremy D. Zucker, Colin J. Brislawn, Carrie D. Nicora, Sarah J. Fansler, Kurt R. Glaesemann, Kevin Glass, and Janet K. Jansson, "Moleculo Long-Read Sequencing Facilitates Assembly and Genomic Binning from Complex Soil Metagenomes," *mSystems* 1(3) (2016): e00045-16, doi:10.1128/mSystems.00045-16.

15. National Park Service, *A Complex Prairie Ecosystem*, accessed June 16, 2016, at https://www.nps.gov/tapr/learn/nature/a-complex-prairie-ecosystem.htm.

16. F. S. Earle, *Southern Agriculture* (New York: Macmillan, 1908).

17. Elaine Ingham, "Soil Food Web," Natural Resources Conservation Service, not dated, accessed June 15, 2016, at http://www.nrcs.usda.gov/wps/portal/nrcs/detailfull/soils/health/biology/?cid=nrcs142p2_053868.

18. Sara Wright, "Glomalin—Soil's Superglue," *AgResearch Magazine*, October 1997, accessed June 15, 2016, at http://agresearchmag.ars.usda.gov/1997/oct/glomalin; USDA/Agricultural Research Service. "Glomalin Is Key to Locking Up Soil Carbon," *ScienceDaily*, July 2, 2008, www.sciencedaily.com/releases/2008/06/080629075404.htm>.

19. accessed June 15, 2016, at https://www.youtube.com/watch?v=9uMPuF50CPA.

20. National Resource Conservation Service, "History of NRCS," not dated, accessed August 13, 2016, at http://www.nrcs.usda.gov/wps/portal/nrcs/main/national/about/history/.

21. Timothy Keller. *Lord of the Earth* (audio sermon), December 10, 2000, From the series *Genesis—The Gospel according to God*, accessed August 12, 2016, at https://www.youtube.com/watch?v=BrbSET3IJS8.

22. The Holy Bible, *English Standard Version* (Wheaton, IL: Crossway, 2011).

23. Tara Isabella Burton, "Pope Francis' Radical Environmentalism," *The Atlantic*, July 11, 2014, accessed August 13, 2016, at http://www.theatlantic.com/international/archive/2014/07/pope-franciss-radical-rethinking-of-environmentalism/374300/.

24. A. Wezel, S. Bellon, T. Dore, C. Francis, D. Vallod, and C. David, "Agroecology as a Science, a Movement and a Practice: A Review," *Agronomy for Sustainable Development* (2009), doi:10.1051/agro/2009004.

25. E. Lichtenberg, "Some Hard Truths about Agriculture and the Environment," *Agricultural and Resource Economics* 33 (2004): 24–33.

26. Upton Sinclair, *I, Candidate for Governor: And How I Got Licked* (Berkeley: University of California Press, 1994.

27. John Horowitz, Robert Ebel, and Kohei Ueda, *"No-till" Farming Is a Growing Practice,* November 2010, ERS Report Summary, accessed August 15, 2016, at http://www.ers.usda.gov/media/135319/eib70_reportsummary.pdf.

28. C. Milton Coughenour and Shankariah Chamala, *Conservation Tillage and Cropping Innovation: Constructing the New Culture of Agriculture* (Ames: Iowa State University Press, 2000).

29. Ag Land Lease, "No-Till," Oklahoma State University, accessed August 16, 2016, at http://aglandlease.info/production-practices/no-till/.

30. David R. Montgomery, "A Case for No-Till Farming," *Scientific American,* June 30, 2008, accessed August 16, 2016, at http://www.scientificamerican.com/article/a-case-for-no-till-farmin/.

31. Catherine Greene, "Organic Market Overview," May 26, 2016, Organic Agriculture, Economic Research Service, US Department of Agriculture, accessed August 19, 2016, at http://www.ers.usda.gov/topics/natural-resources-environment/organic-agriculture/organic-market-overview.aspx.

32. Diamond Dallas Page, *DDP Yoga Program Guide,* 2011, 15.

33. *The Joe Rogan Experience* (podcast), September 5, 2016, episode 842: Chris Kresser.

34. Will Durant, *Our Oriental Heritage,* vol. 1 of *The Story of Civilization* (New York: Simon and Schuster, 1954).

35. Patrick N. Allitt, "Lecture 3: Natives and Newcomers," *American Religious History,* The Great Courses, The Teaching Company.

36. Michael Frassetto, *The Great Medieval Heretics* (New York: BlueBridge, 2007).

37. Lucius Annaeus Seneca, Letter 122, *Letters from a Stoic* (New York: Penguin Classics, 1969).

38. Patrick Grim, "Lecture 17: A Genealogy of My Morals," *Questions of Value,* The Great Courses, The Teaching Company.

39. Eryn Bell, F. Bailey Norwood, and Jayson L. Lusk, "Are Consumers Willfully Ignorant About Animal Welfare?" *Animal Welfare* 26 (2017): 232–402.

40. Jaime Morgan, "Break Down the Walls: Punk and Animal Rights," *National Geographic TV Blogs,* May 24, 2012, accessed September 2, 2016, at http://tvblogs.nationalgeographic.com/2012/05/24/break-down-the-walls-punk-and-animal-rights/.

41. Morgan, "Break Down the Walls," .

42. Will Boisseau and Jim Donaghey, "Nailing Descartes to the Wall: Animal Rights, Veganism and Punk Culture," *Anarchism and Animal Liberation: Essays*

on *Complementary Elements of Total Liberation*, edited by Anthony J. Nocella II, Richard J. White, and Erika Cudworth (Jefferson, NC: McFarland, 2015); Jayson Lusk, "Who Are the Vegetarians?," *JaysonLusk.com*, September 30, 2014, accessed September 2, 2016, at http://jaysonlusk.com/blog/2014/9/30/who-are-the-vegetarians.

43. Boisseau and Donaghey, "Nailing Descartes."

44. accessed September 2, 2016, at http://www.mcspotlight.org/case/pretrial/factsheet.html.

45. Franny Armstrong (codirector and producer) and Ken Loach (codirector), *McLibel* (documentary), 2005; Paul Lewis and Rob Evans, "McLibel Leaflet Was Co-written by Undercover Police Officer Bob Lambert," *The Guardian*, June 21, 2013, accessed September 2, 2016, at https://www.theguardian.com/uk/2013/jun/21/mclibel-leaflet-police-bob-lambert-mcdonalds.

46. "The Daily Show and The Colbert Report Finish . . . ," press release from Comedy Central, April 4, 2013, *The Futon Critic*, accessed September 2, 2016, at http://www.thefutoncritic.com/ratings/2013/04/04/the-daily-show-and-the-colbert-report-finish-1q-2013-as-number-1-and-number-2-among-adults-18-49-and-all-key-young-demos-795303/20130404comedycentral01/.

47. The Humane Society of the United States, "Ag-Gag Laws Keep Animal Cruelty behind Closed Doors," accessed December 19, 2017, at http://www.humanesociety.org/issues/campaigns/factory_farming/fact-sheets/ag_gag.html?referrer=https://www.google.com/.

48. Minxin Pei, "The Real Reason behind Shuanghui's Purchase of Smithfield," *Fortune*, June 4, 2013, accessed September 16, 2016, at http://fortune.com/2013/06/04/the-real-reason-behind-shuanghuis-purchase-of-smithfield/.

49. Trent Loos, *The Best of Trent*, 2nd ed., (self-published, 2012), 34.

50. Carolyn Dimitri, Anne Effland, and Neilson Conklin, *The 20th Century Transformation of U.S. Agriculture and Farm Policy*, Economic Research Service, United States Department of Agriculture, 2005.

51. Kirk Johnson, "Bring a Yoga Mat and an Open Mind. Goats Are Provided," *New York Times*, November 20, 2016; "This Relaxing New Yoga Class Is Full of . . . Goats?!" Popsugar Entertainment, September 15, 2016, accessed June 13, 2017, at https://www.youtube.com/watch?v=N7gTbeBqrzg; "See Why These Cute Little Goats Are the Latest Yoga Craze," *National Geographic*, June 2, 2017, accessed June 13, 2017, at https://www.youtube.com/watch?v=NiVhWBsXdh8.

52. Dan Nosowitz, "Is Goat CrossFit the Next Logical Step after Goat Yoga? You Decide," *ModernFarmer.com*, June 12, 2017, accessed June 19, 2017, at http://modernfarmer.com/2017/06/goat-crossfit/?utm_source=Modern+Farmer+Newsletter&utm_campaign=23e87a9571-Newsletter_June_20_Mon&utm_medium=email&utm_term=0_e8a89c7e43-23e87a9571-75443901&mc_cid=23e87a9571&mc_eid=a45706d583.

53. Alison Luterman, "What We Came For," *The Sun*, Issue 250, October 1996, 3.

54. Information accessed on June 9, 2016, at http://www.agrobot.com/products.html; Ilan Brat, "Goodbye Field Hand, Hello Fruit-Picking Robot," *Wall Street Journal*, April 24, 2015, B1.

55. "Bacchus to the Future," *The Economist*, November 30, 2013, 14.

56. Lise Rathke, "Robots Put Down Roots on Smaller Dairy Farms," *Tulsa World*, September 13, 2015, A8.

57. "World's Largest Meatpacking Firm Wants to Test Out Robot Butchers," National Public Radio, January 5, 2016.

58. Dan Nosowitz, "The World's First Robot Farm Requires No (Human) Farmers at All," *Modern Farmer*, October 7, 2015.

59. Kaleigh Rogers, "Self-Driving Cars Are Coming, but Self-Driving Tractors Are Already Here," *Motherboard*, June 23, 2016, accessed September 9, 2016, at http://motherboard.vice.com/read/self-driving-cars-are-coming-but-self-driving-tractors-are-already-here-ai-artificial-intelligence.

60. Don Paarlberg and Philip Paarlberg, *The Agricultural Revolution of the 20th Century* (Ames: Iowa State University Press, 2000).

61. John Stancavage, "The Henry Ford of the Pecan Industry," *Tulsa World*, June 14, 2014, accessed June 9, 2015, at http://www.tulsaworld.com/businesshomepage1/john-stancavage-the-henry-ford-of-the-pecan-industry/article_d0549fea-af30-57d1-b8af-5a6a7bfe1325.html.

62. "Robot used to round up cows is a hit with farmers," BBC, Technology, November 2013, accessed September 8, 2016, at http://www.bbc.com/news/technology-24955943.

63. Laurissa Smith, "Robots Capture Pollination Problems in Orchard Research," *ABC Rural*, April 19, 2016, accessed September 8, 2016, at http://www.abc.net.au/news/2016-04-19/robots-in-horticulture-crops-1904/7339266.

64. Anthony Funnell, "Robots and the Future of Agriculture," ABC Radio National, November 25, 2015, accessed September 8, 2016, at http://www.abc.net.au/radionational/programs/futuretense/a-swarm-of-agbots/6968940.

65. Patrick Canning, *A Revised and Expanded Food Dollar Series*, Economics Research Service, US Department of Agriculture, Economic Research Report No. 114, February 2011.

66. Kelsey D. Atherton, "Autonomous Tractor Concept Take the Farmers Out of Farming," *Popular Science*, September 1, 2016.

67. Jon Fingas, "Google AI Builds a Better Cucumber Farm," *Engadget.com*, August 31, 2016, accessed September 9, 2016, at https://www.engadget.com/2016/08/31/google-ai-helps-cucumber-farm/.

68. Jacob Bunge, "Farmers Harvest Homegrown Tech," *Wall Street Journal*, April 19, 2016, B1.

69. Andrew Curry, "Archaeology: The Milk Revolution," *Nature* 500(7460) (July 31, 2013).

70. Heidi G. Parker et al., "Genetic Structure of the Purebred Domestic Dog," *Science* 304(5674) (2014): 1160–64.

71. Joseph Stromberg, "Kale, Brussels Sprouts, Cauliflower, and Cabbage Are All Varieties of a Single Magical Plant Species," *Vox*, February 10, 2015, accessed May 11, 2017, at https://www.vox.com/xpress/2014/8/6/5974989/kale-cauliflower-cabbage-broccoli-same-plant. Evelyne Bloch-Dano, *Vegetables: A Biography* (Chicago: University of Chicago Press, 2012).

72. Garrett G. Fagan, "Lecture 33: Aurelian, Diocletian, and the Tetrarchy," *Emperors of Rome*, The Great Courses, The Teaching Company, 16:25.

73. Lyudmila Trut, Irina Oskina, and Anastasiya Kharlamova, "Animal Evolution during Domestication: The Domesticated Fox as a Model," *BioEssays* 31 (2009): 249–360.

74. Michael Cummings, *Human Heredity: Principles and Issues*, updated ed. (New York: Brooks/Cole, 2006).

75. Francis Galton, "Regression towards Mediocrity in Hereditary Stature," *Journal of the Anthropological Institute* 15 (1886): 246–63; Prakash Gorroochurn, "On Galton's Change from 'Reversion' to 'Regression,'" *American Statistician* 70(3) (2016): 227–31.

76. Trut, Oskina, and Kharlamova, "Animal Evolution during Domestication.

77. Amanda Kastrinos, "Delicious Mutant Foods: Mutagenesis and the Genetic Modification Controversy," *Genetic Literacy Project*, June 12, 2016, accessed May 16, 2017, at https://geneticliteracyproject.org/2016/06/12/pasta-ruby-grapefruits-why-organic-devotees-love-foods-mutated-by-radiation-and-chemicals/.

78. US Food and Drug Administration, "The FDA Takes Step to Remove Artificial Trans Fats in Processed Foods," news release, June 16, 2015, accessed May 16, 2017, at https://www.fda.gov/newsevents/newsroom/pressannouncements/ucm451237.htm.

79. Nicole Miller, "Jumping Gene Enabled Key Step in Corn Domestication," *University of Wisconsin–Madison News*, September 25, 2011.

80. James Angstman, "Not Your Grandfather's GMOs: An Interview with Dr. Dan Voytas," *Science in the News*, August 10, 2015, Graduate School of Arts and Sciences, Harvard University.

81. Kathiann Kowalski, "Silencing Genes—to Understand Them," *Science News for Students*, March 27, 2015, accessed May 30, 2017, at https://www.sciencenewsforstudents.org/article/silencing-genes-understand-them.

82. Loredana Guglielmi, "Genome Editing Successfully Treats Leukaemia," *Bionews*, January 25, 2017, accessed May 22, 2017, at http://www.bionews.org.uk/page_764553.asp; James Gallagher, "Designer Cells Reverse One-Year-Old's Cancer," BBC News, November 5, 2016, accessed May 22, 2017, at http://www.bbc.com/news/health-34731498. Claire Maldarelli, "Doctors Successfully Treat Two Babies with Leukemia Using Gene-Edited Immune

Cells," *Popular Science*, January 27, 2017, accessed May 22, 2017, at http://www.popsci.com/doctors-successfully-treat-two-babies-with-leukemia-using-gene-edited-immune-cells.

83. "Lettuce rejoice! Scientists grow longer lasting salad," *ScienceDaily*, University of Southampton, April 10, 2014, accessed April 16, 2014, at www.sciencedaily.com/releases/2014/04/140410083347.htm.

84. Rongxia Guan, Yue Qu, Yong Guo, Lili Yu, Ying Liu, Jinghan Jiang, Jiangang Chen, Yulong Ren, Guangyu Liu, Lei Tian, Longguo Jin, Zhangxiong Liu, Huilong Hong, Ruzhen Chang, Matthew Gilliham, and Lijuan Qiu, "Salinity Tolerance in Soybean Is Modulated by Natural Variation in GmSALT3," *Plant Journal* 80(6) (2014): 937, doi:10.1111/tpj.12695.

85. Kenneth Chang, "A Genetic Fix to Put the Taste Back in Tomatoes," *New York Times*, January 30, 2017.

86. "The New Green Revolution: A Bigger Rice Bowl," *The Economist*, May 10, 2014.

87. Krissa Welshans, "NIR Light Finding Wheat's Potential," *Feedstuffs*, February 2, 2015, 20.

88. Sarah Lewin, "The Culture of Germination," *Scientific American*, May 2015, 26.

89. Anne Fitzgerald, "Ames Firm's Collapse Reflects Troubles of an Industry Iowa Counts On for Jobs," *Des Moines Register*, January 15, 2006; "Phytodyne, Inc. Gains $5 Million Investment from Iowa Values Fund," PR Newswire, February 19, 2004, accessed May 26, 2017, at http://www.prnewswire.com/news-releases/phytodyne-inc-gains-5-million-investment-from-iowa-values-fund-71722772.html.

90. Elizabeth Pennisi, "The Plant Engineer," *Science* 353(6305) (September 16, 2016): 1220–24. (b)

91. "Intellectual Property: A Question of Utility," *The Economist*, August 8, 2015, 50–52.

92. Elon Musk, "All Our Patent Are Belong to You," *Tesla.com*, June 12, 2014, accessed May 26, 2017, at https://www.tesla.com/blog/all-our-patent-are-belong-you; "Episode 551: The Case against Patents," *Planet Money*, July 9, 2014. National Public Radio.

93. Dan Charles, May 2013, "The Curse of Fertilizer," *National Geographic*.

94. Jan Willem Erisman, James Galloway, Zbigniew Klimont, and Wilfried Winiwarter, "How a Century of Ammonia Synthesis Changed the World," *Nature Geoscience*, September 2008.

95. Hager, Thomas. 2008. *The Alchemy of Air* (New York: Broadway Books, 2008).

96. *The World Food Prize*, "About Norman Borlaug," accessed May 26, 2017, at https://www.worldfoodprize.org/en/dr_norman_e_borlaug/about_norman_borlaug/.

97. Malavika Vyawahare, "World's Largest Vertical Farm Grows without Soil, Sunlight or Water in Newark," *The Guardian*, August 14, 2016; Michael J. Coren, "The Price of LEDs Is Falling So Fast It's Profitable to Farm in New Jersey

Nightclub," *Qz.com*, June 17, 2016. Vanessa Wong, "Inside the Computerized Lettuce Factory of the Future," *BuzzFeed News*, March 3, 2017.

98. Ian Frazier, "The Vertical Farm," *New Yorker*, January 9, 2017.

99. Jake Naughton, Niko Koppel, and Guglielmo Mattioli, "A Vertical Farm Grows in Newark," *New York Times*, May 15, 2017, accessed September 5, 2017, at https://www.nytimes.com/video/nyregion/100000005080478/aerofarm-vertical-newark.html.

100. "Shrimp Down, Lobster Up: Is There a Connection?," *Scientific American*, January 9, 2014, accessed May 28, 2017, at https://www.scientificamerican.com/article/shrimp-down-lobster-up-is-there-a-connection/.

101. "Slavery and Seafood: Here Be Monsters," *The Economist*, March 14, 2015, 62.

102. "Marine management: Net positive," *The Economist*, July 16, 2016, 13.

103. Ariel Schwartz, "I Tried 'Shrimp' Made in a Lab—and Now I'd Consider Ditching the Real Thing," *Business Insider*, February 5, 2016, accessed May 28, 2017, at http://www.businessinsider.com/new-wave-foods-lab-made-shrimp-2016-2.

104. John Lyons and Yifan Xiw, "Karmic Battle Takes Place on Shanghai River," *Wall Street Journal*, May 30, 2017. A1.

105. Tyson Foods web site, accessed June 1, 2016, at http://ir.tyson.com/investor-relations/investor-overview/tyson-factbook/.

106. Rowan Jacobsen, "The Biography of a Plant-Based Burger," *Pacific Standard*, September–October 2016, 34–41.

107. "Food Technology: Plant and Two Veg," *The Economist*, February 4, 2017, 57.

108. Karandeep Virdi, "Report Shows Growth in Organic Dairy Market," *Feedstuffs*, June 5, 2017, 25.

109. Lindsay Marchello, "Shocker: Dairy Industry Urges FDA to Crack Down on Milk Alternatives," *Reason*, March 6, 2017, accessed March 13, 2017, at http://reason.com/blog/2017/03/06/dairy-industry-calls-on-fda-to-crackdown.

110. Rebecca Rupp, "The Butter Wars: When Margarine Was Pink," *The Plate* at National Geographic, August 13, 2014, accessed June 12, 2017, at http://theplate.nationalgeographic.com/2014/08/13/the-butter-wars-when-margarine-was-pink/.

111. "Food technology: Plant and Two Veg," *The Economist*, February 4, 2017, 57.

112. Frank Newport, "In U.S., 5% Consider Themselves Vegetarian," *Gallup*, July 26, 2012, accessed June 1, 2017, at http://www.gallup.com/poll/156215/consider-themselves-vegetarians.aspx.

113. F. Bailey Norwood, Pascal A. Oltenacu, Michelle S. Calvo-Lorenzo, and Sarah Lancaster, *Agricultural and Food Controversies* (New York: Oxford University Press, 2015).

114. Anna Starostinetskaya, "Obama Says Drop Meat to Fight Climate Change," *VegNews.com*, May 11, 2017, accessed June 2, 2017, at http://vegnews.com/articles/page.do?pageId=9472&catId=1.

115. Jayson L. Lusk and F. Bailey Norwood, "Some Vegetarians Spend Less Money on Food, Others Don't," *Ecological Economics* 130 (2016): 232–42.

116. Showfat Shafi, "Meet the 'Toilet Man' of India," *Al Jazeera*, August 21, 2015, accessed June 8, 2017, at http://www.aljazeera.com/news/2015/08/meet-toilet-man-india-150820085220487.html.

117. Pramit Bhattacharya, "88% of Households in India Have a Mobile Phone," *Livemint.com*, December 5, 2016, accessed June 8, 2017, at http://www.livemint.com/Politics/kZ7j1NQf5614UvO6WURXfO/88-of-households-in-India-have-a-mobile-phone.html.

118. Shafi, "Meet the Toilet Man."

119. Paul Hawken and Tom Steyer, *Drawdown* (New York: Penguin, 2017).

120. Georgios A. Kintiras, Javier Gadea Diaz, A. J. van der Goot, and Georgios D. Stefanidas, "On the Use of the Couette Cell Technology for Large Scale Production of Textured Soy-Based Meat Replacers," *Journal of Food Engineering* 169 (2016): 205–13.

CHAPTER 3

1. Charles, Larry (director); Cohen, Sacha Baron, Alec Berg, David Mandel, Jeff Schaffer (writers and producers); and Anthony Hines, Scott Rudin, and Todd Schulman (producers), *The Dictator*, 2012, distributed by Paramount Pictures.

2. USDA Office of Communications, *Food Desert Locator*, May 2, 2011, Food and Nutrition Service, US Department of Agriculture, accessed June 17, 2017, at https://www.fns.usda.gov/tags/food-desert-locator.

3. Marissa Martinelli, "John Oliver Wants to Fix Gerrymandering So That Even Racist Grandmas and Quidditch Players Get a Fair Say in Government," *Slate.com*, April 10, 2017, accessed June 17, 2017, at http://www.slate.com/blogs/browbeat/2017/04/10/john_oliver_talks_gerrymandering_on_last_week_tonight_video.html.

4. Marianne Bertrand and Sendhil Mullainathan, "Are Emily and Greg More Employable Than Lakisha and Jamal? A Field Experiment on Labor Market Discrimination," *American Economics Review* 94(4) (2004): 991–1013.

5. Shankar Vedantam, "Researchers Examine Race Factor in Car Crashes Involving Pedestrians," *Hidden Brain* (podcast), February 15, 2017, National Public Radio, accessed June 17, 2017, at http://www.npr.org/2017/02/15/515336658/researchers-examine-race-factor-in-car-crashes-involving-pedestrians.

6. J. Weston Phippen, "'Kill Every Buffalo You Can! Every Buffalo Dead Is an Indian Gone,'" *The Atlantic*, May 13, 2016, accessed June 17, 2017, at https://www.theatlantic.com/national/archive/2016/05/the-buffalo-killers/482349/.

7. Community Forum on Black Liberation and the Food Movement: Panel, November 29, 2016, accessed June 19, 2017, at https://www.youtube.com/watch?v=SvtorZnOQ1I, 46:00.

8. Community Forum on Black Liberation and the Food Movement, 44:25.

9. Lori Eanes, "Full Harvest Farm in Oakland," *Backyard Roots* (blog), accessed June 19, 2017, at http://www.backyardrootsbook.com/full-harvest-farm-in-oakland/.

10. "Marijuana: The Gateway Plant to Urban Farming," Movement Generation Justice & Ecology Project, accessed June 19, 2017, at http://movementgeneration. org/marijuana-the-gateway-plant-to-urban-farming/.

11. Community Forum on Black Liberation and the Food Movement, 46:40.

12. Wiley Rogers, "Full Harvest Farm," *GROW: Foods, Jobs, Community* (blog), June 29, 2014, accessed June 19, 2017, at http://www.plantingjustice.org/blog/ full-harvest-farm.

13. AJ+, *Black Panther-Inspired Urban Farming* (video), October 23, 2015, accessed June 19, 2017, at https://www.youtube.com/watch?v=3l3hMeeVSIo.

14. BYAmedia, *"When I Come Here, I'm Free": Youth Voices in Urban Agriculture*, December 2, 2016, accessed June 19, 2017, at https://www.youtube.com/ watch?v=eqCPqWSczhg. University of California; Rob Bennaton (web page), accessed June 19, 2017, at http://ucanr.edu/Find_People/?facultyid=24164.

15. Oakland University, "Campus Student Organic Farm," Not dated, accessed June 17, 2017, at https://oakland.edu/biology/organic-farm/.

16. Iyana Robertson, "The Inspiring Story behind the Viral Video of Black Kids Rapping about Farming," *BET.com*, December 15, 2017, accessed June 19, 2017, at http://www.bet.com/music/2016/12/15/kids-rapping-about-farming-video. html; "Grow Food Lyrics," *Genius.com*, not dated, accessed June 19, 2017, at https://genius.com/Appetite-for-change-grow-food-lyrics.

17. Michaeleen Doucleff, "Hipsters off the Hook: The Truth behind Abandoned Backyard Chickens," *The Salt* (blog), July 11, 2013, National Public Radio, accessed June 19, 2017, at http://www.npr.org/sections/thesalt/2013/07/10/200699728/ hipsters-off-the-hook-the-truth-behind-abandoned-backyard-chickens.

18. Global Oneness Project, *The People's Grocery* (video), not dated, accessed June 19, 2017, at https://www.globalonenessproject.org/library/films/peoples-grocery.

19. Amanda Suutari, "USA—California (Oakland)—The People's Grocery: Bringing Healthy Food to Low-Income Neighborhoods," EcoTipping Points Project: Models for Success in a Time of Crisis, May 2006, accessed June 19, 2017, at http:// www.ecotippingpoints.org/our-stories/indepth/usa-california-oakland-people- grocery-healthy-food.html.

20. Sarah Jones, "Class-Conflict Cuisines," *The Nation*, October 30, 2017, 28–31.

21. Monica M. White, "'A Pig and a Garden': Fannie Lou Hamer and the Freedom Farms Cooperative," *Food and Foodways* 25(1) (2017): 20–39.

22. Karissa Lewis, "Black Land and Its Role in the Liberation of Black People," *Huffington Post*, February 24, 2017, accessed June 29, 2017, at http://www. huffingtonpost.com/entry/black-land-and-the-liberation-black-people_us_ 58b05447e4b0780bac289b9c.

23. National Congress of American Indians, *Tribal Nations and the United States: An Introduction*, accessed June 29, 2017, at http://www.ncai.org/tribalnations/intro- duction/Tribal_Nations_and_the_United_States_An_Introduction-web-.pdf.

24. John Rodgers and Amory Starr, "On Discourses and Social Movements," *Journal of Developing Societies* 11 (1995): 74.

25. Seattle Police Department After Action Report, April 4, 2000, accessed July 4, 2017, at http://media.cleveland.com/pdextra/other/Seattle%20PD%20after%20action%20report.pdf.

26. WTO coverage, KIRO TV, accessed July 4, 2017, at https://www.youtube.com/watch?v=B2mAOpTdTKs; Four Days in Seattle: The 1999 WTO Riots, plus news stories one week later, accessed July 4, 2017, at https://www.youtube.com/watch?v=pFamvR9CpYw&t=338s.

27. Amory Starr, *Naming the Enemy: Anti-corporate Movements Confront Globalization* (New York: Zed Books, 2000).

28. Norwood et al., *Agricultural and Food Controversies.*

29. Amory Starr, *Afterglobalization* (radio broadcast), May 19, 2005, A-infos Radio Project, L.A. Sound Posse.

30. Amory Starr, "The New Imperialism," Socialist Scholars Conference, New York, April 13, 2002, accessed July 5, 2017, at http://amorystarr.com/the-new-imperialism/. Starr, *Naming the Enemy.*

31. Krissa Welshans, "Brazil Meat Industry Reeling from Scandal," *Feedstuffs*, April 3, 2017, 3.

32. USDA Office of Communications, "USDA on Tainted Brazilian Meat: None Has Entered U.S., 100 Percent Re-inspection Instituted," Press Release No. 0025.17.

33. "Q&A: Horsemeat Scandal," BBC News, April 10, 2013, accessed July 12, 2017, at http://www.bbc.com/news/uk-21335872.

34. "Food Demand Survey (FooDS)—January 2015," *JaysonLusk.com*, January 15, 2015, accessed July 7, 2017, at http://jaysonlusk.com/blog/2015/1/15/food-demand-survey-foods-january-2015.

35. Tyler J. Klain, Jayson L. Lusk, Glynn T. Tonsor, and Ted C. Schroeder, "An Experimental Approach to Valuing Information," *Agricultural Economics* 45 (2014): 635–48.

36. American Meat Institute, *Media Teleconference* (slides), July 9, 2013, accessed July 7, 2017, at https://www.meatinstitute.org/index.php?ht=a/GetDocumentAction/i/92227.

37. Joel L. Greene, "Country-of-Origin Labeling for Foods and the WTO Trade Dispute on Meat Labeling," Congressional Research Service, December 8, 2015, 7-5700, RS22955.

38. Norwood, F. Bailey and Ted C. Schroeder. "Usefulness of Placement Weight Data in Forecasting Fed Cattle Marketings and Prices," *Journal of Agricultural and Applied Economics* 32(1) (2000): 63–72.

39. Iowa Public Television, "1980s Farm Crisis," not dated, accessed July 7, 2017, at http://site.iptv.org/mtom/classroom/module/13999/farm-crisis.

40. Kurt Lawton, "Taking a Look Back at the 1980s Farm Crisis and It's [*sic*] Impacts," *Corn + Soybean Digest*, August 22, 2016, accessed July 10, 2017, at http://www.cornandsoybeandigest.com/marketing/taking-look-back-1980s-farm-crisis-and-its-impacts.

41. Azzeddine Azzam and John R. Schroeter, "Concentration in Beef Packing: Do Gains Outweigh the Losses?," *Choices*, First Quarter 1997.

42. National Cattlemen's Beef Association, "National Cattlemen's Association," not dated, accessed July 12, 2017, at http://www.beefusa.org/national-cattlemensassociation.aspx.

43. World Trade Organization, "The WTO in Brief: Part 1," not dated, accessed July 12, 2017, at https://www.wto.org/english/thewto_e/whatis_e/inbrief_e/inbr01_e.htm.

44. Nathan Halverson, "How China Purchased a Prime Cut of America," *Reveal*, January 24, 2015, accessed July 10, 2017, at https://www.revealnews.org/article/how-china-purchased-a-prime-cut-of-americas-pork-industry/.

45. David Harvey, *A Brief History of Neoliberalism* (New York: Oxford University Press, 2007).

46. Iain Bruce, *The Real Venezuela: Making Socialism in the 21st Century* (London: Pluto Press, 2008); George Ciccariello-Maher, *Building the Commune: Radical Democracy in Venezuela* (New York: Verso, 2016).

47. Bruce, *The Real Venezuela*. Ciccariello-Maher, *Building the Commune*.

48. Food and Agriculture Organization of the United Nations, "World Food Situation," accessed June 21, 2017, at http://www.fao.org/worldfoodsituation/foodpricesindex/en/; Food and Agriculture Organization of the United Nations, *The State of Food Insecurity in the World* (Rome: FAO, 2010).

49. Ned Resnikoff, "Detroit's Secret Weapon against Food Insecurity," *MSNBC. com*, July 25, 2014, accessed June 22, 2017, at http://www.msnbc.com/msnbc/detroit-gardening-weapon-against-food-insecurity.

50. USDA Office of Communications, "USDA Announces New Support to Help Schools Purchase More Food from Local Farmers," December 2, 2014, Food and Nutrition Service, US Department of Agriculture, accessed June 22, 2017, at https://www.fns.usda.gov/pressrelease/2014/026014.

51. Elizabeth Fitting, "Cultures of Corn and Anti-GMO Activism in Mexico and Colombia," *Food Activism: Agency, Democracy and Economy*, ed. Carole Counihan and Valeria Siniscalchi (New York: Bloomsbury, 2014).

52. "US Dollar to Venezuelan Bolivar Exchange Rate," *YCHARTS.com*, accessed June 26, 2017, at https://ycharts.com/indicators/venezuelan_bolivar_exchange_rate.

53. Fabiola Zerpa, "My Venezuela Nightmare: A 30-Day Hunt for Food in a Starving Land," *Bloomberg.com*, July 18th, 2016; John Otis, "Facing Severe Food Shortages, Venezuela Pushes Urban Gardens," National Public Radio, February 16, 2016; "Food and Venezuela: Let Them Eat Chavismo," *The Economist*, June 20, 2015, 36. David Luhnow and Jose De Cordoba, "Venezuela's Sinister Turn," *Wall Street Journal*, June 24-25, 2017, C1; Carlos Jasso, "Animals Starving in Venezuela Zoos," July 12, 2016, *NationalGeographic.com*; "Venezuelan On Daily Life amid Protests: 'We Need to Be Here to Fight,'" *All Things Considered*, June 22, 2017, National Public Radio, accessed June 28, 2017, at http://www.npr.org/

2017/06/22/533989376/venezuelan-on-daily-life-amid-protests-we-need-to-be-here-to-fight; Kegal Vyas and Sara Schaefer Munoz, "Venezuelans Risk Crossing Sea to Get Basics," *Wall Street Journal*, June 24–25, 2017, A8; Meredith Kohut, "Desperate for a Cure," *National Geographic*, July 2017, 74–79.

54. Christina Schiavoni and William Camacaro, "Special Report: Hunger in Venezuela? A Look beyond the Spin," July 11, 2016, *Food First*, accessed December 12, 2017, at https://foodfirst.org/special-report-hunger-in-venezuela-a-look-beyond-the-spin/; Frederick Mills and William Camacaro, "Venezuela Takes Control of Its Border as Bogota and Caracas Bring Their Cases to UNASUR," August 31, 2015, Council on Hemispheric Affairs, accessed December 12, 2017, at http://www.coha.org/venezuela-colombia-border-dispute/; Lucas Koerner, "Venezuela Recognized by FAO for Halving Malnutrition," June 8, 2015, *VenezuelaAnalysis.com*, accessed December 12, 2017, at https://venezuelanalysis.com/news/11410; Rachael Boothroyd Rojas, "UN Expert: No Humanitarian Crisis in Venezuela," December 6, 2017, *VenezuelaAnalysis.com*, accessed December 12, 2017, at https://venezuelanalysis.com/news/13533.

55. "Venezuela: The World's Worst-Performing Economy" (video), *Al Jazeera English*, February 27, 2016, accessed June 28, 2017, at http://www.aljazeera.com/programmes/countingthecost/2016/02/venezuela-world-worst-performing-economy-160227103201996.html; "Venezuela Land Reform Criticized," *Al Jazeera English*, December 27, 2009, accessed June 28, 2017, at https://www.youtube.com/watch?v=c8i4Pin-KqI.; "Venezuela: On the Edge," *Al Jazeera English*, July 21, 2017, accessed June 28, 2017, at http://www.aljazeera.com/programmes/peopleandpower/2016/07/venezuela-edge-160718091013652.html "Property Rights in Venezuela: Life, Liberty and Property," *The Economist*, August 31, 2010; Zerpa, "My Venezuela Nightmare," ; "Venezuela: The Angry 80%," *The Economist*, October 1, 2016, 35; "Food and Venezuela: Let Them Eat Chavismo," *The Economist*, June 20, 2015, 36; Eric Boehm, "Venezuela Arrests Bakers for Making Rolls, Claims They Were Waging 'Economic War' against Country," March 22, 2017, *Reason.com*; "Free Exchange: Self-Inflicted Wounds," *The Economist*, April 8, 2017, 68; Francisco Toro, "Disaster Déjà vu in Venezuela," September 2016, *Reason.com*, 39–41; "Venezuela: The Revolution at Bay," *The Economist*, February 14, 2015, 31; "Venezuela's 'Economic War': Everything Must Go . . . ," *The Economist*, November 16, 2013, 42; Juan Forerok, "Venezuela Is Starving," *Wall Street Journal*, May 6–7, 2017, , A1; Anatoly Kurmanaev and Mayela Armas, "Venezuela's Congress Is Stripped of Its Powers," *Wall Street Journal*, March 31, 2017, A7; "Venezuela: Army Rations," *The Economist*, August 6, 2016, 27; Harriet Alexander, "Venezuelan Farmers Ordered to Hand over Produce to State," *The Telegraph*, July 21, 2015; Richard Washington, "Venezuela Calls for Mandatory Labor in Farm Sector," *CNBC*, July 29, 2016, accessed June 28, 2017, at http://www.cnbc.com/2016/07/29/venezuela-calls-for-mandatory-labor-in-farm-sector.html; "Venezuelan on Daily Life amid

Protests: 'We Need to Be Here to Fight,'" *All Things Considered*, June 22, 2017, National Public Radio, accessed June 28, 2017, at http://www.npr.org/2017/06/22/533989376/venezuelan-on-daily-life-amid-protests-we-need-to-be-here-to-fight; "As Venezuelan Go Hungry, the Military Is Trafficking in Food," *All Things Considered*, January 9, 2017, National Public Radio, accessed June 28, 2017, at http://www.npr.org/sections/thesalt/2017/01/09/508986586/as-venezuelan-go-hungry-the-military-is-trafficking-in-food; "Did Venezuela Reinstate Slavery—or Find How to Grow More Food?," *telesur.com*, August 4, 2016, accessed December 12, 2017, at https://www.telesurtv.net/english/news/Did-Venezuela-Reinstate-SlaveryOr-Find-How-to-Grow-More-Food-20160804-0032.html.

56. Tony Leys, "ISU Researcher to Test Altered Bananas," *Des Moines Register*, August 2, 2014.

57. Kendal Gast, "Genetically Modified Bananas Spark Controversy," *Iowa State Daily*, February 23, 2016.

58. International Institute of Tropical Agriculture, "Banana & Plantain," not dated, accessed May 18, 2016, at http://www.iita.org/banana-and-plantain.

59. Hannah Dankbar, Rivka Fidel, Ahna Kruzic, Jackie Nester, and Becca Nixon, "Letter: Jeopardizing ISU students' Health and Uganda's Future?," *Ames Tribune*, September 20, 2015.

60. Bridget Mugambe, "AFSA Open Letter Opposing Human Feeding Trials Involving GM Banana," December 9, 2014, Alliance for Food Sovereignty in Africa; Bridget Mugambe, *The Global Struggle for Food Sovereignty: A Discussion with African Food Leaders and Farmers* (video), October 26, 2014, accessed April 15, 2016, at http://www.youtube.com/watch?v=ztQKRmsnIRE.

61. *Wakeup*, not dated, accessed June 1, 2016, at http://wakeupsummer.com/index.php/rokgallery?slug=imperial-palace-tokyo&catid=17&id=17:more-than-700-people-pack-vandana-shiva-lecture.

62. Presentation by Vandana Shiva at Iowa State University, March 11, 2015, accessed June 2, 2016, at http://www.isutransgenicbanana.com/resources/.

63. Pamela White, "Letter: ISU deans support researcher," *Ames Tribune*, March 28, 2015, Opinion.

64. Rachel Schurman and William A. Munro, *Fighting for the Future of Food: Activists versus Agribusiness in the Struggle over Biotechnology* (Minneapolis: University of Minnesota Press, 2010).

65. Theresa Papademetriou, "Restrictions on Genetically Modified Organisms: European Union," March 2014, Library of Congress, accessed May 18, 2016, at https://www.loc.gov/law/help/restrictions-on-gmos/eu.php.

66. Caitlin Deaver, "Keystone XL Pipeline: Student Activists Protest Construction," *Iowa State Daily*, September 23, 2013.

67. Andrea Basche, Angie Carter, Hannah Dankbar, Rivka Fidel, Ahna Kruzic, Jackie Nester, Becca Nixon, Gabrielle Roesch-McNally, and Jen Tillman, "Letter: Public Dialogue on Transgenic Banana Needed," *Ames Tribune*, April 20, 2015, Opinion.

68. IRB document posted to website, accessed June 6, 2016, at http://www. isutransgenicbanana.com/resources/; Tony Leys, "Iowa Trial of GMO Bananas Is Delayed," *Des Moines Register*, January 12, 2015, accessed June 6, 2016, at http:// www.desmoinesregister.com/story/news/health/2015/01/12/isu-genetically-modified-bananas-trial/21663557/.

69. Anonymous, "A Controversial GMO Study Is Going Bananas," February 25, 2016, *Munchies*, accessed June 7, 2016, at https://munchies.vice.com/about.

70. Tony Leys, "ISU Still Plans GMO Banana Trial, Despite Controversy," *Des Moines Register*, February 17, 2016; "Vitamin A Equivalence of the Provitamin A in Biofortified Bananas," *ClinicalTrials.gov*, August 2016, accessed June 26, 2017, at https://clinicaltrials.gov/ct2/show/NCT02702622?term=banana+iowa+state&rank=1.

71. Wendy McElroy, "Henry Thoreau and 'Civil Disobedience,'" 2005, *Thoreau Reader*, accessed May 18, 2015, at http://thoreau.eserver.org/wendy.html.

72. Susan Campbell Bartoletti, *Black Potatoes: The Story of the Great Irish Potato Famine, 1845–1850* (Boston: Houghton Mifflin, 2001).

73. www.leafandroot.org.

74. David Gumpert, "Raids Are Increasing on Farms and Private Food-Supply Clubs—Here Are 5 Tips for Surviving One," July 15, 2010, *Grist.com*, accessed July 17, 2017, at http://grist.org/article/food-five-tips-for-surviving-a-raid-on-your-farm-or-food-club/full/.

75. Town of Blue Hill, Maine, Ordinances and Amendments, Local Food and Community Food Self Governance 2011, Section 5, Local Food and Community Self-Governance Ordinance of 2011, passed April 1, 2011, accessed July 17, 2017, at http://www.townofbluehillmaine.org/uploads/1/5/1/9/15195878/local_food_and_community_food_self_governance_2011.pdf.

76. Baylen Linnekin, "USDA Wrongly Targets Wyoming's Food Freedom Act," October 8, 2016, *Reason.com*.

77. Reason staff, "What's the Federal Government's Beef with State Meat Processing Rules?," June 17, 2017, *Reason.com*.

78. Jennifer Mitchell, "Maine Law Lets Municipalities Regulate Food," July 8, 2017, *Weekend Edition*, National Public Radio, accessed July 21, 2017, at http://www.npr.org/2017/07/08/536125062/maine-law-lets-municipalities-regulate-food.

CHAPTER 4

1. National Gardening Association, *Garden to Table: A 5 Year Look at Food Gardening in America*, 2014, *Garden.org*, accessed August 11, 2017, at https://garden.org/special/pdf/2014-NGA-Garden-to-Table.pdf.

2. Dancing Rabbit Ecovillage, "Cutting Our Carbon Footprint," accessed August 7, 2017, at https://www.dancingrabbit.org/about-dancing-rabbit-ecovillage/eco-living/cutting-our-carbon-footprint/.

3. See the series of polls at http://www.gallup.com/poll/206030/global-warming-concern-three-decade-high.aspx?g_source=CATEGORY_CLIMATE_CHANGE&g_medium=topic&g_campaign=tiles.

4. Accessed August 14, 2017, at http://www.walterscott.lib.ed.ac.uk/biography/chronology.html.

5. World Health Organization "10 Facts on Polio Eradication," April 2017, accessed August 14, 2017, at http://www.who.int/features/factfiles/polio/en/.

6. Roberta H. Anding, "Lecture 23: Dietary Approaches to Weight Management," *Nutrition Made Clear*, The Great Courses, The Teaching Company.

7. Lara R. Dugas, Stephanie Kliethermes, Jacob Plange-Rhule, Liping Tong, Pascal Bovet, Terrence E. Forrester, Estelle V. Lambert, Dale A. Schoeller, Ramon A. Durazo-Arvizu, David A. Shoham, Guichan Cao, Soren Brage, Ulf Ekelund, Richard S. Cooper, and Amy Luke, "Accelerometer-Measured Physical Activity Is Not Associated with Two-Year Weight Change in African-Origin Adults from Five Diverse Populations," *PeerJ* 5 (2017): e2902, doi:10.7717/peerj.2902; Herman Pontzer, "Exercise Paradox," *Scientific American*, February 2017, 28–31.

8. E. Hemmingsson, K. Johansson, and S. Reynisdottir, "Effects of Childhood Abuse on Adult Obesity: A Systematic Review and Meta-analysis," *Obesity Reviews* 15(11) (2014), doi:10.1111/obr.12216; E. Hemmingsson, "A New Model of the Role of Psychological and Emotional Distress in Promoting Obesity: Conceptual Review with Implications for Treatment and Prevention," *Obesity Reviews* 15(9) (2014): 769, doi:10.1111/obr.12197.

9. E. M. Taveras, M. W. Gillman, M.-M. Pena, S. Redline, and S. L. Rifas-Shiman, "Chronic Sleep Curtailment and Adiposity," *Pediatrics* 133(6) (2014): 1013, doi:10.1542/peds.2013-3065.

10. Barbara H. Fiese and Kelly K. Bost, "Family Ecologies and Child Risk for Obesity: Focus on Regulatory Processes," *Family Relations* 65(1) (2016): 94, doi:10.1111/fare.12170; Rachel Tumin and Sarah E. Anderson, "Television, Home-Cooked Meals, and Family Meal Frequency: Associations with Adult Obesity," *Journal of the Academy of Nutrition and Dietetics* 117(6) (2017), doi:10.1016/j.jand.2017.01.009; Daphne C. Hernandez and Emily Pressler, "Gender Disparities among the Association between Cumulative Family-Level Stress & Adolescent Weight Status," *Preventive Medicine* 73 (2015): 60, doi:10.1016/j.ypmed.2015.01.013; T. Østbye, R. Malhotra, M. Stroo, C. Lovelady, R. Brouwer, N. Zucker, and B. Fuemmeler, "The Effect of the Home Environment on Physical Activity and Dietary Intake in Preschool Children," *International Journal of Obesity* 10 (2013), doi:10.1038/ijo.2013.76.

11. Peter Dolton and Mimi Xiao, "The Intergenerational Transmission of Body Mass Index across Countries," *Economics & Human Biology* 24 (2017): 140, doi:10.1016/j.ehb.2016.11.005.

12. Centers for Disease Control and Prevention, "Childhood Obesity Facts," Not dated. accessed August 14, 2017, at https://www.cdc.gov/obesity/data/childhood.html.

13. Rachana Bhatt, "Timing Is Everything: The Impact of School Lunch Length on Children's Body Weight," *Southern Economic Journal* 80(3) (January 1, 2014): 656–76.

14. Leah Frerichs et al., "Influence of School Architecture and Design on Healthy Eating: A Review of the Evidence," *American Journal of Public Health* 105(4) (April 1, 2015): e46–e57; Leah Frerichs et al., "The Role of School Design in Shaping Healthy Eating-Related Attitudes, Practices, and Behaviors among School Staff," *Journal of School Health* 86(1) (2016): 11–22; Brian Wansink, "Environmental Factors That Increase the Food Intake and Consumption Volume of Unknowing Consumers," *Annual Review of Nutrition* 24 (2004): 455–79.

15. Martin Caraher, Annie Seeley, Michelle Wu, and Susan Lloyd, "When Chefs Adopt a School? An Evaluation of a Cooking Intervention in English Primary Schools," *Appetite* 62 (2013): 50–59; Leann Lipps Birch, Linda McPhee, B. C. Shoba, Edna Pirok, and Lois Steinberg, "What Kind of Exposure Reduces Children's Food Neophobia? Looking vs. Tasting," *Appetite* 9(3) (1987): 171–78; Helen Coulthard and Dipti Thakker, "Enjoyment of Tactile Play Is Associated with Lower Food Neophobia in Preschool Children," *Journal of the Academy of Nutrition and Dietetics* 115(7) (2015): 1134–40; E. Roche, J. M. Kolodinsky, R. K. Johnson, M. Pharis, and J. Banning, "School Gardens May Combat Childhood Obesity," *Choices* 2017, Quarter 1, accessed September 17, 2018 at http://www.choicesmagazine.org/choices-magazine/theme-articles/transformations-in-the-food-system-nutritional-and-economic-impacts/school-gardens-may-combat-childhood-obesity; University of Florida Institute of Food and Agricultural Sciences, "Gardening as a Child May Lead College Students to Eat More Veggies," *ScienceDaily*, September 19, 2016, accessed September 17, 2018, at www.sciencedaily.com/releases/2016/09/160919110301.htm.

16. A. Hammons and B. H. Fiese, "Is Frequency of Shared Family Meals Related to the Nutritional Health of Children and Adolescents? A Meta-analysis," *Pediatrics* 127 (2011): e1565–e1574.

17. T. T. Huang, D. Sorensen, S. Davis, L. Frerichs, J. Brittin, J. Celentano, et al., "Healthy Eating Design Guidelines for School Architecture," *Preventing Chronic Disease* 10 (2013): 120084, doi: http://dx.doi.org/10.5888/pcd10.120084.

18. Shawn McMahon and Jessica Horning, "Living Below the Line: Economic Insecurity and America's Families," Wider Opportunities for Women, Fall 2013, accessed September 8, 2017, at http://www.wowonline.org/wp-content/uploads/2013/09/Living-Below-the-Line-Economic-Insecurity-and-Americas-Families-Fall-2013.pdf.

19. http://www.tulsarealgoodfood.org/rgfamilygrocers, accessed September 14, 2017.

20. Becki McAnnally, "Rolling Stores, Not the Rolling Stones—Could They Return?," *Alabama Pioneers*, accessed September 17, 2017, at http://www.alabamapioneers.com/rolling-stores-return/.

21. Eva Jacobs and Stephanie Shipp, "How Family Spending Has Changed in the U.S.," *Monthly Labor Review*, March 1990, accessed September 17, 2017, at https://www.bls.gov/opub/mlr/1990/03/art3full.pdf; Eliza Barclay, "Your Grandparents Spent More of Their Money on Food Than You Do," *The Salt*, March 2, 2015, National Public Radio, accessed September 17, 2017, at http://www.npr.org/sections/thesalt/2015/03/02/389578089/your-grandparents-spent-more-of-their-money-on-food-than-you-do.

22. Claudia Prat, Neeti Upadhye, and Guglielmo Mattioli, "A Free Food Forest in the Bronx," *New York Times*, September 8, 2017, accessed September 8, 2017, at https://www.nytimes.com/video/us/100000005396311/swale-food-forest-bronx-permaculture.html?playlistId=100000004687548&region=video-grid&version=video-grid-thumbnail&contentCollection=The+Daily+360&contentPlacement=0&module=featured-videos&action=click&pgType=Multimedia&eventName=video-grid-click.

23. Alexandria Levine, "A Forest Floats on the Bronx River, with Free Produce," *New York Times*, July 7, 2016, accessed September 8, 2017, at https://www.nytimes.com/2017/07/07/nyregion/a-forest-floats-on-the-bronx-river-with-free-produce.html?mcubz=1&_r=0.

24. "The League S03E06: Yobogoya! Will Destroy Ya," December 4, 2011, *Fantasy Football Fools*, accessed September 8, 2017, at http://www.fantasyfootballfools.com/culture/the-league-s03e06-yobogoya-will-destroy-ya/.

25. Brian Barth, "Farming the Forest Floor," *Modern Farmer*, Fall 2016, 56–64.

26. Jennifer Levitz, "Foragers Draw Outcry, 'Stop Eating My Yard!'" *Wall Street Journal*, April 2, 2017, A1.

27. See her website, amorystarr.com.

28. Nadia Schilling, "Google Predicts a Plant-Based Revolution!" *In Defense of Animals*, June 8, 2016, accessed August 30, 2016, at https://www.idausa.org/google-predicts-plant-based-revolution/.

29. Aruni Nan Futuronsky, *Recovering My Voice* (Bloomington, IN: iUniverse, 2008), chap. 16, Kindle location 1476.

30. Futuronsky, *Recovering My Voice*, chap. 16, Kindle location 1482.

31. Lauren Brande, "About the Alcoholics Anonymous (AA) 12-Step Recover Program," April 29, 2013, *Recovery.org*, accessed August 31, 2017, at http://www.recovery.org/topics/alcoholics-anonymous-12-step/.

32. Meera Nanda, "Not as Old as You Think," *Open*, February 12, 2011, accessed August 31, 2017, at http://www.openthemagazine.com/article/living/not-as-old-as-you-think.

33. Durant, *Our Oriental Heritage*.

34. Durant, *Our Oriental Heritage*.

35. https://www.youtube.com/watch?v=pofiS_2Mzlo.

36. Remark made on *The President Show*, May 18, 2017.

37. KayLoni L. Olson and Charles F. Emery, "Mindfulness and Weight Loss: A Systematic Review," *Psychosomatic Medicine*, 2014, doi:10.1097/PSY.0000000000000127.

38. Christian H. Jordan, Wan Wang, Linda Donatoni, and Brian P. Meier, "Mindful Eating: Trait and State Mindfulness Predict Healthier Eating Behavior," *Personality and Individual Differences* 68 (2014): 107–11. Lori I. Kidd, Christine Heifner Graor, and Carolyn J. Murrock, "A Mindful Eating Group Intervention for Obese Women: A Mixed Methods Feasibility Study," *Archives of Psychiatric Nursing* 27 (2013): 211–18; Gayle M. Timmerman and Adama Browm, "The Effect of a *Mindful Restaurant Eating* Intervention on Weight Management in Women," *Journal of Nutrition Education and Behavior* 44(1): 22–28; Kelsie L. Hendrickson and Erin B. Rasmussen, "Effects of Mindful Eating Training on Delay and Probability Discounting for Food and Money in Obese and Healthy-Weight Individuals," *Behavior Research and Therapy* 51 (2013): 399–409; Monica Beshara, Amanda D. Hutchinson, and Carlene Wilson, "Does Mindfulness Matter? Everyday Mindfulness, Mindful Eating and Self-Reported Serving Size of Energy Dense Foods among a Sample of South Australian Adults," *Appetite* 67 (2013): 25–29.

39. Zaynah Khan and Zainab F. Zadeh, "Mindful Eating and It's [*sic*] Relationship with Mental Well-Being," *Procedia—Social and Behavioral Sciences* 159 (2014): 69–73.

40. Charles Spence, *Gastrophysics: The New Science of Eating* (New York: Viking Press, 2017).

41. Stephen Dubner, "Save Me from Myself: A New Freakonomics Radio Podcast," February 2, 2012, *Freakonomics.com*, accessed September 7, 2017, at http://freakonomics.com/podcast/save-me-from-myself-a-new-freakonomics-radio-podcast/.

42. Spence, *Gastrophysics*.

43. Spence, *Gastrophysics*.

44. Tony Duff, *Oryoki and the Oryoki Chant* (Kathmandu, Nepal: Padma Karpo Translation Committee, 2008).

CHAPTER 5

1. Austin Harrington, "Lifeworld," *Theory, Culture, & Society* 23(2–3) (2006): 341–43.

Index

Printed in the USA/Agawam, MA
October 16, 2019

740279.004